Everything You Need To Know About Men…

…You Can Learn From Dogs.

By Diane Klumb

Lulu Press

ISBN_____

© 2007 by Diane Klumb

All rights reserved under International and Pan-American Copyright Conventions. Published in The United States by Lulu Press. No portion of this book may be reproduced, stored in a retrieval system or transmitted by any means, electronic, mechanical, photocopying, recording or otherwise without the written permission of the author. Although every precaution has been taken in preparation of this book, the publisher and author assume no responsibility for errors or omissions. Neither is any liability assumed for damages resulting from the use of the information herein.

This book is dedicated to...

   ...every woman who has ever asked herself:

"What the hell was I thinking!?"

Contents

	Introduction	11
1.	This Whole Pack Thing	17
2.	Pack Order, Genes, & Biochemistry	37
3.	Alphas	89
4.	Betas	111
5.	Junkyard Dogs	127
6.	Retrievers	145
7.	Perpetual Puppies	161
8.	Sentinels	181
9.	Omegas	203
10.	Leglifters (PitBulls & Specials)	219
11.	Fearbiters	247
12.	Lone Wolves	259
13.	The Final Chapter	281
	Acknowledgements	293

"Fear of the dangers of anthropomorphism has caused ethologists to neglect many interesting phenomena, and it has become apparent that they could afford a little disciplined indulgence."
-Robert Hinde, 1982

"You can't always get what you want, but if you try sometimes, you just might find you get what you need."
- The Rolling Stones, 1968

Introduction

Before you read this book, you need to understand two things.

First, I did absolutely no actual *research* before I wrote this; so don't expect footnotes or anything - it's pretty much written off the top of my head, which is the way I do everything.

Second, I am not an expert in the fields of ethology, psychology, biochemistry, genetics or, come to think about it, much of anything at all. (This is primarily due to my having taken the scenic route through college, at which Multiple Unnamed Institutions of Higher Learning I still owe library fines accruing steadily since the late sixties, and probably now exceeding the GNP of several small third-world countries.)

However, for reasons I have a hard time explaining, even to myself, I have actually been showing and breeding dogs since the days when Lyndon Johnson's beagles scampered around the South Lawn. Consequently I've spent the better part of my life in the more or less constant company of both dogs and men and, although I don't consider myself an expert on either subject by a long shot, under those circumstances one would have to have the IQ of an *artichoke* not to notice the basic similarities.

That, as it happens, the sole extent of my "expert status" on the subject.

So don't quote any of this stuff in scientific journals, or use it in a term paper or anything, or you'll end up looking really stupid, which may bother you a whole lot more than it does me.

You may also have noticed that this book is published by an Alternative Method, rather than by the traditional publishing route. There are two main reasons for this as well:

The first reason is that I don't handle rejection well *at all*, and John Grisham's first (and possibly best) book was turned down by something like *seven houses*, for God's sake, so I figure I don't have the proverbial snowball's chance in hell of publication of *this* particular book by that route, especially since the publishing industry is a pretty male-dominated field, and this is not a book men are probably going to be excited about.

I mean, how can somebody keep sending the same manuscript out time and time again? All I know is I'd be totally wiped out by the first rejection slip, start hitting the Hostess Snowballs pretty hard to make myself feel better, never get around to sending it out again, and the ultimate result would be that I'd be fat and you wouldn't be reading this. A lose/lose scenario if I ever saw one.

And anyway, as Dial Press so kindly explained to George Orwell when they declined *Animal Farm* back in 1944: "There is not much demand for animal stories in the USA." (*These* are the people deciding what America reads?)

The second reason is that publishing *has* changed radically, though admittedly not always for the better, since Billy Faulkner's time.

The days of some poor tortured genius with a bottle of cheap bourbon at his elbow pounding out a manuscript on the old Smith-Corona, and then sending it off to a New York publishing house to be critiqued, cleaned up, typeset, bound, and hyped are totally gone, thanks to computers.

In today's Brave New World of desktop publishing, virtual inventory, and print-on-demand sales any idiot with spell-check and a bottle of cheap bourbon at his elbow can disseminate whatever silliness he so chooses to gazillions of unsuspecting readers via the internet without subjecting himself to some anal-retentive editor in Manhattan criticizing his syntax. *And he can keep all the money, too.*

God bless America.

DO NOT READ THIS BOOK. . .
         IF YOU HAVE A Y CHROMOSOME.

A while ago (actually, it was right about the time Dubya was more or less elected for the first time, which constitutes "a while ago" unless you are an adolescent, in which case "a while ago" is last Thursday) I wrote a column for a well-known dog magazine - which I have been doing every month for many years except when I forget - about male pack order and politics that was titled "WARNING: Do Not Read this Column if You Have a Y Chromosome". I swear that was the *exact* title of the column.

I was absolutely amazed at how many men read it.

I simply could not comprehend why, until I found actual photographs of the X and Y chromosomes. Here's what they look like, honest to God:

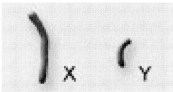

Explains a lot, doesn't it?

The human genome, it turns out, has roughly 30-40,000 genes contained within it, spread out among 23 pairs of chromosomes. You know how many of those genes are on the Y chromosome? Maybe 80. That's *eighty*. Out of thirty or forty *thousand* genes, I kid you not. And we've been letting these guys run the *planet* ...amazing.

But, I'll try again, for all the good it will do:

DO NOT READ THIS BOOK. . .
         IF YOU HAVE A Y CHROMOSOME.

I'm *only* telling you this for your own good. This book was *written* for women. For example, you may notice that the print is pretty big. This is not a mistake, nor does it reflect an effort to make the book appear fatter (women don't *like* things to appear fatter, with the possible exception of their husband's ex-wife) - it's *demographics.*

The Baby Boom being what is was, statistical odds are that *many* women reading this book will be looking at forty (either back at it with fondness or toward it with horror, depending on which end of said Boom you may have entered the world) but either way, I have no desire to be the cause of *any woman* having to finally take that God awful field trip over to Walgreen's to get a pair of reading glasses because, as an experience, it's demoralizing as hell.

Men look Distinguished, Professorial, and somehow *important* when they pull a pair of wire-rimmed reading glasses out of their shirt pocket to examine something, kind of like a jeweler pulling out a loupe to examine the quality of a diamond, or a Victorian robber baron pulling a gold watch out of his vest-pocket to see if the train is late. Women, on the other hand, might as well just hang a sign around their necks saying

"MENOPAUSE IS RIGHT AROUND THE CORNER."

So, the print is nice and big. It also has a lot of information in it that men are probably better off not knowing because it, frankly, puts them at a little bit of a disadvantage.

Now, if you *are* a guy *(Hint: Does the restroom you usually use have urinals in it? You're probably a guy...)* and you are still reading, you might as well keep going, because it's pretty clear you suffer from what is generally referred to by elementary school teachers as "Problems Following Simple Instructions" and there's no way I can stop you anyhow but, I *am* warning you - you are *not* going to be entirely comfortable, and I *certainly* wouldn't read it in public, like on an airplane or anything, because you'll end up looking like an insecure *dweeb*, like one of those guys caught reading Helen Gurley Brown's **Sex And the Single Girl** back in the Sixties... at least to women.

If you *still* are having a hard time with that Following Instructions thing (which is probably, now that I think about it, a glitch on the Y chromosome over which you have no control) and you consequently find yourself caught red-handed in spite of my warnings, you *can* try a couple of these semi-lame excuses, which will probably be just slightly better than anything you can come up with on your own at a moment's notice, though I *really* don't see why I should be helping you out...

OK, Let's do a run-through:

You're on the plane, you didn't listen to my instructions, so you're reading this book and the flight attendant saunters over and says:

"*OH! I see you're reading* **Everything You Need to Know about Men** *(dissolves in giggles)... So...what do you think YOU are?*"

At which point all female heads in the vicinity swivel to hear your answer...

Frankly, you're already a dead man, but you don't know it yet.

So you can try: *"My wife musta stuck this in my briefcase as a joke - I had no idea what it was about."*

Or, *"The person sitting here before me must have left it on the seat..."*
Or, *"Oh...gee...Guess this isn't the new Sky Mall?..."*

(Hint - Any of these will work better if you can also manage that slow, endearing, lopsided grin that Harrison Ford has gotten so much mileage out of over the years, by the way...)

Or - this one is actually my personal favorite - you can try to bluff your way through by being Joe Cool:

"Oh, I'm just reviewing it for Esquire."

(Another Hint - although this last excuse is the least lame, and doesn't require the HF grin to pull it off effectively, on a plane the size of, say, a Boeing 727, no more than three guys can use it per flight, or you'll all get caught...so get your stories straight back at the gate first. It is conceivable, although unlikely, that you could all be reviewing it for *different* magazines, but *not* all the same one.)

Here's the *real* problem with guys reading this book - and after this *I'm going to stop talking to you:*

Almost all men start out thinking that they are Alphas, even if they practically have "LEGLIFTER" tattooed on their foreheads.

I have no idea why this is, but it's probably caused by yet another gene on the Y Chromosome, right next to the one that makes all men, no matter what their age, weight, or level of fitness, *honestly believe they look good shirtless.*

Odds are, you're probably not, and you probably don't.

Get OVER it.

1

Man's Best Friend - This Whole Pack Thing

The age-old bond between man and dog (about which much has been written over the years), and their behavioral similarities (about which absolutely *nothing* has really been written until now), are both based on a single premise:

Both men and dogs are essentially descended from pack-hunting predators.

What's a predator?

Well, discounting all the negative social and cultural connotations, it's simply an animal who relies on the hunting, killing, and devouring of other animals (generally those lower on the food chain, for practical reasons) as his main source of nutrition. Some predators, like cats, are *obligate carnivores*, which means that, left to their own devices, they eat meat exclusively while others, like dogs and man, are a little more open-minded.

By comparison, animals that rely on carrion (which is meat someone *else* has killed) as their main source of nutrition are referred to as *scavengers*. That may not sit comfortably with those of us who regularly buy our carrion at the butcher shop, but it's true nonetheless...

Those herbivores who rely mainly on green stuff and whose existence provides sustenance for predators are generally referred to as *prey,* while those who eat pretty much anything, like bears and skunks, are omnivores, and are generally neither predators nor prey. (True omnivores, for the record, have by and large never felt much need to organize themselves at all. They are also characterized by the fact that many of them smell pretty awful, which may have a bearing on their solitary habits, though I doubt anyone's done any serious research on that.)

As a rule of thumb, predators are pretty easy to spot in the Animal Kingdom - their eyes are generally on the *front* of their heads, whereas animals whose longevity depends on their ability to avoid ending up as someone *else's* lunch generally have their eyes on the *sides* of their heads so as to better watch their asses while they are merrily munching their salads. Predators also have canine teeth (between the incisors and the premolars) which are very efficient for tearing flesh from bone, and relatively short digestive tracts.

Cows, for example, are *not* predators, and in spite of their bulk, are pretty *low* on the food chain. Cows, you may have noticed, are all pretty wide between the eyes (which is what gives them that *bovine* look as well as good peripheral vision) and they don't have canine teeth. They don't need 'em.

Being herbivores, they have teeth entirely designed for eating herbage. Mother Nature did not *intend* for cows to hunt and kill other animals or to eat a meat-based diet at all, (which is why cows also have multiple stomachs and we don't) and when man tried to one-up her in that department by adding ground-up dead cows to cattle feed to raise the protein levels we ended up with Mad-Cow Disease, pretty much reinforcing that (once again) Mother Knows Best, we're idiots, and it's a miracle we haven't yet wiped ourselves off the planet.

There are two kinds of predators, basically - solitary predators like tigers, and pack-hunters, like the ancestors of dogs and men. Being a solitary predator requires patience, cunning, and finesse. (Which probably explains the age-old affinity of women for cats, but that's another book entirely...)

Pack hunting requires camaraderie, organization and order, with order playing a major role. It also requires a pack.

Let's define "pack", here. And the *best* way to do that is by referring to a dictionary, which I have discovered beats the hell out of randomly pulling definitions out of one's posterior.

I firmly believe with enough dictionaries at one's disposal, one can win *any* argument. I own a ridiculous number, especially if you count those written in languages in which I am not the least fluent - but then you never really know when you are going to get in an argument with a Hungarian, do you...and who wants to be caught at a disadvantage? Just because they wouldn't let us join the Boy Scouts is no reason not to Be Prepared.

That particular personal peculiarity notwithstanding, it *is* a good idea to keep *Webster's* pretty much within reach at all times, as it's Suitable for Everyday Use in solving garden-variety domestic disputes. If one *really* wants to be sure of one's verbal ground, however, I strongly suggest the Big Kahuna, the Mother of All Dictionaries, the Last Word On Our Mother Tongue - *The Oxford Universal*...because, to give the devil his due, the Brits *invented* the language, after all, whereas we just bastardized it.

So the Big Kahuna it is:

> **Pack** *(from the Middle English packe, or pakke.)*
> let's try:
> 5. *a number of animals kept or naturally congregating together spec. of hounds, for hunting, or wild beasts (esp. wolves) 1648.*

That works.

I guess pakkes in 1648 were pretty much like packs today, from the sound of it, which just proves that nothing much has changed in the last 450 years unless you count indoor plumbing, which is a Good Thing, especially if you have pakkes of wolves wandering around.

It was the wolf researchers, after all, who coined the term Alpha for the pack-leadership position to begin with, back in the early 1900s, after studying the pack-behavior of wolves in very cold and inhospitable places for months on end. The canine behavioralists borrowed the term from *them* some years later and applied it to domestic dogs, and I'm borrowing it from *those guys* and simply applying it to men, because that's the way things work.

Homo Sapiens, like wolves and hounds, kill more efficiently when operating as a pack, or at least they did before the invention of the high-powered rifle and scope. Those early guys who organized themselves into packs to bring down a mastodon or a wooly mammoth to haul back to the cave lived to pass on the genes that allowed them to do so, while their less pack-oriented brethren did not. Their pack leaders were by definition Alpha Males. It ain't rocket-science and it's not even particularly original, as theories go, but odds are it's historically accurate.

(Let me clue you in on something - *Homo Sapiens* is a recycler by nature. There is no such thing as "original artwork" outside of maybe cave drawings, so don't spend a lot of money on it, and mankind probably hasn't had an original thought in the last several millennia, either. Anyone who *thinks* they've had one is just plain arrogant, and/or hasn't done much reading.)

At any rate, what the wolf-guys found out was:

Packs Have Order.

How'd they figure it out?

Well, day after day the wolf-researchers would hide behind large rocks and watch a pack of wolves trotting off to work single file down their narrow wolf paths, and one day it *finally* occurred to one of them (these are *guys*, remember? The same guys whose powers of observation are such that they can fail to notice changes in their wife's hairstyle, their living room furniture, or their number of actual offspring unless it is actually pointed out to them) that the wolves, *each sporting a unique hair color, for God's sake,* always trotted off to work every morning single file *in the same order.* I swear I am not making this up. (No doubt it was this astute observation which also gave rise to the expression "If you're not the lead dog the view never changes"…)

After spending so much time prostrate on the frozen Tundra peering through binoculars, they were not feeling particularly poetic, so they dubbed this pack-order phenomenon: "Pack Order".

Pack Order is critical to the survival of a pack - if it's upset, nobody eats, the collective sex life of the pack goes to hell in a handcart, nobody remembers to take care of the kids, and the whole pack is ultimately in trouble.

And so in order to ensure that packs operate efficiently, and that pack-animals survive and even continue to evolve, rather than ending up as an evolutionary footnote like the Dodo bird[1], Mother Nature hard-wires each little pack-member, before he pops out of the womb, with all the qualities he needs to take his proper, pre-determined place in the pack. Indeed, for most male pack animals, *the view never changes from the moment of birth*, and women would do well to remember that.

This hard-wiring, in reality, is determined by genes that control the production, reception, and reuptake of hormones such as testosterone, vasopressin, prolactin, and oxytocin, and neurotransmitters lsuch as serotonin and dopamine. A fair amount of research has been done on it, some of which I've actually

---

[1]Evolutionary footnote: The Dodo bird is extinct.

read and understand and none of which I'm going to bother to reference, because even if I *did* include a reference like:

Hidetoshi NARA, Miho INOUE-MURAYAMA, Akiko KOSHIMURA, Akinori SUGIYAMA, Yuichi MURAYAMA, Masami MAEJIMA, Yuko UEDA, Hideyuki ITO, Ettore RANDI, Heui-Soo KIM, Ji-Hong HA, Hitoshi KITAGAWA, Yukari TAKEUCHI, Yuji MORI, Toshiroh IWASAKI, Mitsuo MORITA, Katuaki ÔTA, Shin'ichi ITO **Novel polymorphism of the canine dopamine receptor D4 gene intron II region** Animal Science Journal, *Vol. 76 Issue 1 Page 81 February 2005*

...let's face it, nobody's gonna go look it up anyway, so I'd just be showing off, and if I'd wanted to write a boring doctoral dissertation on the subject I would've put a lot more work into this whole project.

A lot of this research on pack status and biochemistry, by the way, was done on primates as well as wolves, and this has led to some erroneous but hopeful conclusions about human Alpha males and sexuality. (This stuff was written mostly by *men,* of course, who seem particularly enamored with the fact that Alpha status in some of the lesser primates comes with the perk of unlimited sexual access to females. Hope springs eternal, I guess...)

For the most part I prefer the wolf research, and not only because the dominant wolves seem more inclined than lesser primates to keep their pants on.

Although we admittedly share much of our genome with primates, they are NOT the genes that control our taste in food. *Those* genes we share with canines. I mean, give your average guy the choice between a plate of fresh, warm, red meat and a plate of bananas, assorted leaves, and termites, and every guy *I* know is gonna go for the rib eye...let's face it - the "Fruit and Insect Plate" is just not a popular menu item with your garden-variety human male, who'd put it in much the same category as chicken salad on a croissant, which you may have noticed is rarely served by guys at male social events like

Superbowl parties. ("Hey, Joe, wanna toss me another chicken salad on a croissant and a cold Bud outta the cooler there?")

By and large, the same holds true for dogs, who would rather drink out of *the toilet* than eat fruit and bugs.

Actually, dogs would probably rather drink out of the toilet than an actual water bowl if we let them, so maybe that's a bad analogy. For the record, GUYS would probably drink out of the toilet too if we let them - and much to their mothers' horror, many a toddler has tried...these, I might add, are invariably little-boy toddlers. Hence the fairly recent and much-heralded invention of toddler-proof toilet-seat locks, which also allow little-boy toddlers an excellent opportunity to hone their little-boy engineering skills by trying to get them open...

But anyway, simple common sense tells us that if we are looking at Human Male Pack Order, it makes more sense to look hardest at the order of *hunting* packs. (That's also probably why man's best friend is a canine, rather than a primate ...I mean, unless he's a professional organ-grinder, don't you think a guy with a pet monkey is a little...*weird?*)

Now, at first blush, logic would indicate that these pack-order genes are on the Y Chromosome (also known by molecular geneticists as the Guy Chromosome), maybe right next to the Remote Control gene, but I personally suspect they're not.

Why not? Simple. The piddley Y chromosome, along with whatever paltry amount of useful genetic material it contains within its 80 or so genes, is passed *totally intact* from father to son. (Although female gender is dependant upon inheriting two X chromosomes, males have one X and one Y, and so must pass the same Y to each male offspring)

That Y, in fact, is the "male line of descent" that kings worried about so much in days of old, and it is that single chromosome which was used to determine that one Thomas Jefferson, esteemed author of the Declaration of Independence, founder of the University of Virginia, and third president of these United States, does indeed have descendants whose maternal ancestors most likely were not eligible to join the Daughters of the American Revolution, much less the United Daughters of the Confederacy.

So, if the genes for Alpha status were all on the Y chromosome, for example, an Alpha male would only produce Alpha sons, creating complete domestic and global chaos, and the whole system would fall apart. And statistically there'd have to be a *whole* lot more Alpha males out there than seems to be the case from cursory observation.

I'm pretty sure I remember reading somewhere (I'm too lazy to go look it up so you'll have to take my word for this one) that in any species, dominant males make up less than 5% of the population, which pretty much matches what I'd guess just by looking around....

It simply makes more *sense* that they'd be scattered around the genome a little, and at least some of them would be on the *X chromosome*, where there is more possibility of variation in male offspring during meiosis, which certainly appears to be the case. (Of course, as far as I can tell, with the exception of the discovery that the gene controlling the production of testosterone, a critical player in male pack order, actually *is* located on the X chromosome, and the fact that in most social species high-ranking males are the sons of high-ranking females, it appears that to date that no one has done any serious research on this including me, so at best it's a theory, and one admittedly based on fairly sketchy logic, but it is, at this time at least, unchallenged by the entire scientific community, if for no other reason than sheer lack of interest.)

So what does this hypothesis mean in plain English?

It means a man's status in life is to a large extent determined by his mother.

Duhhhhhhhhhhhh...!

Even though it's really no longer necessary for the procurement of a decent high-protein meal, the formation of packs is still absolutely necessary for human male survival, *or at least they are hard-wired to still think it is*, and so men form themselves into packs at every opportunity, starting very early in life, like with Cub Scouts.

Packs are a Guy Thing, start to finish.

Although we are also very social animals, women simply do not form tightly structured packs like men do, and women who've been through Basic Training were quick to point this out to me.

Admitting women into the military was, as it almost always is when women are admitted to anything previously considered a Male Domain, mostly a matter of adding a couple of gender-specific bathroom facilities, sans urinals, and complete with coin-operated Feminine-Hygiene Product Dispensers. *Voila!* Instant Gender Equality. (This is, in reality, about as effective as achieving *racial* equality by scraping the words COLOREDS and WHITES off the wall above a couple of water fountains in Mississippi, but that's totally beside the point we want to make here.)

The time-honored, carefully researched, and essentially brutal Military Method that quickly and efficiently transforms dopey post-adolescent raw male recruits into a single Lean, Mean, Fighting Machine with a collective consciousness and a naturally evolved Pack Order simply does *not* have the same effect on women.

Throw a bunch of women together, subject them to intense psychological and physical stress, and they will emerge at the other end tougher, individually more confident, and undoubtedly *knowing a whole lot more about each other.*

But are they an organized male-type pack, with a leader and a well-defined chain of command? Naahh...they're just a bunch of women who have to function in a hostile work environment, which, as we all know, *is just not all that much of a novel experience for us.*

Why don't women form structured packs like guys do? Because *women* are simply not pack-hunting predators - they never were. In our early hunter/gatherer days, men were the hunters, and women were the gatherers. Because of this, women, like females of most other species (hyenas being the notable exception), carry lower baseline levels of testosterone, the "competition hormone", then males do, and higher baseline levels of oxytocin, the "tend and befriend" hormone responsible for cooperation. (For the record, Mars, god of War, most likely carried a boatload of the former, while Venus, goddess of Love, no doubt carried high levels of the latter. The ancient Greeks and Romans clearly knew their biochemistry...)

Anyhow, men are essentially hunters, and women are essentially gatherers, which is the way it's been since our early days. If you doubt this for a moment, my advice to you is:

Take a man shopping.

Men who wouldn't know a Purdy side-by-side from a sawed-off Remington go through a mall at Christmas like they're on safari. They shop for groceries like they're clearing the Great Plains of buffalo, filling their carts as they go. (If men ever start grocery shopping in packs, we're in serious trouble....)

Gathering is a selective process, if you think about, for example, picking strawberries. Hunting is not. You pretty much have to kill it first and *then* drag home whatever you got, for better or worse. (With wild game, it's often worse.) Which goes a long way to explain some of the presents women have received from their mates over the years.

Men hunt, women gather.

And although we women may inherit those pack-hunting genes on our respective X chromosomes and pass them on, like Xq28 (the gene which may incline certain of our sons to be attracted to Floral Design as a career choice), we simply don't *express* them.

There's a big difference, by the way, between *learning* a specific behavior and *expressing the genes* for a specific behavior, as anyone who's trained gun dogs (or taught chickens to play the piano) can tell you.

This was the source of debate between Skinner's *operant conditioning* adherents and Whitman's *ethologists,* who believe that the secrets to behavior are found in the genes - in other words, the Nature vs. Nurture argument. Once the molecular geneticists entered the fray, things started looking up for the ethologists...

In fact, the old gun dog trainers, who rarely held degrees in molecular genetics and wouldn't know an exon from Exxon, have long used a single succinct sentence to express this difference between learned and inherited behaviors, of which I am inordinately fond:
"You can train a pig to point, but that don't make him a pointing dog."

And although women can *learn* to lead one if we have to and could certainly hunt efficiently if the need to do so were to arise, highly organized male-type hunting packs are just... well...not inherently *us*, ya know?

But men love 'em. Here's a brief list of male-designed packs, each with their own pack order, offered in no apparent order other than how they popped into my head while I was typing, and by no means complete:

Human Male Packs- Some Examples:

The Boy Scouts of America
The US Senate and House of Representatives
The Loyal Order of Moose
The US Army, Navy, Air Force, and Marines
The Democratic Party
The Wednesday Night Bowling League
The Holy Roman Catholic Church
Teamster Locals
The American Kennel Club
The US House of Representatives
The Rosicrucians
The National Rifle Association
The Republican Party
The Third Reich
The Knights of Columbus
The Knights of the Round Table
The US Supreme Court
The NFL
General Motors Corporation
Halliburton

Well, I could go on and on, but you get the idea...men just have this weird and somewhat annoying *need* to form packs. Some are entirely social and downright silly, probably reflecting the need of men to form packs outside the work (i.e. "hunting for food") environment, which may be fairly static in an industrialized nation such as ours, and some control pack behavior on a national or even global scale.

Now, you may have noticed that some of these packs now accept women, more or less grudgingly, but if you want to be part of one, bear in mind you'll have to assume one of the pre-existing male pack positions rather than getting to make up one of your own, and odds are, it ain't gonna be Alpha...unless of course you're Nancy Pelosi.

Because they have this inborn pack-order thing, whenever a group of men gather, a pack will almost automatically form, after a little prerequisite ritualistic posturing. It doesn't matter what the situation is - if you leave six men together stuck in an *elevator* for an hour, a pack will form, and someone will shortly be in charge of Getting Everyone Out. This guy is the Alpha, and everybody in the elevator knows it.

(Women in that situation will probably use the same time to share vital information - like where did you get that *great* haircut? - and maybe a couple stories about their kids. Standing on each other's shoulders to climb up onto the *top* of the thing seems a little dangerous and stupid, to say nothing of *greasy* with all those cables and stuff up there. You push the emergency call button, and sooner or later, it will get fixed - that's what elevator-repairmen are for. Why on earth would anyone need to be *in charge*?)

But whenever men are gathered in any group, the same pack status positions will always emerge, no matter what their ages, occupations, or bank accounts. In fact, one of the things I've noticed over the years is that those particular criteria factor in very *little* when packs form outside the corporate environment. In a stuck elevator, for example, an Alpha bricklayer outranks a Beta CEO any day, no matter *whose* card is platinum, and every other guy in there instinctively knows it . This is much more primitive stuff, and it takes more than the pricey cut of a suit to cut it, so to speak.

And *speaking* of speaking, it is worth noting that men instinctively and unerringly determine each other's innate pack status position without speaking. Maybe it's subtle posturing, maybe it's pheromones, hell if I know. Whatever it is, women can surely sense it too.

The ability to recognize an Alpha is probably instinctive because Alphas are necessary to the welfare and survival of the pack, as well as being the animals Mother Nature intended to do most of the breeding. (The latter is no doubt why women find them attractive.)

It's the rest of the pack (the other 95%) that's confusing, though, so let's get down to sorting them out.

Outside of a dog, a book is man's best friend. Inside of a dog, it's too dark to read. - Groucho Marx

After all this talk about predators and wolves, it is important to remember that it is the *domestic dog* with whom man shares a special bond, not the wolf. In fact, until fairly recently a good deal of mankind considered the total eradication of *Canis Lupus* from the planet a sort of Moral Imperative, due to their occupation of the same relative position on the food chain. (A lot of western sheep-ranchers still feel this way, in fact...)

Not so *Canis Familiaris*, with whom *Homo Sapien* has been sharing his hearth, home, and the occasional chili dog, for the last 20,000 years. Modern Man and Modern Dog are soul mates and best friends. Why? Because both are essentially domesticated animals with some weird genetic memory of past wildness, and this equally weird leftover neurological hard-wiring from those days.

In truth, your average Labrador Retriever has no more need for his pack-hunting instincts than does your average stockbroker when it comes to keeping his belly full. Both can generally obtain their full daily requirement of protein, calcium, vitamins, and minerals without actually *killing* anything. But they both still *have* those pack instincts in full measure - they are born with them, and they will die with them. This is a Good Thing. It means we don't have to crawl around on the frozen tundra watching wolves in order to understand men - *we can simply observe the domestic dog.*

Which, as it happens, I've been doing for years and during which time I've made the following Entirely Casual and Unscientific Observation:

ALL men (and all dogs) will inevitably fall into one of the following predetermined Pack Status Personalities, which from here on out we'll refer to as a guy's (or a dog's) PSP:

Alphas
Betas
Retrievers
Leg Lifters (Pitbulls & Specials)
Junkyard Dogs
Perpetual Puppies
Sentinels
Omegas
Fear Biters
Lone Wolves

Understanding what and *who* they are, and how little control they actually have over it, will go a long way to unraveling the mystery that is both men and dogs. And, as my daughter pointed out, it also explains why a lot of relationships are doomed from the start: **You simply picked yourself out the *wrong dog,* girlfriend.**

What is *amazing* is how accurate PSP is, and how men in each group display exactly the *same* character traits and idiosyncrasies, regardless of age, education, socioeconomic status, or anything else that should matter.

It is also interesting to note that some ethnic groups tend to produce more males from a given PSP than one would logically expect, which is no doubt caused by the same geographic distribution of genes that inclines different ethnic groups to different mutations of the APOE gene, which largely determines one's predisposition for heart disease.

It could also quite possibly be the result of deliberate selection over the years on the part of women. For example, a Jewish friend of mine who has bred show dogs for decades and certainly understands pack order explained to me that if you want to find any number of Jewish Alpha males you'll have to go to Tel-Aviv. According to her, Jewish women in this country deliberately select *away* from that gene, the same way show breeders select away from bad tailsets, because Alphas are simply too hard to groom and handle, whereas in Israel they are probably necessary for the survival of the state. I have absolutely *no idea* whether or not this is true, but it's a fascinating theory.

Carried to its idiotic extreme, it could also explain the puzzling preponderance of LegLifters among men of Mediterranean and Latin descent as simply the result of the traditional cultural tolerance of those women for obnoxious macho behavior in males...hence, they don't weed 'em out of the gene pool - in fact, so great is their tolerance for Leglifters, they actually *marry* them and bear their children.

And what is *also* amazing is that there is so little consensus among women about which PSP is the most *desirable* in a mate, once they are introduced to the concept and can easily sort out the men in their lives.

A lot of women prefer Betas, and by and large they *do* make the most reliable husbands and often the best fathers, which can outweigh their tendency toward erectile dysfunction - less of a problem since the invention of Viagra, certainly. Others confess to a lifelong weakness for Junkyard Dogs, or Retrievers.

Other women can only find true happiness with a Perpetual Puppy. (They are playful, loving, and easy to handle, but you have to keep an eye on them at all times, which many women find exhausting. On the other hand, if you know you have a tendency to be a little...well...*controlling*...these are your boys, no doubt about it - they not only tolerate it, they actually *appreciate* their wife being in charge.)

I've not met a sane woman yet who actually *wants* a Fear Biter, although some women are stuck with one before they figure it out. (If you are wondering just who these guys are, I'll give you a hint - *relationships with them all too often end with a restraining order.*) They are sometimes hard to identify out of the gate, but the ability to do so before you get involved with one can save you a *lot* of grief in the long run.

The advantage of understanding Pack Order, and being able to identify a guy's PSP, is that you can also figure out which one is best suited to your own personality and lifestyle *before* you waste a lot of time shopping around in the dark and end up making a stupid mistake.

In other words, one should ideally choose a man pretty much the same way you'd intelligently choose a *dog* - which, I might point out, women tend to be *better* at. (Which probably explains why a lot of women can have two husbands and three relationships go south over the lifespan of one dog....)

When it comes to both men and dogs, you'd better like what's there before you commit to it, because there is *no chance whatsoever* of changing his PSP - it's pretty much hard-wired in. What you see is what you get. Forever.

So...what follows is a rundown on the different PSPs, starting off with the biochemistry responsible for them.

Understanding the hard-wiring behind male behavior is critical to understanding men - in fact, high schools should make it a required science course for girls, the way they used to require Home Economics. The divorce rate in the next generation would positively plummet, because girls would have the tools to make better choices the first time around. So don't skip that section.

However, if you're single and out there in the trenches, understanding biochemistry won't help you actually identify a guy's PSP in a crowd, or even on a date if it comes down to that - unless of course the date involves an unplanned disaster, like a train wreck or a hurricane or something, in which case you can pretty much guess their PSP by how they deal with it.

What single women *really* need is to be able to simply *look* at a guy and make an educated guess as to his PSP before they end up giving out their actual home phone number to a Leg Lifter by mistake (unless, of course, the personality traits of a Leg Lifter float your particular boat) so the last section is a Field Guide for handy reference, starting out with Identifying Plumage.

Did you ever wonder exactly *why* some guys are clotheshorses, and some could care less?

Me neither. But there *is* a reason, and there are clues here that can help you figure out what kind of a guy he *really is* (in other words, his PSP) simply by what he puts on in the morning, assuming it's not an actual *uniform*.

As far as guys in uniform go, there are cut-and-dried rules and emblems of rank specific to the military. These are easily learnable if one is particularly interested.

If, on the other hand, the uniform involves a paper hat, or a chicken costume, and the guy is past high-school age, it's a different story entirely....

In reality, *every* guy wears a uniform of one sort or another, whether he is reading the Sunday paper at home, applying for a job, or going out on a date, and his uniform denotes his rank in the universal male pack just as clearly as stripes, oak leaves, or stars on his shoulders would, if you know how to read the fine print.

Each chapter also includes a little bit about each PSP's Habitat. A man's home may indeed be his castle, but it also reveals a whole lot about his pack status.

Most women have had the unnerving experience at least once in their lives of walking into the apartment of a guy they've been dating for a while and finding something decidedly different than what they'd been expecting...sometimes way better, sometimes frighteningly worse.

If, for example, it looks like something out of Architectural Digest, you're probably dating a Special, which may or may not be OK depending upon your personal taste.

On the other hand, if there are odd newspaper clippings taped all over the walls and a decided odor of decaying protein that he doesn't seem to notice, you're in the den of a Lone Wolf, and my advice is to *get out of there immediately* - in fact, run, don't walk, and call a cab from your cell phone when you're a couple blocks away.

Assuming he's single, how a guy lives is *definitely* related to his PSP.

And if he's already living with another woman, what the hell are you wasting your time for? Any guy YOU can steal can (and most probably will) be stolen in turn by someone else down the road, and you can take that to the bank...it's part of his PSP.

Also included is a brief rundown on career preferences (some are very revealing, some decidedly less so), taste in cars and other toys, political leanings, marriage and parenting potential, and (last but not least) the Mating Habits of the various PSPs.

Although there is probably not a man on the planet who will appreciate the publication of this information, a guy's PSP is indeed directly related to what you can expect in bed, *and* what Mother Nature gave him to work with in that department...

One note about gender preference, since we're on the topic of mating habits - every guy has a PSP, and it is *entirely* unrelated to his taste in sexual partners. There are gay Alphas and there are straight Specials, although there may well be less of the first and, unfortunately (as these guys are usually gorgeous), more of the latter. Pack-status and sexual preference are caused by entirely different genes, and some day some bright young molecular geneticist is going to publish a research paper proving it - until that happens, just take my word for it, because I Know I'm Right.

Although there is little consensus among women regarding which PSP is overall the most desirable in a mate, the last two PSPs - Fear Biters and Lone Wolves - pretty much cover the guys no sane woman wants to get stuck with. They are included in the Field Guide for the same reason you'd include any other dangerous animal - the better you are at identification, the less likely you are to get too close. If you start seeing the red flags that indicate the guy you are dating may be a FearBiter, for example, my best advice is to get the hell out of there as soon (and as carefully) as you can.

Lone Wolves, a wholly (or unholy) scary group, are in a class pretty much by themselves. These guys are total and complete loners for the most part, and that in itself should be a cautionary sign since, romantic notions aside, the Lone Wolf represents a lethal genetic anomaly in a species whose very existence depends upon the ability to function as a member of a pack.

These include the fellows whose neighbors show up on the six o'clock news saying "*Gee, he seemed like such a nice man*", while in the background you can see guys in navy blue FBI windbreakers standing around while guys from Forensics with masks over their noses haul those creepy big black bags out of his house. Sometimes it *really* pays to know what you're dealing with before you get involved.

2

Pack Order, Genes, and Biochemistry

*Remember, Ginger Rogers did everything Fred Astaire did...
and she did it backwards and on high heels.
-Ann Richards*

In order to understand male pack order, women really do need to understand a little 21st-century molecular genetics and a little biochemistry. (It's not that hard, trust me...especially if we do it backwards and on high heels.)

The reason so few women understand this stuff, I have come to realize, is simply because most of the guys involved in these fields are really boring writers.

None of them can speak plain English, and most of them are highly uncomfortable drawing even the most obvious conclusions, especially when sex is involved. This is most likely because, with a few notable exceptions, most of the cutting-edge scientists out there are males, Omegas, and probably half of them suffer from Aspberger's Syndrome. In fact, I personally know an absolutely brilliant biochemist who is so socially dysfunctional he can't *ride* in a car, much less drive one, for God's sake...and although he's a real sweetheart I seriously doubt he's getting laid on a regular basis.

To be fair, it's probably also because they are careful scientists and have been taught not to extrapolate data or draw conclusions, but rather to just publish their findings and leave the ex-

trapolation and conclusions to politicians and pharmaceutical companies. Since I am not a scientist by any stretch of the imagination, luckily I have no such reservations…

So let's take a minute here and learn a little genetics and biochemistry, girl-style. It will be worth it in the long run - as somebody really famous whose name I have forgotten once said, *"We only fear that which we do not understand."*

Besides, once you understand the basic concepts and terminology, you can easily apply them to each PSP, and I won't have to keep repeating myself.

In the last few years, science has made great strides in understanding that most psychological disorders are caused not by cold mothers or penis envy or a bunch of other really stupid Freudian bullshit, but rather by biochemical imbalances that are often the result of simple gene mutations.

One well-studied human pedigree in the Netherlands, literally awash with murderers, rapists, arsonists, and other assorted criminals and crazies over the last two hundred years, was discovered to carry a rare mutation in a gene related to abnormal serotonin function in the brain. But only in the males. Honest to God.

And the late Frances Crick (one of the guys who won a Nobel Prize for unraveling the mystery of the DNA helix back in 1952) predicted that in the future, psychologists would have degrees in neurobiology. Odds are good he was right.

Most recently, the current crop of bright young gene-jockeys have been identifying genetic mutations that clearly don't represent pathology so much as they are associated with simple *personality differences.*

Discounting serious early neglect or abuse (which actually can permanently alter brain function by burning out receptor molecules and resetting the emotional thermostat in the amygdala), whether one is basically shy or outgoing, laid-back or high-strung, nasty or nice, appears to be largely dependent upon one's genetics, not only one's environment, which is certainly good news for parents. (Of course, since you *inherited* those genes from your parents, they're not totally off the hook.)

Ironically, any dog breeder with a couple litters under her belt already *knows* this, which is probably why women from the dog-show world are so quick to accept the whole concept of inherited human male pack order.

In addition to physical characteristics, every breeder has seen very specific personality traits of a sire they didn't even *own* displayed in offspring he's never laid eyes on, which pretty much discounts the environmental theory unless you're a total idiot, which most dog breeders are not. Many a gorgeous stud dog has ceased to be popular when other breeders realized he passed his nasty disposition on to his kids, along with his good looks.

In fact, the heritability of personality in dogs is clearly borne out by the differences in the personality traits between various breeds - the genes that determine the personality of your average Border Collie are very different than the ones that determine the personality of your average Pug and, no matter how much work you put into the project, your average Pug is never going to be any good at herding sheep. (Nor will he be particularly interested doing so.)

In fact, we dog breeders have deliberately selected for these different personality traits over the last couple hundred years (long before the discovery of molecular genetics) which is why we have all these different, and remarkably specialized, breeds in the first place.

If you want to create a breed to retrieve ducks out of the icy Chesapeake Bay, for example, you select for entirely different physical and personality traits than you would if you wanted to create a breed with which to hunt quail in Texas, where heavy muscle and a waterproof coat, the stubborn mental toughness of a Missouri mule, and a natural desire to retrieve are not nearly as important as speed, independence, tolerance for heat, and super-developed scenting ability.

And whether a particular pup of any breed is inherently dominant or submissive, a social butterfly or a wallflower, easily startled or bulletproof, stubborn or biddable, is readily determined by 7 weeks of age, which is, not coincidentally, when pack order starts to reveal itself within a litter. Along with physical characteristics, breeders select breeding stock based on whichever personality traits they desire to perpetuate.

Since *homo sapiens* shares over 95% of his genome with *canis familiaris* (as well as with other primates and many rodents, which is where most of the actual lab research has been done), it should not come as much of a surprise that many of the exact same "personality-forming" genes exist in humans.

As genetics clearly affects the male personality, and hence the male PSP, we really need to understand it so, here we go:

Genetics 101, Girl-style

Contrary to what you may have read, genes are *not* blueprints - genes are actually more like *recipes*.

This is good news for women, who are generally better at reading recipes than blueprints anyway. Whereas blueprints are complex plans for producing totally inorganic things like skyscrapers and engines, recipes are simple instructions for producing *organic* things, like cakes. And puppies. And babies.

Genes are no more than the recipes for the various proteins, hormones, and enzymes that the body uses for all sorts of things you need to develop from a one-celled embryo into a complex vertebrate, and to function from the moment of conception until the day you finally cash in your chips. Everybody inherits two versions of each recipe, one from each parent. Sometimes they are the same, and sometimes they are very different.

Over the years, the genetic "recipes" for some dishes have ended up with lots of variations, sort of like all the recipes for chicken salad in the South.

Here in the land of Sweet Tea it seems like every woman of voting age is required by law to have two good recipes for that luncheon staple in her recipe file, handed down for generations by the women on each side of her family, and although they are all very different, they're all chicken salad.

This phenomenon adds diversity to both the human gene pool and to the buffet table at Southern social gatherings. These recipes are organized into 23 separate sections called *chromosomes*, and are passed from one generation to the next in a recipe file called the *genome* - each human genome contains some thirty thousand or so recipes, two for each dish.

Although everybody has two, each parent passes only one recipe for each dish to each child they produce (this process, called *recombination,* keeps the whole recipe file from doubling in size with every generation, which would become unwieldy to haul around after awhile), and which one you get is largely a matter of luck, unfortunately - nobody gets to pick and choose. (Picking and choosing is the idea behind genetic engineering, which makes people a little queasy for some reason that I cannot fathom...personally, I wish I'd been genetically engineered to have longer legs.)

So half of your personal recipe file, or genome, comes from your mother's file, and the other half comes from your father's, with the recipes randomly selected. Their files each represent half of each of *their* parents' files, and so on all the way back to Lucy.

I'll give you a case in point - my husband's grandmother had the sort of metabolism that allowed her to eat like a truck-driver her entire life without ever gaining a pound, probably the result of a few recipes being altered somewhere along the line. (This most likely happened through a mistake in the copying - like writing 'baking powder' instead of 'baking soda', which as we all know will yield very different results when the next person makes the dish.) And although she, unfortunately, didn't display this metabolism herself, his mother inherited these altered recipes in her personal file, and passed them to her son, who can eat pretty much whatever he wants and stay lean. He in turn, in a cruel twist of fate, passed them to his son (in whom they exist largely unappreciated) and not his daughter, who got stuck instead with the metabolism (passed on from me) that allows one to assume the proportions of a major household appliance on a mere thousand calories a day.

Although I'm sure from the standpoint of evolutionary biology, the second metabolism would be handier for women in times of famine, and would therefore actually provide a biological advantage for the species (which is no doubt why the damned genes are still around), we don't happen to LIVE in those times, and so my poor daughter got screwed, and like me, has to rely on (yuck) diet and exercise to keep from looking like a refrigerator. Mother Nature can really be a bitch!

Now, many of these recipes are pretty versatile, sort of like the recipe for making a good basic sauce, and can be used in lots of different dishes and served lots of different ways. (Mother Nature is also very economical.)

Slight variations in the recipes can create entirely different results, as can variations in the number and distribution of their *receptors*.

Receptors are simply protein molecules on various cells in different parts of the body to which chemicals produced by the genes attach themselves - it's like what you pour the sauce over. (The fact that you get different results should not come as a big surprise to any woman who knows her way around a kitchen...Lobster Thermifor is rarely mistaken for Creamed Chipped Beef on toast, although the sauce used in both is essentially the same - in genetics the lobster and the chipped beef would be the receptors.)

The various dishes produced by these genetic recipes are the basis for *biochemistry.* Biochemistry shouldn't be scary for women - all cooking and baking is basically biochemistry, so we've all been practicing it for years without even knowing it - we're just working with different *ingredients* here.

Biochemistry 101, Girl-style

In addition to building very different cells throughout the body, the enzymes produced by genes are precursors to all of the hormones and neurotransmitters in the body. This is important to know because most of what determines a guy's PSP is dependent upon the different levels of the various hormones and neurotransmitters in the male brain at any given point in time.

Hormones are a group of chemical substances in the body with which most of us are pretty familiar, and the fact that they affect brain function as well as lots of other systems will hardly come as a big surprise to any woman who's ever had PMS.

What *is* a surprise is that several hormones generally thought to be unique to women are also produced in fair quantities by *men*.

For example, *prolactin,* long known to be necessary for the production of breast tissue and lactation (hence the name), is found at nearly equal blood levels in some men as well, although most of them don't need a bra nor do they lactate (which would actually be handy in some cases around 2AM...) In addition to stimulating milk production prolactin, it turns out, also functions as a neurohormone in the brain, where it is a strong determiner of "nesting" behavior in males in virtually every species in which it's been studied - in fact, the gene necessary for its synthesis might well be called the 'home-improvement gene', honest to God. High prolactin levels in men are also a fairly common cause of erectile dysfunction. See why you need to read this chapter???

The other chemical substances that you need to know about, *neurotransmitters*, are simply specialized molecules in the central nervous system (or CNS in geek-speak) which allows nerve cells to communicate with one another. These tiny molecules are responsible for thought, appetite, mood, impulse control, sex drive, and even, in the case of serotonin, for all physical motion.

Now, everybody produces these hormones and neurotransmitters, and everyone has receptor molecules in different parts of the brain to receive them, which in turn causes neurons to fire, resulting in thinking as we know it.

It's the variation in both the *production* levels of the various chemicals and the *number and distribution of their receptors* that creates differences in thinking, and consequently in behavior.

What follows are descriptions of the major brain chemicals that determine male pack order, their basic function, and the PSPs in which they affect critical personality traits.

Serotonin (5-HT)

Of the thirty or so neurotransmitters identified to date, serotonin is definitely the 500-pound gorilla, much as testosterone is the 500-pound gorilla of male hormones. There are at least 14 different known receptors located in the CNS just for serotonin alone - *the serotonin system is the largest single system in the brain*, and influences the widest range of functions in the body.

In the brain, serotonin is critical to the regulation of mood, sleep, appetite, and sexuality - in other words, it covers a lot of the really important stuff! Which is probably why Serotonin Deficiency Syndrome, a condition in which there are inadequate levels of serotonin in the brain, manifests as depression, anxiety, sleeplessness, weight gain, lack of libido, and migraines....

I know, I know... and, yes, it's probably underdiagnosed. Although the research on it has been around for over a decade now, most doctors have never even heard of it. As a group, they really need to read a little more, and maybe play golf a little less....)

The body produces the serotonin it needs to function from *tryptophan,* an essential amino acid. Grossly simplified, it's basically a two-step process - first the body converts a portion of the tryptophan provided by the diet into *5-hydroxy L-Tryptophan,* or 5-HTP, which is then converted to serotonin. (Serotonin, in turn, is converted by the body into *melatonin,* another neurohormone, which regulates the body's circadian rhythm, determining sleep/waking patterns. When serotonin levels in the brain are low, you have a hard time sleeping through the night...sound familiar?)

When serotonin levels in the CNS drop to nearly zilch, the ability to move around pretty much ceases. This is a safety mechanism that all species share, and is responsible for the universal tendency of all animals to literally "freeze" when faced with imminent threat, which can be a Good Thing if you are an opossum, or a Bad Thing if you're behind the wheel of a car and halfway across a very high suspension bridge in heavy traffic.

A good deal of human misery is probably caused by the fact that our serotonin system, which we share with most other complex vertebrates, is about 10,000 years out of date...like Pack Order, it hasn't evolved much from our early hunter/gatherer days.

In animals such as, oh say, clams, who are not exactly the Rocket Scientists of the Wild Kingdom, serotonin is responsible primarily for physical motion, but doesn't really affect thought patterns all that much. This is because clams, who do not appear to have particularly deep thoughts or waste a lot of time worrying about politics or religion, have a pretty rudimentary central nervous system and do not even *possess* a cerebral cortex, which is where rational (or "executive") thought takes place.
We should not make fun of them for this deficiency, though… God knows there are days when it looks like a decided evolutionary advantage.

Unlike the uncomplicated world of clams, though, ours is a complex social species with a reasonably well-developed cerebral cortex, and serotonin is responsible for both physical and mental impulse control.

In the cerebral cortex, serotonin modulates the effects of the other neurotransmitters - what it does is literally *prioritize* the importance of messages being sent by other neurotransmitters before action is automatically taken on them.

In addition to preventing Road Rage, this ability to prioritize neural impulses creates the sense of rational calm and general well-being typical of Alphas, who are characterized by both annoyingly high impulse control and correspondingly high serotonin levels. Why Alphas? Although most people associate Alpha status with high testosterone, it's more likely serotonin that determines it.

In fact, in several social species, the females are attracted to males with the highest serotonin levels; in addition to choosing them as mates over their high-testosterone brethren, these wise girls will actually assist those males (no doubt the biological basis for the "women's vote") in achieving and maintaining the Alpha position, clearly preferring their calm and low-key leadership style over the more aggressive physical dominance of the high-testosterone males.

In all species studied, serotonin levels are associated with pack status right across the board, and in some (the vervet monkey is the one in which they have actually tried this) simply artificially raising serotonin levels in a male was sufficient to raise his status position within the group, sometimes even to that of Alpha. (In more complex societies like ours, it's probably not enough, or every guy on Prozac would be an Alpha, and Lord knows they're not...)

It's important to remember that serotonin levels will normally vacillate some, especially in Alphas, who are probably by necessity more serotonin-sensitive than pack members with less responsibility. The fact that serotonin levels rise and fall in response to external environmental factors is a safety mechanism which can be critical to survival; there are times when it is entirely appropriate to be hyper-alert, worried, or even depressed - it's an intelligent reaction, and allows us to recognize and deal with crisis situations quickly when the need arises.

When serotonin levels stay high no matter what, the result is the Alfred E Neuman Syndrome - you know: "What, me worry?" This response is more typical of Perpetual Puppies than Alphas. The inability to immediately grasp and deal with a threat on the part of an Alpha wolf (or a Commander-In-Chief for that matter), can spell disaster for the entire pack. There are lots of self-confident dodos in the world, but they don't necessarily make good leaders. An effective leader needs intelligence and quick unerring judgment as well as the simple calm self-confidence provided by high serotonin levels alone.

When it comes to serotonin, it's the *baseline* levels that really matter, and when serotonin levels are chronically low, clinical depression can result, as well as inappropriate aggression and lack of impulse control.

Most anti-depressants currently in use (Prozac, Paxil, and the like) are SSRIs- Selective Serotonin Re-uptake Inhibitors. What they do is prevent the reuptake of serotonin within the brain, allowing it to stay in there longer so it is available to its many receptors. (Why not just pop a couple serotonin capsules, I'll bet you're wondering…it won't work. Can't cross the blood/brain barrier- serotonin is only produced in the brain itself.) When an SSRI actually works, it gives the person taking it the sense of calm confidence and general well-being that Alphas are pretty much born with. But as everybody probably knows, it doesn't always work, and there are several reasons for this.

The first one is so simple it's actually *stupid* - the body makes serotonin from 5-HTP, which is made from tryptophan, and the body can't make tryptophan - it's an essential amino acid, which means you have to eat it. (It's found in largest quantities in high-protein foods like meat and eggs.) An SSRI can't *keep* serotonin in the brain if serotonin is not being *produced* in the first place. Duhhh.

It's also worth knowing that very little of the tryptophan you eat is converted to serotonin on a *good* day, and even less when you are under stress. Tryptophan goes first to the liver, where a lot of it is converted to *kynurenine*, a powerful muscle stimulant - when the system is kicked into 'stress mode' by a perceived threat, cortisol causes even *more* tryptophan to be converted to kynurenine as part of the flight-or-fight response, which makes even *less* available for the production of 5-HTP, which is what the brain needs to make serotonin.

This actually makes good biochemical sense if you think about how old the serotonin system is… if you've got a saber-toothed tiger on your tail, you really don't need to feel GOOD about yourself right then - you need immediate muscle response so you can boogie on out of there ASAP. It makes a lot less sense if you're sitting at your desk in front of a computer screen.

The ingestion of carbohydrates actually helps facilitate the ability of tryptophan to make it into the brain, which explains why everybody feels so mellow after Thanksgiving dinner - turkey is one of the world's great sources of tryptophan, and the rest of the dinner is pretty much carbohydrates. (That's also why a lot of people crave carbohydrates when stressed, just for the record...the body is trying to produce more serotonin. When serotonin levels in the brain are high, the desire for carbs goes way down.)

And research has shown that a low-protein, low-cholesterol diet will actually cause serotonin levels to fall, and anxiety and aggression levels to rise correspondingly. So clearly nutrition matters when it comes to serotonin levels, which probably explains why I've never, *ever,* met a high-PSP male who was a vegetarian - they are, to a man, "red meat-and-potatoes" kind of guys, and red meat-and-potatoes is the simplest recipe for serotonin production. (And, of course, a lot of high-status males are hunters, which is pretty incompatible with a vegan lifestyle...)

After that it gets a little more complicated.

Some of us, it appears, are more efficient at producing 5-HT than others, even given the same raw material (tryptophan) to work with.

As researchers at Duke found out, there are at least two variations on the TPH2 gene, which contains the recipe for the enzyme that regulates 5-HT production. A fair number of people appear to be carrying a gene mutation that causes them to produce maybe 50-80% less serotonin than people who don't carry it and it's pretty clear from Duke's research that this gene puts its lucky owner at risk for clinical depression. People with this gene mutation were also least likely to respond to SSRIs, not surprisingly.

Besides the genes that are responsible for more or less serotonin *production,* there appear to be mutations in the 5-HT *receptor* genes as well. Two of these genes have been studied fairly extensively by producing what are called "knockout" mice. (In order to find out what a gene's function actually *is,* researchers genetically engineer mice with that particular gene disabled, or "knocked out", and look at the differences between them and "wild type" mice, with normal gene function.) So what did they find?

Some Very Interesting Stuff. Knocking out one (a receptor gene called 5-HT1B) produced abnormal territorial aggression along with a high attraction to - and tolerance for - alcohol. (None of these behaviors were found in wild-type mice, but God knows they are common enough in humans...) A knockout of the other receptor they looked at (5-HT2C) led to obesity, caused entirely by an inability to control appetite rather than a metabolic disturbance. These knockout mice were chronic overeaters - again, not a trait found in wild-type mice, but probably reflective of current US obesity rates. And that's only two of at least *14 different 5-HT receptors identified to date.*

In other words, how one responds to a deficiency in serotonin is largely dependent on one's personal hard-wiring. (This 'hard-wiring' is actually the number and distribution of, and variations in, the 5-HT receptors one has. All of which is largely determined by genes.)

In addition to genetics and nutrition, the research on the 5-HT1B receptor touches on another important factor that affects serotonin (as well as several other neurotransmitters and hormones), and that is *ethanol* - aka grain alcohol - the key ingredient in beer, wine, and distilled spirits.

You probably already know that, for better and/or worse, alcohol consumption affects a significant aspect of human social activity, and also that there are genetic factors involved. About a gazillion studies of twins (involving twins raised by their natural parents and those raised by adoptive parents) have proven that alcohol abuse has high heritability, which really doesn't surprise anyone I know.

But what you probably *don't* know is that by virtue of alcohol's biochemical action on various hormones and neurotransmitters, it is also a key player in male pack order.

And not just in humans. In every species studied, those animals which are most highly attracted to alcohol (and not surprisingly most likely to abuse it) carry significantly lower baseline levels of serotonin than those who are not. (Gee, maybe it's got something to do with that 5-HT1B receptor?)

The simple fact is that alcohol temporarily raises 5-HT levels in the brain, which those genetically predisposed to low levels have probably figured out, and then causes them to fall even lower, which they obviously *haven't* figured out. (Biochemically, ethanol blocks the conversion of tryptophan into 5-HTP in the liver.)

One of the most fascinating studies done on alcohol, pack status, and serotonin has been going on for over thirty years on the island of St Kitts, home to some 40,000 vervet monkeys who over the last few centuries have developed a particular fondness for rum, which is produced in quantity on the island.

The notion that man is the only creature who finds merit in getting shit-faced is an absurdly speciest one, by the way - it is absolutely ASTOUNDING how many animals will deliberately choose to ingest both fermented and hallucinogenic plant matter entirely on their own in the wild - it would appear that the desire to tinker with one's inherent brain chemistry is hardly unique to humans...but, as it turns out, almost nothing IS.

Led by two researchers from McGill University to study both the behavioral and genetic roots of alcohol abuse, highly controlled experiments on the rum-drinking vervet population there has revealed a lot of interesting stuff.

Like their human cousins, most of the vervets are pretty much "social drinkers"- although there are variations in the amount of alcohol consumed, most prefer their alcohol mixed with water or juice (not surprisingly, it is generally the females who prefer their drinks sweetened), they rarely drink alone or before noon, and they rarely drink to excess, even when alcohol is readily available. (In short, they exhibit a reasonable degree of *impulse control*.)

These monkeys exhibit all the same alcohol-induced behavior variations that people do - some turn into comedians, some become belligerent, and some turn into regular lounge lizards, hitting on all the females. In other words, a troop of vervet monkeys with access to rum pretty much resembles your average human cocktail party. These social drinkers represent about 80% of the vervet population, along with a few teetotalers thrown in for good measure.

The other 20% are classified as "abusive" rather than "social" drinkers. These monkeys prefer their liquor straight, rather than mixed with water or juice. Whenever alcohol is available, they drink it - even in the morning, or when they are alone. And they consume it steadily, drinking until they fall asleep or pass out, whichever comes first. The next day they get up and do the same thing all over again. *In short, they exhibit little or no impulse control.* And these are the animals with the lowest baseline serotonin levels, and the lowest pack status. (They are also statistically more likely to be males.)

The Alpha male vervets, who not surprisingly have the *highest* serotonin levels, are decidedly NOT found in the abusive 'binge-drinking' group, although a lot of the Alphas apparently are not teetotalers, either. *(Maybe when you've got a boatload of serotonin - and impulse control - to begin with, you can neurologically "afford" to reduce it some without ending up with a lampshade on your head or facedown in the gutter...?)*

One of the most interesting phenomena observed, from a pack status point of view, is that the Alpha animals will literally 'cut off' the alcohol supply by pouring out the rum when they decide the low-ranking pack members have had enough, which reflects altruism, Alpha-style. (No doubt if the drunks possessed car keys they'd confiscate them as well...)

What all this tells us, in a nutshell, is that these gene variations affecting serotonin (and alcohol consumption) are clearly significant in determining pack status. And, although environmental deprivation can certainly alter their expression (peer-raised vervets tend to carry lower serotonin levels than those raised by their mothers) it's pretty obvious that the genes themselves are inherited. Leadership and impulse control, like depression and alcoholism, tends to run in families.

Vasopressin (AVP)

Beware the young and healthy guy who has to get up two or three times in the middle of the night to pee - *you might as well kick him to the curb right now, because sooner or later, he's gonna cheat on you, and you can take that to the bank.*

The reason for this is a little-known hormone called vasopressin (AVP for short), and the more you know about it, the better off you'll be...trust me. A hormone long-known for its role in kidney function, where it's responsible for the concentration of urine (which is why some guys can go literally forever without peeing), AVP more recently was discovered to have an important role in the brain as well.

Actually, *important* doesn't begin to cover it. We're talking about **THE COMMITMENT GENE**, here...the holy grail of all sane women.

The story starts with the prairie vole, an obscure little wild mouse that no one would really give a rat's ass about **except that they are completely and totally monogamous**, which is even rarer in rodents than in men.

I really need to point out here that this observation was first brought to light by...a woman. Figures.

The prairie vole chooses a mate, spends one entire night having wild mouse sex (we're talking maybe *30 or 40 times* here), after which they are bonded for life. In fact, should his mouse wife meet an untimely end, the male prairie vole will most likely spend the rest of his life celibate. Bless his little heart!

His first cousin, the montane vole, on the other hand, is typically promiscuous. Like the worst date you've ever been on, the montane vole mates quickly (and generally only once) with whoever is handiest and then abandons her to raise the resulting offspring alone. In fact, should he run into her again, he's unlikely to even recognize her. (A total jerk, in other words. The animal kingdom is full of 'em.)

What's odd is that the prairie vole and the montane vole (who maybe only ten people on the planet can tell apart by just looking at them) are almost identical genetically as well...Almost.

The only difference genetically between the monogamous prairie vole and the promiscuous montane vole is in the vasopressin receptors in the brain. Although the AVP receptors themselves are the same in both species, there are *major* differences in the number and distribution of them.

This *(try to stay with me here, because this is very important stuff!!)* is because there is a difference in the actual gene that *produces* the receptors - the prairie vole has an extra chunk of DNA in the "promoter switch" upstream to the receptor gene, while the montane vole does not. (This "insertion" varies in length among wild prairie voles, from 350 to 550 letters, but apparently no one's determined if the mice with the longest chunks are the most faithful, which I'd be willing to put a couple of bucks on, myself...) This variation apparently determines the number of AVP receptors each vole has, and where the receptors are going to be located.

Turns out that is the only difference between the two species.

Now, sex causes vasopressin to be released into the male brain, where it acts as a neurotransmitter. In the monogamous voles, the receptors are located in the same parts of the brain where addictive drugs act - the so-called "reward" or "pleasure" regions.

The male prairie vole actually becomes addicted to his mate. I love it.

Now, these guys didn't get PhDs because they were *stupid* - of *course* they looked at people to see if the same genes were there, too. (Being good scientists, they also compared other monogamous species, including primates, with their promiscuous cousins for good measure, found the same differences in the receptor gene, and even made a transgenic mouse to see if they were right. They were.)

Turns out that sex causes vasopressin to be produced in the *human* brain as well. And the vasopressin receptors, which are also exactly the same, are found in the exact same parts of the brain as they are in...ta da...

the monogamous prairie vole.

It *also* turns out that human males have the same "monogamy insertion" on their promoter that the prairie vole has and, also like the prairie vole, *there are significant variations in the length of it from one guy to another...* Like there's a woman on this earth who would find that surprising.

So, yes Virginia, it looks very much as if there is a commitment gene, although you'll never get anyone with a PhD to come out and actually put that in print. (They're probably afraid women will start demanding a gene test for it prior to walking down the aisle, or even getting into *bed* if they've got any brains at all...)

But what this *also* tells us is that, although God knows it often doesn't seem like it, *ours really is basically a monogamous species.* This is consistent with the "testicular size" theory, which I think I first read about in one of Matt Ridley's books and which I've always personally liked.

Testicular size theory? OK, OK...here it is - in a nutshell, so to speak:

The bigger the testicles, the more promiscuous the male. For example, the average guy chimp, among the most highly promiscuous of primates, has testicles roughly *three times* the size of your average human guy's, when adjusted for body size. "Balls like a Brahma bull" is not just an idle expression, either - your average bull has a lot of cows to inseminate even on a slow day.

This theory, which is pretty well-accepted among the sort of people who actually study this stuff for a living, (both in evolutionary biology and in practical animal husbandry) applies to different species, though, and I have no idea if it holds for humans, although I strongly suspect it does, based entirely on anecdotal evidence provided by the women I asked, when they stopped laughing long enough to think about various men they've known and their respective anatomical differences. (Hey, do your own survey if you don't believe me... but my advice is to stick with asking women - men seem a little reticent about discussing the size of their testicles and whether or not they cheat on their wives, I found....)

Testicular size notwithstanding, if ours was a truly promiscuous species, the most successful and powerful males would have *harems,* and last time I looked, Bill Gates and Warren Buffet, both of whom have all the earmarks of Alphas, have each claimed only one wife apiece, although both could probably afford several more...

The truth is, although harems have certainly existed in isolated groups throughout history, they've simply never caught on with the general population - in fact, we tend to view monogamy as a measure of a man's character, as poor Bill Clinton found out the hard way. No pun intended.

So anyhow, the "vasopressin connection" seems to hold for all monogamous species they've looked at so far, and probably represents some pretty good science. The "getting up to go the bathroom connection", on the other hand, is entirely anecdotal and once again based entirely on a loose survey I did of women who've been married to both cheating bastards and faithful partners, but to date it's running 100% accurate as a predictor, so as far as I'm concerned, you can use it with a fair amount of confidence.

My favorite piece of anecdotal evidence, by the way, is the absolutely legendary ability of our most famously monogamous president, Jimmy Carter, to make it through interminable summit meetings without ever having to excuse himself to go to the bathroom. I mean, think about it - this president's bladder control was so impressive people have actually COMMENTED on it in print. Lucky for Rosalynn.

The other fact that leads me to believe I'm right is that there is a synthetic version of vasopressin available as a nasal spray which has been used successfully for years in the treatment of...........I'm not making this up......... *bed-wetting.*

So, would getting hold of this stuff (it's available online under the trade name Desmopressin) and squirting it up the nose of your average no-good cheating hound dog before spending the night with him cause him to become less likely to stray afterwards? I actually have *no idea*, sorry - as far as I know, no one's actually tried it as a treatment for promiscuity, and it would be completely and totally irresponsible of me to suggest it.

Now, in the human world, monogamy is definitely related to pack order and, as a group, Alphas are the winners here, hands-down. The same is true of wolves, where generally the Alpha wolf breeds only with highest-ranking female in the pack. Like the prairie vole,

Alphas in these species are both psychologically and physically addicted to their mates - once that pair-bond is formed, they're stuck for life. (For better or worse, as the old saying goes.)

Now, being guys (which of course makes even the best of them, by definition, dumber than prairie voles) this does not mean these males might not want to cheat (what poor Jimmy Carter referred to as a man "lusting in his heart" in his politically unfortunate Playboy interview back in the 70s), it just means that if they *do* actually try lusting anywhere *except* in their hearts, *they simply can't get it up...* no doubt a humiliating experience they most likely will not wish to repeat.

This does not mean to imply that monogamy is the sole province of Alphas, or that there aren't monogamous males to be found in all of the other PSPs, because in spite of the unfortunate variations in the length of that repeat, ours is a genetically monogamous species, but there is really no PSP other than Alpha that I know of for which monogamy is an actual *qualification*. (Hey, maybe they have the longest repeats, how should I know...or maybe they just have the best impulse control. Anyway, somebody should fund a study on it...)

So that's pretty much all you need to know about vasopressin, except possibly for the fact that high levels of vasopressin will cause males to become aggressive toward other males (the biological basis for male jealousy), and that its production is effectively blocked by two chemical substances - our old friend ethanol, and surprisingly, caffeine.

The clear take-home message here is that if a guy got genetically short-changed in the monogamy department to begin with, hanging around coffeehouses or knocking a few back after work at the neighborhood pub probably isn't going to improve his track record any...

In terms of practical genetics, it's also worth noting that although monogamy appears to be alive and well in the wolf, in the domestic dog the trait has been deliberately selected *against* by breeders. A handsome stud dog who will willingly mate with only one female on the planet is not likely be a popular fellow in the world of show dogs, where everybody wants a piece of his DNA to improve their line.

Because of this, the gene for *promiscuity* has actually been selected for in dogs over the years, resulting in the fact that the average domestic dog, far from being monogamous like his cousin the wolf, will now attempt to screw anything, including a cat or a chair leg, given the opportunity. (And, not coincidentally, a lot of domestic dogs have pretty big testicles for their size, if you stop to think about it. And most male dogs pee constantly. So there.)

Which all suggests to me that the "monogamy gene" is pretty easily lost in a species and it's up to us as women to see that it's not lost in ours. As experienced dog breeders know all too well, once you've lost a desirable gene in your line, it's damn hard to get it back.

Prolactin (PRL)

If the gene responsible for generous distribution of vasopressin receptors is the 'commitment' gene, then surely the gene responsible for the production of prolactin must be the 'nice' gene - what an absolute *sweetheart* of a hormone this is!

Prolactin, of course, is the hormone responsible for breast development and lactation in women. In both sexes, however, it also acts as a neurotransmitter in the brain, where it also facilitates care of the young, albeit a little less directly than in the production of milk. (This makes exquisite sense, since prolactin is found in animals other than mammals - like for instance birds, who don't produce milk but obviously still need to feed their young, as well as build nests and sit on eggs...raising baby birds is a tremendous amount of work.)

Species in which males carry the highest prolactin levels after mating are the ones in which males share responsibility for nest-building and rearing of the young. In species like penguins, where each male makes a significant individual investment in the rearing of his own young, male prolactin levels are higher than they are in species like wolves, where rearing of the young is a responsibility shared by the entire pack. In fact, in some species, females are actually hard-wired to instinctively choose mates based upon their aptitude for nest-building and feeding of the young rather than their physical superiority or leadership ability. (We've traditionally not been one of them, unfortunately...)

Prolactin levels in males, like serotonin, will vary based on circumstance - in the wild, they tend to be lowest during the mating season, when testosterone is highest, and they tend to rise after mating, when testosterone levels fall. (This is actually true in people, too.) The higher the prolactin level, and the lower the testosterone, the less likely a male is to get into fights with other males and court other females, and the more likely he is to take an active role in child rearing and to have a greater interest in all things domestic - in humans, the simple act of holding an infant has been shown to raise a man's prolactin levels, in fact.

But just like everything else in the world if some is good, more is not necessarily better; at least not when it comes to baseline levels. As with serotonin, it's the *baseline* levels of PRL that are significant in pack order. And baseline levels vary considerably. Dominant males are generally low in prolactin, which is why the house can fall down around them before they get around to doing anything about it, while less dominant males, who carry higher baseline levels, are actually helpful in the domestic department as a rule.

Differences in prolactin levels also explain why some men are naturally good with babies while others can't ever seem to get the hang of carrying one with one arm no matter how hard they try, much less changing an actual *diaper* without having it fall off a couple minutes later. As with vasopressin, a smart woman doesn't need a blood panel to gauge a man's prolactin level - there are several easier ways to determine it should she be interested in doing so:

In general, the higher the baseline prolactin level, the nicer the guy, the sweeter his smile, and often the less ...umm... *well-endowed* he is apt to be. (The good news is that at least two of the three can actually be determined in a restaurant on the first date without being unceremoniously chucked out by the maitre'd.)

The reason we know this (not the part about being chucked out of the restaurant, I just made that up) is because of a medical condition known as Hyperprolactinemia, a condition in which baseline prolactin levels are abnormally high. Because PRL mediates the effects of testosterone (and vice-versa), hyperprolactinemic men are singularly lacking in annoying male aggression, and are often excessively, genuinely *nice*. (The most severely affected are positive *doormats*.) Like all low-testosterone men, they have crinkles around their eyes, and sweet smiles that turn up at the corners. They are also often characterized by what the medical profession calls hypogonadism, which is a nice way of saying they have smaller-than-average penises and testicles, and they often suffer from impotence problems.

Hyperprolactemia can have many causes - it can be the result of a tumor on the pituitary gland, it can be a side effect of many common prescription drugs, which raise prolactin levels, or it can be genetic.

A friend of mine remembers the possibly NICEST guy she ever dated, who explained to her well before they ever ended up in bed that all the men in his family had unusually small penises. (That actually turned out an understatement…MICROSCOPIC would probably have been a better description, according to her.)

Now, of course, she realizes that all the men in his family probably suffered from an hereditary form of Hyperprolactinemia, which also explains his overall niceness and sweet smile. She figures she probably should have married him - he, no doubt, made some smart girl a wonderful husband, microscopic penis notwithstanding.

Because prolactin levels can be accurately measured in the blood, and prolactin is a major contributor to male impotence, and we all know who runs the research world, it should come as no surprise that there's actually a fair amount of serious scientific research that's been done here. *And a lot of it is stuff women really need to know.*

PRL is normally released in what is referred to as a 'prolactin surge' immediately after orgasm (it's also worth knowing that orgasm with a sexual partner will release 400% more prolactin - *that's not a typo* - than an orgasm brought about by masturbation, although I keep wondering where they got the volunteers for that study) and is responsible for the "male refractory period", which is the down-time immediately after orgasm when an erection is pretty much a physical impossibility.

In the brain, prolactin blocks the further release of dopamine (the neurotransmitter responsible for arousal and for orgasm itself) and produces the feeling of sexual satiation. This feeling of satisfaction, along with the physical inability to achieve erection, lasts until prolactin levels return to normal - about an hour on average across the board, although it varies considerably. Hyperprolactinemic men are more or less permanently stuck in the refractory period - their baseline prolactin levels are more like those found immediately after orgasm, which is probably why they are so nice, come to think about it...

Another study (where do they *find* these volunteers???) came up with an average refractory time of around 19 minutes for a group of healthy normal 26-year-old males, except for one extraordinary subject, *who had absolutely no refractory period, and could achieve a second erection and subsequent orgasm (with ejaculation) within two minutes of the previous one.*

Turned out this fellow produced no 'prolactin surge' at all - his levels stayed the same no matter what. And although I'm sure all the girls in the lab were scrambling for this guy's phone number, the truth is, he'd be very poor husband material - with that pitiful PRL response, odds are he'd never be able to change a damn light bulb. Or a diaper.

So anyhow, in the wild, the rise in prolactin levels after mating is responsible for what is called "nesting behavior". In humans, this nesting behavior translates to infant and child care, housekeeping, home-maintenance, and home-improvement, which we all know some men are way better at than others.

The PSP that probably most reliably displays these high-prolactin traits is the Beta, which explains why a lot of women (especially those who find having sex several

times a day with a guy who won't help around the house annoying) think they make the best husbands.

On the other hand, both my husband and my son-in-law, otherwise intelligent men, whose personal prolactin levels probably hover somewhere between pitiful and non-existent on a good day, have concluded through some bizarre leap of logic that this research all points unequivocally to the fact that...

HOME-IMPROVEMENT ACTUALLY CAUSES IMPOTENCE...

which they have both suspected all along, and they think Home Depot should post warning signs on their doors. Sigh.

Since male prolactin levels tend to rise with age, the refractory time normally gets longer as men get older. By middle age, the refractory period after orgasm for a fairly healthy man can actually last for days rather than nineteen minutes - a fact of life that seems to bother men a whole lot more than it bothers women and, no doubt, accounts for the popularity of Viagra. Which is probably why a lot of guys help more around the house as they mature, and are often better husbands and fathers the second time around. (Alphas as a group seem to be pretty immune to this aging thing, by all accounts. I suspect they are born with so little prolactin to start with, they'd have to be well over *ninety* before they reached levels that improved their nest-building instincts much.)

Dopamine (DA)

I can't get no satisfaction...
  cause I try... and I try...and I try...and I try.
    The Rolling Stones, 1965

Dopamine is one of the most-studied and least-understood of the neurotransmitters. It is synthesized in the body in a series of steps from the amino acid tyrosine and is utilized in several parts of the brain. A crucial part of the basal ganglia motor loop, it is responsible for fluidity of movement - Parkinson's disease results from an insufficiency of dopamine caused by the death of DA neurons in the nigrostriatal pathway.

Dopamine is critical to rational thought - Schizophrenia involves what is basically a little-understood screw-up in the DA pathway in the prefrontal cortex and is characterized by irrational thought patterns. It is also an integral player in the brain's "reward system"- dopamine largely regulates desire, arousal, and pleasure, all functions of the *limbic* (or emotional) brain, which is not exactly where higher "executive brain function" takes place.

Dopamine also functions as a neurohormone, preventing the constant release of the hormone prolactin, with which it maintains what appears at first to be a fairly adversarial relationship. The largest single natural release of dopamine the body can produce on its own occurs at the precise moment of orgasm (which pretty much tells you everything you need to know about dopamine!), after which point prolactin takes over - remember the prolactin surge? DA is responsible for feeling arousal and pleasure, and PRL for feeling satiation, or satisfaction, immediately thereafter.

If prolactin is the Nice Boy of the hormone world, then dopamine is by definition the Bad Boy...without prolactin he'd be in serious trouble all the time - it appears that without prolactin, dopamine simply doesn't know when to quit. Prolactin and dopamine really work pretty well together.

Research has shown that the same DA levels experienced with orgasm can be attained artificially with drugs like cocaine and heroin (which explains a lot about their appeal) - the only problem is, it's not followed by a natural PRL surge, so when the dopamine levels fall, there's no feeling of satiation, which provides a sort of natural brake for the body's "pleasure system". Rats trained to push a lever to receive an injection of dopamine will just keep pushing that lever over and over, without sleeping, eating, or drinking, until they fall over. (I'm not sure if anyone has actually tried following the dopamine injection with a prolactin injection, but it would probably be an interesting experiment - my guess is, those rats would smile, roll over, fall asleep for a while and then wake up hungry, but what do I know?)

Dopamine is implicated in male pack order primarily because of one of its many receptors - DRD4, which is located on human chromosome 11, to be exact. Variations on this single gene appear largely responsible for two phenomena which directly affect pack status - *altruism* and *risk-taking*.

Altruism

Altruism, believe it or not, is hardly unique to humans - it's a trait found in many social animals. Altruism, in short, is a 'pro-social' behavior - putting the good of other pack members above self-interest. In most social animals, it's the high-status PSPs and the Sentinels who are most likely to display altruism automatically - they are simply hard-wired to help other pack members, even those who are neither their mates nor their offspring.

But why?

Evolutionary biologists have been interested in the genetic basis for altruism since the sixties, when they began studying the phenomenon in many species. They were puzzled by the continued existence of what was clearly a gene that did not directly benefit individual survival.

This has caused me to conclude that most evolutionary biologists are complete idiots.

Altruism still exists because in social species, it helps to ensure *the survival of the entire species in the long run.* Duhhh. (I'm guessing, like most scientists, few evolutionary biologists have ever served in the military, because those guys have understood this concept forever - it's what Basic Training is all about.)

Solitary animals, like bears, are rarely altruistic - there is simply no *need* for them to be altruistic. Their individual survival does not depend on the survival of other bears, since they don't hunt in packs, or rely on numbers for protection from predators. Bears can be entirely self-centered and self-absorbed and the species will still do just fine.

This pro-social behavior we call altruism has been linked to a specific short stretch of DNA in the D4DR receptor gene that actually *promotes* dopamine release. The simple act of doing something that benefits someone else, even if there is no one around to witness it, gives the altruist a release of dopamine - probably not as much as with an actual orgasm, but certainly enough to incline him to do it again sometime.

Once you get the release of dopamine, prolactin kicks in, and so the rush of pleasure is followed by a feeling of satisfaction. Altruists, in other words, are hard-wired to experience both pleasure and satisfaction simply by helping others, and so are motivated by a release of dopamine to do it from a very early age.

The least complicated form of altruism is what evolutionary biologists refer to as "reciprocal altruism", and it's best characterized by a single line that anyone who's ever lived in the northern half of the United States is familiar with - namely:

"*You need a jump, there?*"

In the north, any normal person will stop, haul the jumper cables out of the trunk, and jump-start any perfect stranger's dead car battery without a second thought. Nor will they expect more than a simple thanks for doing so.

In fact, in most cases, the proper Winter Jump Etiquette calls for both parties to grin at each other once they hear the engine turn over, return the cables to the appropriate trunk, and both drive off with a wave. (If it's too cold to grin safely without causing your teeth to freeze, an "OK" sign with the thumb and forefinger is considered an acceptable alternative.) Excessive conversation, effusive thanks, or offers of cash are all indications that a guy's Not From Here.

This sort of casual altruism is summed up by the old adage "what goes around comes around", since anyone with more than three functioning brain cells who attempts to actually operate a motor vehicle when it's *twenty-two below zero* knows that sooner or later they will be in the same boat, and there's no sense in tempting Karma in that regard.

This type of altruism is simple *pro-social behavior* at its best, and everyone benefits. Simple reciprocal altruism is the basis for coalition building in all social species, and is also the basis for good foreign relations policy. It also makes us feel pretty good about ourselves. (When we were kids, it was called the Golden Rule, *everyone* practiced it, and the world was, frankly, a nicer place.)

Now, altruism comes in several other flavors, and each one is most likely determined by levels of the other hormones that influence the various PSPs.

High-serotonin altruism is rarely of the warm and fuzzy variety - it's the result of a cool rational assessment of what's best for the survival of the entire pack, (as opposed to any particular individuals within it, including oneself), and a willingness to take the heat for the resulting decision. It's the hallmark of real leadership and, like monogamy, it's a requirement of the Alpha PSP.

The quintessential example of this high-serotonin altruism is without a doubt the decision made single-handedly by Presi-

dent Harry Truman back in 1942 to send the Enola Gay and her ghastly payload to destroy the Japanese city of Hiroshima when Hirohito simply refused to surrender to Allied forces after the fall of the Third Reich...despite repeated threats by the Allies that his refusal to do so would result in that country's destruction.

After examining all possibilities, including a wholesale invasion of Japan, Truman decided that a demonstration of the destructive capability of these new and terrible weapons was the fastest way to end the war and to ultimately save human lives on both sides, which it did - Japan surrendered within the week, finally ending World War II. And once that extremely difficult decision was made, Harry Truman swore he never lost a moment's sleep over it. Truman, who kept a sign in the Oval Office that read THE BUCK STOPS HERE, was without question an Alpha.

Hirohito, unfortunately for the residents of Hiroshima and Nagasaki, was not. A Leglifter to the end, this idiot refused to surrender unconditionally after being warned of, and then witnessing the total instantaneous destruction of Hiroshima and, ONCE AGAIN ignoring the warning, witnessed the total and instantaneous destruction of Nagasaki three days later, after which point he finally gave up. (Damn good thing, too, because unbeknownst to him, Truman had played his whole hand and was at that point completely out of nukes - he'd have had to resort to firebombing, the less spectacular but equally effective method by which both sides had previously demolished perfectly good cities along with their inhabitants. War is stupid.) Like any real Alpha, Harry Truman did what he had to do and took the heat for it. This is, after all, the man who coined the phrase "If you can't stand the heat, get out of the kitchen." High-serotonin altruism at its best. And Harry, bless his heart, was totally addicted to Bess.

High-oxytocin altruism, on the other hand, is motivated primarily by compassion (empathy) for one's fellow man, especially those less fortunate than oneself, and is the most easily recognized. It is often motivated by an emotional (rather than an intellectual) assessment of given situation and so is directed by the limbic brain rather than the prefrontal cortex. Most commonly exhibited by people like Mother Teresa and those who vote a straight Democratic ticket, it's the hallmark of Retrievers, who are invariably among the kindest of men.

High-testosterone altruism generally results in feats of heroism, and tends to be of the spectacular variety - these are the guys who will risk their own lives to save someone else's without a moment's thought. (It's the "without a moment's thought" part that clues us to the presence of testosterone - action without undue reflection is pretty much the signature of T.) This form of heroic altruism is generally practiced by Junkyard dogs, who will often make a career of it, by Leglifters, and by Alphas and Retrievers generally as an option of last resort. Among high-testosterone males, altruism can start to look a lot like a competitive sport.

The final, and probably the least-recognized, form of altruism is *high-cortisol altruism*. These are the guys, and they exist in many species, who will risk all to warn the rest of the pack of imminent danger. Extremely pro-social behavior, it's primarily found in the ranks of the Sentinels, and like high-testosterone altruism, it's often their actual job. Investigative and combat journalism both fall into this category.

There's another form of "altruism" that bears mentioning, which is not really altruism at all, and that's what is generally known as *Philanthropy.* (In this context, it is always spelled with a capital P.) Unlike true altruists, who get a dopamine release from the behavior itself, the Philanthropist derives satisfaction only from the recognition of the behavior by others, which in turn raises his status within the group. These guys will never do anything that benefits someone else unless they get press for it.

'Altruism' of this sort is really a pretty sophisticated form of leg-lifting, and is mostly practiced by LegLifters and Lone Wolves.

Good news for the planet: It's been estimated that probably two-thirds of the population worldwide carries at least one copy of a short repeat on the D4DR receptor gene, which inclines them to altruism of one sort or another. This really isn't all that surprising - as with all pack animals, the widespread distribution of this gene variation is pretty much necessary to long-term survival of *homo sapiens* as a species.

Novelty-Seeking and Risk-Taking

Oddly, a long repeat on that same DRD4 receptor gene is associated with another personality trait entirely - novelty-seeking. It is alternately referred to as the "risk-taking" or "thrill-seeking" gene, but neither of those are particularly accurate, as each of those traits requires a particular brain chemistry in addition to the novelty-seeking gene itself.

People with this variation have a harder time getting a dopamine release, and without it, there is no surge of prolactin, and hence - no satisfaction. So these people will do things normal people wouldn't think of doing, from babyhood on, in search of novel stimuli.

The incidence of this trait varies from country to country (not surprisingly, it's higher in the US than many other countries), but if you want to see a bunch of them standing all in one place, just visit any amusement park and take a look at the people standing in line, positively panting, to get on roller coasters with names like the Screaming Vomit, or the Heart Attack. These people actually represent a subgroup - they are the very high-testosterone 'thrill-seekers', every one of them - all ages, sizes and shapes, all standing in line for a dopamine rush.

(In fact, a friend of mine who loves them actually told me that for her, the 'roller-coaster rush' is exactly like an orgasm. Egads.) These people are also attracted to 'extreme sports' - in fact, they are attracted to extreme *everything*.

Babies carrying this gene, it has been noted, are more alert than babies who don't carry it. From an early age, they are much more curious, more easily bored, and tend to have less tolerance for mind-numbingly "stupid", repetitive stuff...like schoolwork. (A lot of ADHD people carry this mutation, not surprisingly.)

Now, scientists automatically started looking for this gene in segments of the population suffering from personality disorders and substance-abuse problems (a couple of groups with, no doubt, some serious deficits in their serotonin systems), and failing to find it with the degree of regularity they expected, some have started to question the whole premise of a causative gene-mutation at all.

This is so stupid it boggles the mind, but completely understandable considering...

Scientists, as a group, are among those men *least* likely to carry this mutation. They have, almost to a man, infinite tolerance for stupid repetitive nitnoid tasks, which is how they got PhDs in the first place. And what do they know about the inability to tolerate that which is colossally boring? *These are some of the most boring human beings on the planet, which is why nobody reads their stuff.* So it's entirely understandable that they would expect to find a gene that makes people so very different from themselves primarily among social misfits, criminals, and drug-addicts. Stupid, but understandable.

Common sense should tell us that coupled with high serotonin and a high IQ, "novelty-seekers" are the people who have moved civilization forward over the last 10,000 years. Throw some testosterone in there and a guy would probably sail to the edge of the earth to see if it was maybe round. Or maybe he'd skipper a PT boat in the South Pacific during WWII, write a book called *Profiles in Courage*, get himself elected as the first Irish Catholic President, engage in a pissing contest with Nikita Khrushchev and take the planet to within inches of total nuclear destruction, *win it*, and then get shot in the head because he insisted on riding in an *open convertible* through Dallas, Texas…

If researchers really wanted to find that particular genetic combination in spades within a single successful family, they really ought to start by looking in Hyannis Port.

It is the 'novelty-seeking' gene variant *combined* with high testosterone levels which causes the personality trait we think of as **risk-taking,** because testosterone, by virtue of its own actions on the brain, is a facilitator of risk. Does the fact that these two variations exist on the same gene mean a risk-taker cannot be an altruist? *Not at all.*

Each and every one of us carries *two* genes at each locus, remember? One recipe from each parent. So it's certainly possible to have both gene variations in one's personal genome - they are not mutually exclusive.

Altruism is basically a pro-social behavior, which is about helping others. Risk-taking, or the more accurate 'novelty-seeking', is hardly the opposite of that - the opposite of *pro-social behavior* would be *antisocial behavior* (the province of Fearbiters and Lone Wolves), and there's nothing intrinsically anti-social about novelty-seeking (or even risk-taking) behavior.

In fact, if it weren't for risk-taking altruists, who would make an actual *profession* out of rescuing all the idiots who ignore weather forecasts and end up clinging desperately to tiny overturned sailboats in a hurricane, or buried in an avalanche under six feet of snow on the side of a mountain somewhere?

Now, these search-and-rescue guys (usually high-status PSPs) are very high-testosterone risk-takers, and what they do is very physical, but you can be a lower-testosterone risk-taker just as easily - all risk is not physical by a long shot. Carrying a copy or two of the novelty-seeking gene with average testosterone levels might incline one to day-trading, for example. Lots of risk, which gives them a dopamine release, without jumping out of a perfectly good airplane hoping your chute will open. Playing the stock market, or even internet poker for that matter, both give the same sort of enjoyment from risk-taking that skydiving does. In fact, the existence of this gene is pretty much responsible for the existence of modern Las Vegas.

The PSPs most likely to display real physical risk-taking in spades, though, are Junkyard dogs, with LegLifters probably running a close second. (Both high-testosterone guys, the difference between them is largely a matter of altruism and IQ - the latter group usually carries less of both.) Low-testosterone men with the novelty-seeking gene are probably not risk-takers at all - they just have short attention spans, and flit from one career to another without being very focused. Lone Wolves, *who are totally devoid of altruism*, are also by definition risk-takers. In fact, their inability to release dopamine through any behavior other than total dominance over others is what makes them Lone Wolves.

So for purposes of determining PSP, the importance of dopamine is really in its relationship to pleasure and satisfaction. From a woman's viewpoint, it's worth knowing that some PSPs are pretty easily pleased and satisfied, while for others, through no fault of their own, pleasure and satisfaction are harder to achieve. Not surprisingly, the second group tends to blow through more wives in their lifetime, which it helps to know right out the gate.

Testosterone (T)

If hormones had the power of speech, odds are pretty good that Testosterone's vocabulary would be pretty much limited to:

Ooh-Rah!

Odds are also pretty good that Testosterone would be unsure of how to actually spell it.

I, in fact, wasted much more time than was probably strictly necessary wading through innumerable Jarhead websites (both official and unofficial) trying to ascertain the correct spelling, to no avail. As was helpfully pointed out on one of them, where the battle still rages, this is probably because Marines are not very good at writing things down. (In fact, there often seems to be a direct inverse relationship between T levels and spelling ability...)

For those who might not be aware of it, *Ooh-rah!* is the unofficial battle cry of the Marine Corps. And as every Jarhead knows, it comes not so much from the larynx as from the gut and right up through the diaphragm. Sort of like belching.
It basically means yes.

EXAMPLE:
Marine Sergeant: *Are you Jarheads ready to kick some serious Iraqi ass?*
Marines: **Ooh-rah!**
Marine Sergeant: *I can't HEAR you...*
Marines: **Ooh-rah!!!**
Marine Sergeant: *I STILL can't hear you...*
Marines: **Ooh-rah!!!!**

Now, in all honesty, testosterone has gotten a pretty bad rap in recent years especially among women, who rarely carry enough of it to belt out a good **Ooh-rah!** even were they so inclined. (*The exception here would, of course, be female Ma-*

rines, a particularly tough, high-T group of women for the most part.)

In fact, silly as it may seem, testosterone is perceived as so dangerous by our very own government that it is actually classified as a Schedule III Controlled Substance right along with methamphetamine, and you need a license to produce it even for your own personal use - a Federal Law virtually no one pays any attention to, as far as I can tell. But without testosterone there would be no men and no sex, so it really can't be *all bad.* So let's see what testosterone is responsible for besides facial hair...

Almost everything I know about testosterone, incidentally, I learned from the late James McBride Dabbs, a professor of psychology who spent his entire academic career at Georgia State studying this one hormone. He developed a saliva test for measuring T levels, which allowed him, and innumerable grad students, to look at its effects in a wide segment of the population, both male and female, over the years. He even wrote a great book on the subject that every woman should read - it's called **Heroes, Rogues and Lovers**. *What I didn't learn from James Dabbs, I learned from Dave Barry, who also knows a lot about testosterone, and also wrote a great book on the subject - it's called* **Dave Barry's Complete Guide to Guys**.

Although this is really, *really,* hard to believe, testosterone and estrogen, the two primary sex hormones, are actually almost identical biochemically. Both start out as cholesterol, which is converted by enzymes in the testes, ovaries, and the adrenal glands into testosterone. Testosterone is then converted by the enzyme aromatase - *which removes a single carbon molecule* - into estrogen.

So the entire difference between all that is male and all that is female on this planet comes down to a single molecule of carbon. Who *knew*?

Both sexes produce estrogen and testosterone - the basic difference between men and women is that women produce more estrogen, and men produce *way* more testosterone - on average, about 10 times as much. However (according to James Dabbs anyway) it's also possible to carry high levels of both testosterone *and* estrogen, which is true for both stallions and professional football players, honest to God. (It is also true in rattlesnakes, although I honestly can't imagine why…)

Physically, testosterone is responsible for the qualities we usually think of as masculine - strength, quick muscle response, thicker skin (and skull), and fat carried primarily in the stomach area (the ubiquitous 'beer gut'), where it can be easily converted to energy - all qualities which are advantageous in hunting, competing for available females, and defense of territory. Estrogen, on the other hand, is responsible for those qualities we usually think of as feminine - stamina, strong immune function, and fat storage in the hips and buttocks (where as we all know it's only accessible in times of complete famine) - all of which are advantageous to successfully producing and raising offspring.

But like most other hormones, testosterone acts directly on the brain as well, where is responsible for a whole lot of stuff, *every bit of which is critical to PSP.*

In the brain, testosterone is active primarily in the limbic brain (the hypothalamus, amygdala, and hippocampus) none of which are involved in what neurobiologists call "executive function." (This is probably why there are so few really high-testosterone executives.) As a neurohormone, T is linked to dominance-seeking and sex drive, as well as spatial memory (high-testosterone males have a built-in GPS), and increased focus (which is why most men are incapable of multi-tasking) - all of which, like muscle, are advantageous in hunting, competing for available females, and defending territory. (Are you starting to see a pattern here?)

Testosterone's ability to increase focus, incidentally, is precisely why it is a facilitator of risk, and why it is a component of risk-taking behavior. Testosterone promotes *action*, not reflection.

Now, there's a feeling (especially among men) that if *some* testosterone is good, *more* must be somehow better, but surprisingly, that has not been borne out by research. Although high testosterone levels provided distinct advantages in our hunter-gatherer days (it's that part about hunting, competing for available females and defending territory), in actual fact, men with *average to low T levels* are more successful in the modern world. By and large, they are more likely to have college educations, to have higher-paying careers, and far more likely to describe themselves as "happily married", and more likely to *stay* married, than men with the highest testosterone levels. They also have more patience and smile more.

The dominance-seeking tendencies, as well as the physical energy, that high levels of testosterone provide are advantageous in today's society only when combined with the mediating influences of a high IQ and high serotonin - both have a 'civilizing' effect, and generally allow high-testosterone males to make it through the educational system in spite of their impatience, dislike of inactivity, and their problems with authority. Assuming they can get through high school and college, the energy, aggression, and focus provided by testosterone can be real attributes in certain professions. (Defense attorneys, for example, have higher T levels than other lawyers - in fact, their levels are similar to the average construction worker's.) And without high-testosterone men, our Armed Forces would be in serious trouble, from the top on down. Of course, altruism helps here, too - all that muscle and energy is better when harnessed for the good of the pack than for sheer self-interest.

Of course testosterone levels affect pack order a lot, though not the way most people expect. To begin with, there's a big difference between *dominance,* which is a position, and *domi-*

nance-seeking, which is the personality trait associated with high testosterone levels in both men and women. (Write that down somewhere.)

The dominant (ie. highest-ranking) male in a pack may not necessarily be the male with the strongest dominance-seeking tendencies - in fact, in many species, including ours, odds are pretty good he's not. (This is borne out by the fact that with few notable exceptions, men with the highest T levels are rarely the most successful in modern society, where the impulse control provided by high serotonin levels will generally get you farther.)

Testosterone drives the urge to dominate, but without the intelligence and/or social skills needed to achieve and maintain a position of dominance in anything but the most primitive society, the result is likely to be frustration and often resulting aggression on the dominance-seeker's part.

Every criminologist worth his salt knows that the high testosterone/low serotonin/low IQ "cocktail" that some men display is a sure-fire recipe for incarceration. Our maximum security prisons are full of 'em. (Non-violent criminals tend to have significantly lower T levels than the most violent ones.) High testosterone and low serotonin combined with both high cortisol and noradrenaline levels generally produces a Fearbiter.

If they are bright and have reasonable social skills, these guys can often get surprisingly far in life before they ultimately self-destruct...Tricky Dick, who sported a permanent 5 o'clock shadow, a bad case of paranoia, and a nasty temper, was a case in point - as far as I know, the only Fearbiter to actually occupy the Oval Office. It's also probably significant that he was the only occupant of that office to self-destruct before he could finish out his second term.

High testosterone and a *high* IQ combined with very low serotonin levels and no altruism whatsoever is probably the basic biochemical profile of your garden-variety serial killer. (It's a very bad combination, and defines the Lone Wolf.)

On the other hand, pro-social guys with high testosterone, *high* serotonin levels, and an IQ that's less than Mensa-level will generally do OK for themselves - they dominate the construction fields, most professional sports, and believe it or not, Broadway and Hollywood. (Somewhat surprisingly, professional actors were found to have the highest testosterone levels of any occupational group tested except pro football players.) These are the guys that probably fix your transmission, your plumbing and, with a little luck and some good political connections, they can even become President.

And the sex drive provided by testosterone? Again, if some is good, more is not necessarily better - it can actually be a social liability at extremely high levels (generally when combined with low impulse control), which is why some more enlightened countries allow voluntary castration for repeat sexual offenders.

A less drastic but equally effective approach to the problem of protecting society against repeat sexual offenders (and there really isn't any other kind because these guys clearly have some biochemical glitches they can't control) might be the judicious administration of serotonin-enhancing drugs combined with an industrial -strength prolactin implant, but to the best of my knowledge this solution hasn't yet occurred to anybody but me...

Actually, it has been determined that there is no measurable difference seen in either sex drive or sexual performance until testosterone levels are really pretty pathologically low, which produces other health issues as well - the "normal" range for this hormone is pretty wide in both sexes. Otherwise healthy men with T levels that are average or even below average perform just as well sexually as those on the high end of the curve. (This makes sense if you think about it - healthy women, who carry on average *ten times less testosterone than men*, still have a sex drive...Duhhh.) And they're easier to live with, and statistically way more likely to stay married. *In fact*, if anyone ever did a study on it, I'll bet they'd find that guys with average and low-average T levels actually get laid more...let's face it, getting bonked on the head with a club and dragged by the hair back to the cave just doesn't have the appeal for most women that it maybe once had.

OK, so what *about* facial hair? (We might as well leave by the same door we came in through...) Easy. It's simply a *display of testosterone*. Testosterone is a biologically expensive hormone, produced at the expense of both stamina and immune function. In earlier days, facial hair provided an easily-read signal to females that this is indeed a male who could 'afford' it, precisely like the tail plumage on a peacock or the rack on an elk - a biological indicator of virility. To other males, of course, it's a subtle and unspoken threat.

That, incidentally, is why you'll never see a clean-shaven pirate.

Oxytocin (OT)

Oxytocin is a mammalian hormone responsible for uterine contractions and milk letdown, which might make one intelligently wonder what it has to do with male pack order. Not surprisingly, oxytocin is found at highest levels in women during childbirth. (Dog breeders will immediately recognize this hormone as the drug with the trade name Pitocin, which is often administered to bitches during and immediately after whelping.)

For a long time, researchers assumed that oxytocin was only important to females for reproduction. Then it finally occurred to somebody that, Gee whiz, *guys* (none of whom, so far as we know, actually produce babies except indirectly) actually produce this hormone too, so maybe it was worth a look. Which is why nearly all the research on this hormone in men is fairly recent.

Turns out that, besides causing uterine contractions and milk letdown, oxytocin also affects the brain pretty directly, where it acts a neurotransmitter, just like its first cousin vasopressin. (In fact, the genes responsible for the production of these two hormones sit closely together on the same chromosome.)

Oxytocin promotes both social bonding and social memory, and females (what a surprise!) generally produce more of it than males, even when they are not actively engaged in childbirth. The massive amounts of oxytocin produced by females at parturition is largely responsible for formation of the bond between mother and infant, and the oxytocin produced by females during sex causes them to bond with their partners in much the same way that vasopressin does in males - oxytocin receptors are located in the same "reward" areas of the brain. (Oxytocin is the hormone basically responsible for the myriad of emotions lumped into the catch-all category of "love".)

Oxytocin's facilitation of social memory, on the other hand, is probably why, unlike men, women rarely if ever actually forget that they're married, even under extreme stress. It also makes them generally better at remembering faces, and birthdays, and how long they've been married, and how old their kids are. (The fact that men generally carry lower OT levels explains why most of them have been known to forget each and/or all of these things at one time or another...and it's maybe good to know they really can't help it.)

Because of its effects on social behavior, oxytocin has been dubbed the "tend and befriend" hormone.

When faced with stress, the adrenal glands release a surge of hormones responsible for the stress response. Females of most species, when faced with stress, will generally experience the same initial surge of stress hormones that males experience, with the same physical results - an immediate rise in heart rate and blood pressure, dilation of the pupils, etc. But luckily for us, in females it is immediately followed by a surge of oxytocin, which is what makes women immediately pick up the phone and call their girlfriend, their sister, or their mother, rather than just stomping around in a funk. (Most men also rarely report an urge to bake cookies or clean house when stressed, and apparently it's not just because it would be hard to manage while stomping. The cookie-baking urge, along with the housecleaning urge, clearly represents the "tend" part of the "tend and befriend" response.) This tend and befriend response dissipates the stress hormones (primarily cortisol) in the body, which is why women feel a whole lot better after talking about their problems with other women, and feel a strong *need* to do so that men simply do not understand.

This ability of oxytocin to dissipate the negative physical effects of stress through social bonding is one of the reasons why women live longer than men. Men, it turns out, also produce oxytocin under stress, but its effect is in large part inhibited by that 500 pound gorilla, testosterone.

There *is* a way to level the playing field here, though, which allows men the health benefits of oxytocin that women have, although I'm frankly a little conflicted about revealing it. The fact is, sexual intercourse causes both sexes to produce oxytocin (we're talking garden-variety old-fashioned sex with penetration, by the way..."partnered sexual activity excluding intercourse", in the somewhat Victorian language of the authors of the research study, apparently does not yield the same effect) and the oxytocin released by sexual intercourse alone has been shown to provide measurable stress-resistance, including the ability to control blood pressure, that can last up to a week in both sexes. In short, having sex *before* a stressful event can actually make a man more immune to the harmful effects of the stress he's about to encounter. Share this information, or not, as you see fit.

Oxytocin also increases trust, it was found out, via one of the most peculiar scientific experiments I've yet to run across... What they did was divide a group of male volunteers into two groups. They squirted oxytocin up the noses of one group, and water up the other, although no one knew which they got. (This represents good science.) Then they had all the volunteers make 'investments'. The oxytocin-up-the-nose group, it turned out were all much more inclined to trust what their individual 'bankers' told them, and to invest as advised by them, while the control group was not.

The take-home message for women here is that the best time to invest in the stock market is probably not while actively engaged in childbirth. And it probably explains why some guys (who as a group are by and large less trusting than women), are more trusting than others.

Since T levels in men vary a lot from individual to individual, and so do levels of oxytocin, it's not much of stretch to guess that men with less testosterone and more oxytocin are going to have better social-bonding skills, better social memory and be more trusting. These guys are usually Retrievers.

Oxytocin levels probably increase a bit with age as T levels naturally decrease. Which ought to make men both more trusting *and* better able to remember their wives' birthdays as they get older.

Cortisol, Adrenaline, and Noradrenaline

Most people have already heard of these three hormones, all of which are integral to at least a couple of PSPs.

For some reason *cortisol* has been getting a lot of press lately, (mostly in late-night TV ads that claim it's responsible for that "midriff bulge' women can't seem to get rid of) and most people know it has something to do with stress. *Adrenaline* (as in an 'adrenaline rush', which all of us have experienced at one time or another) is technically known in the US as *epinephrine* (and listed in the INN that way) simply because Parke, Davis & Co. slapped a US trademark on "adrenalin" way back when it was first identified and there was legally too much similarity between the two. *Noradrenaline*, the least well-known of the three, is known as *norepinephrine* in the US for presumably the same reason. The whole rest of the world calls them adrenaline and noradrenaline.

Now that we've cleared *that* up, what do these three hormones do? They are all key players in the body's *Fight or Flight Response*. Also called the *acute stress response*, this was first identified by the Harvard psychologist Walter Cannon way back in 1929.

HERE'S WHAT HAPPENS:

The adrenal glands release cortisol, adrenaline, and noradrenaline *in response to a message of imminent threat perceived by the brain.* So, although the effects are entirely physical, the triggering mechanism for the release itself is dependent upon individual brain chemistry.

Cortisol, which is used throughout the body for lots of different things on a daily basis, is diverted into the bloodstream to cope with the emergency at hand, and tends to stay in the body longer at the 'emergency' level before dissipating, leading to what is generally called *chronic stress*. The other two generally dissipate pretty quickly, but all three are released more or less simultaneously in response to a perceived threat.

This release creates a sort of chain reaction in the body. You become more alert, your pupils dilate, your heart rate increases, your blood pressure increases, your immune response and sensitivity to pain are suppressed, you breathe faster, your muscles tense - in other words, the body prepares for fight or flight.

Now, this fight-or-flight response varies from species to species as well as among individuals within each species. Whether one's response is hair-trigger or sluggish mostly depends on where you sit on the food chain.

Your average land tortoise, for example, does not have a hair-trigger flight-or-fight response, simply because it's not critical to his survival. (I mean, *think* about it - which is a two-hundred-pound turtle gonna choose, flight or a fight? Odds are, he'll just stick his head in his shell and wait it out.) Your average *rabbit*, by comparison, wouldn't make it past noon without one and so the response is highly developed in that entire species. (Clearly another difference between the tortoise and the hare...)

Generally speaking, the lower one sits on the food chain, and therefore the more physically vulnerable one is, the more well-developed is this response, for purely practical reasons of survival. In men, the lower the pack status position, the higher the cortisol levels tend to be. (This is a circular sort of thing - the highest PSP males tend to have high serotonin levels, and cortisol blocks serotonin production.)

These reactions all prepare the body for either fighting or fleeing, both of which require a sudden urge of energy. Assuming you're not a land tortoise, *which* particular option one chooses generally depends upon the levels two other hormones - testosterone and noradrenaline. The higher the level of these two hormones in the bloodstream, the more likely one is to choose fight over flight.

The problem with the fight or flight response is really that, like the serotonin system, it made more sense 10,000 years ago. The system is set up for physical action, and 99% of the perceived threats the average person (who is not a professional boxer or in an actual combat situation) is going to face on a day-to-day basis *are not physical threats,* and therefore probably don't require a physical response, unless one is in the habit of either decking one's boss or jumping up and running from the building whenever one is faced with stress on the job. Most reasonably intelligent people will choose Door Number

Three, which is basically to do nothing. This option, known as *behavioral inhibition,* will cause cortisol levels to rise.

Although cortisol levels do go up and down as the situation warrants, like the tortoise and the rabbit, you are *born* with your own particular level of both baseline cortisol levels and your own cortisol response, and there's really not much you can do about it. Even in *fish,* the cortisol levels are higher in the non-dominant males when they are forced to live in a tank with an extremely dominant male.

Cortisol response, in people anyway, has been linked to the APOE gene on chromosome 19, which has several variations - people with two copies of the e4 variant appear to carry higher baseline cortisol levels and are at higher risk for heart attack, stroke, anxiety attacks, and Alzheimer's. (In fact, the e4 variant, which has gotten a lot of media attention, has been dubbed the "heart-attack gene".)

The physical effects that elevated cortisol provides in an emergency - like increased blood pressure and decreased immune response - are advantageous for a short-term burst of action, but if they are not physically 'used up' in short order (which cannot happen when one is sitting at a desk) they become pretty toxic to both the brain and the body, and lead to *chronic stress,* which puts one at risk for a whole lot of physical problems.

The two PSPs most susceptible here are Sentinels, who tend to have high baseline cortisol levels as a group, and Fearbiters, who unfortunately are also saddled with high testosterone and noradrenaline levels.

Noradrenaline, like cortisol, is a two-edged sword. Because it also functions as a neurotransmitter, it is important to brain function, where at ideal levels it heightens attention. (Abnormally low levels of noradrenaline are associated with ADD, not surprisingly.) When levels are too high, however, it leads to an aggressive response to each and every perceived threat, which nine times out of ten is probably a bad idea...and then noradrenaline signals the body to produce more testosterone, which certainly isn't going to make the situation any more warm and fuzzy, either.

Putting All This Science Together

So now you probably know enough about genetics and biochemistry to understand that this PSP stuff really isn't anything a guy has any *control* over, or anything you can change no matter how hard you try...it really is about hard-wiring, which is inherited.

And that's why it's important to be able to identify a man's inherent Pack Status Personality and decide if he's right for you before you invest too much time and effort in him because you are *not* going to change him...as a dog-breeder friend of mine once pointed out: *No matter what you do, in the end you're gonna go out with the same DNA you came in with.*

3

Alphas

No PSP in men or dogs is so often misunderstood as the Alpha personality, which is why a lot of women think they don't *like* Alphas.

A lot has been written about human "Alpha Males' and, frankly, most of it is *flat-out wrong.* The main reason it's wrong is because most stuff about 'Alpha males' is written by *guys.* In fact, I recently read (in an article written, of course, by a guy) that Genghis Khan, J. Paul Getty, and Aristotle Onassis were all Alpha males. *Not a one of them*, as it happens, displayed any of the critical traits of the Alpha personality - me, I'd guess them all for Leglifters.

The PSP *most* people think of as an Alpha is actually the Leglifter.

So why do people confuse Alphas with Leglifters? Mostly because Leglifters go around *telling* everyone they are Alphas - it's part of *being* a Leglifter.

Real honest-to-God Alphas, on the other hand, *don't* go around telling everyone they are Alphas. Unlike Leglifters, they don't feel this uncontrollable *need* to, and they are way too laid-back at any rate to bother. In fact, if it comes right down to it, most of them have never given it a moment's thought.

OK, so given that, how does one identify an Alpha?

In a canine pack, male Alpha status is determined by intelligence, courage, physical superiority, and natural leadership ability. (I didn't just make this up, by the way - I read it in some wolf-research stuff.)

These qualities also define the Alpha personality in men. (This part I figured out myself.) And they are all largely determined by genetics and biochemistry.

Since they were *born* with these qualities, they don't think about them much, and they *sure* as hell don't talk about them. Alphas are not great communicators when it comes to discussing themselves or their feelings. In truth, they'd sooner discuss their own *bowel* habits. (If you really need to know what a man is thinking, or God forbid actually *feeling,* these are definitely *not* the boys for you, and you might as well know that right out the gate.)

So the bottom line is, if a guy *tells* you he's an Alpha, odds are ….

He isn't.

Now, the first three traits - intelligence, courage, and physical superiority - are pretty cut-and-dried, and are fairly easy to identify, but they don't, by themselves, determine Alpha status, because they are also qualities sometimes found in Retrievers, in many Betas, and in nearly all Junkyard Dogs. (LegLifters, for the record, usually have the physical superiority and the courage, but often lack the intelligence factor as well as the leadership traits, so are lower on the food chain, by definition, and are rarely close personal friends of Alphas.)

Natural leadership is predicated on instinctively doing what is best for the pack as a whole, to ensure its survival - in other words, *altruism.*

Altruism is an absolute prerequisite for the Alpha PSP. (These guys most likely have two copies of the recipe for altruism in their personal recipe files…)

In addition to altruism, natural leadership *also* requires an innate ability to inspire the trust and confidence of those around us, which is not quite as common. Others will automatically turn to a natural leader for direction and, as this first starts happening to Alphas about when they join Cub Scouts, by the time they are adults they don't even think about it - it's simply part of who they are. This ability to inspire trust makes it effortless for them to form coalitions from a very early age, which in turn reinforces their leadership position and protects it from outside challenges.

Leadership, for an Alpha, is not a particularly stress-inducing situation, and the recognition of this is probably what inspires trust. It's reassuring to know the guy in charge is not going to come unglued as soon as the shit hits the fan.

Alphas have innate biochemistry which makes them more stress-resistant than most. The reason for this, of course, is our old friend *serotonin* - in virtually all species studied, Alphas maintain the highest levels of serotonin in the brain.

On the other hand, Alphas rarely carry extremely high levels of testosterone. Testosterone, we know, is closely correlated to the trait of "dominance-seeking" in most species, but high levels of testosterone alone are not enough to guarantee Alpha status, nor are they even critical to *achieving* Alpha status. Without the higher testosterone levels, the *desire* to be in a leadership position (which is what "dominance-seeking" means) won't be as high, but desire alone is certainly not enough all by itself to ensure it. It is only when the desire is coupled with intelligence, altruism, stress-tolerance, confidence, and the ability to inspire trust, that Alpha status can be achieved and maintained.

An Alpha who is not heavily endowed with excess testosterone will generally end up in a leadership position in spite of himself. The classic case history of such a man is Harry Truman, a self-avowed "sissy" of a kid whose idea of fun was playing the piano. (In fact, President Truman once told a group of startled White House visitors as he sat down to play that had he not gotten sidetracked into politics, he "would have made a hell of a piano player in a whorehouse.")

Yet starting with his service as an inexperienced Captain in WW I (where the battalion he led saw an incredible amount of combat *and never lost a single man*) every time he reluctantly found himself in a leadership position, he was a natural.

Harry Truman was perfectly happy being an obscure Senator from Missouri when he was literally hand-picked for the presidency. Aware that FDR was dying, the Democratic Party bosses literally strong-armed the reluctant Truman into accepting the nomination for vice-president in 1944.

Truman (who, like most Americans, hadn't a clue FDR was dying) resisted, until Roosevelt himself told him he'd be responsible for the downfall of his party if he didn't accept. With a grumbled "well, why didn't he just say that in the first place?" Truman finally acquiesced.

Eighty-two days after his inauguration, FDR was dead, and Truman found himself President of the United States, an office he had never desired, in the middle of the most terrible war the world had ever seen. He ended the war and was re-elected in 1948, defeating Dewey in the biggest upset in political history, and then went home to Missouri in 1952, saying simply he'd "had enough of Washington" and refusing to run again.

In my experience, very few men actually possess natural leadership quality, and it is what ultimately separates the Alphas from the other high-ranking PSPs. Truth is, the planet just doesn't *need* that many Alphas in any species, and they probably make up less than 5% of the population overall. (That's one in twenty guys you'll meet, to put it in perspective…)

It is important to remember that there is a BIG difference between the Alpha *personality* and the Alpha *position* within a pack, which is why this is in boldface type. Betas, Golden Retrievers, Junkyard Dogs, (and even LegLifters) all can - and in our society, for a wealth of reasons we'll explore later, often *do* - lead packs more or less successfully, both at home and in the outside world, although almost always at far greater personal cost.

On the other hand, it costs an Alpha no more effort to lead than to breathe - both come entirely naturally. These guys don't get ulcers. Although they are genetically incapable of shirking responsibility, they also have a low tolerance for bullshit, combined with a rare ability to differentiate between the two, and they will walk away when they've had enough of the latter. They'll simply go back to Missouri.

As a result of their inborn concern for the welfare of their pack, Alpha males are not intrinsically selfish, nor greedy, nor are they particularly self-indulgent. On the other hand, it's not that they are morally *superior* or anything - although they are by nature altruistic, "personal sacrifice" is not a concept they particularly embrace, nor even give much thought to, because if one has to *think* about it, one is not an Alpha, plain and simple.

They just do the right thing pretty much automatically, and without any soul-searching, because they are hard-wired to do so, in large part because of their genetic ability to easily release dopamine. And they honestly believe anyone else in their position would do the same thing, so it's not like it's a Big Deal or anything…which of course is not true, but there's no sense trying to explain that to them.

Many men can, and do, "rise to the occasion" when necessary and, out of such situations, feats of true courage, altruism, and heroism are born. Alpha males are *born* altruistic and courageous - not foolhardy (those would be Leglifters and Junkyard dogs), but essentially courageous, which Webster defines as "constant readiness to deal with things fearlessly by reason of a stout-hearted temperament or a resolute spirit". Altruism and courage, both physical and moral, therefore costs them nothing, whereas for those less inherently resolute it generally involves far greater personal expense.

Alphas are, surprisingly, a lot more *laid-back* than most women expect, mostly due to their high serotonin levels. When faced with stress, they are more likely to respond with irritation than full-blown anxiety. These guys never have anxiety attacks.

I've never yet met an Alpha who was a party animal. Hardly anyone ever describes one as "a whole lot of fun", either, as these guys take themselves fairly seriously, and abhor looking foolish. Although they actually *can* be very funny (on rare occasions), their collective sense of humor is pretty dry, and they have no affinity for slapstick whatsoever.

Alphas rarely, if ever, get involved in either verbal or actual physical altercations. There's a simple reason for this - their high serotonin levels and resulting impulse control being what it is, they simply never *start* fights, and very few lower-ranking males will ever deliberately start a fight with an Alpha, which is probably the result of some primitive self-preservation instinct more than brains. One of the strangest phenomena I have ever witnessed is the manner in which conflict literally dissolves when an Alpha steps up to the plate. I've seen it happen over and over, and it never fails to fascinate me. Here's what happens:

About three-quarters of the way through a heated group discussion which appears in imminent danger of turning into a brawl (this can be at a school board meeting or in a sports bar, doesn't matter) a guy who heretofore hasn't said much will rise to his full height (sometimes without even standing up, which is amazing), make deliberate eye contact with the arguing parties, and put forth a reasonable suggestion for the resolution of the conflict, using no more volume than absolutely necessary to be heard over the din, and that is the end of it.

I'm willing to bet you have witnessed this phenomenon as well, but had no idea what was happening, or even that anything particularly important *was* happening. (Most people are just relieved that the conflict was resolved.) Here's what *actually* happened:

Pack Order was established. In any social species, chaos turns quickly into to harmony as soon as pack order is established - the Sentinels get their cortisol levels under control, the Leglifters get their testosterone back in their pants, the Fearbiters go back to their corners, and the whole pack calms down. Packs lacking an Alpha personality at the helm tend to be constantly unstable and chaotic.

Another misconception about Alphas is that they make constant eye contact. They don't. When an Alpha makes eye contact, it *means* something. (Write that down somewhere.)

I once watched two Alphas engaged in casual conversation for the better part of an hour, *and they never made eye contact once during the entire conversation.* Not *once*. (I wish I'd filmed the damn thing. Can you imagine two women talking for two *minutes* without eye contact?...of course not.)

Why did these guys not establish eye contact? *They didn't need to.* It was an entirely casual and comfortable conversation between two men of equal status with nothing to prove.

Plumage

Alphas are by definition good physical specimens, because physical superiority is a prerequisite of that PSP. They are generally good-looking, in an ordinary sort of way, although not necessarily drop-dead gorgeous.

(Being drop-dead gorgeous, whether you are male or female, *usually* involves some effort and vanity beyond the physical attributes nature endowed one with, and Alphas are not particularly vain as a group.)

But in both man and dog, you will *never* find an Alpha with a serious "conformation flaw" because it flies in the face of Darwinian theory. In purebred dogs, conformation flaws depend on the written Standard of each particular breed, which you can find at www.akc.org if you are interested. *(For those of you who are ADD, my advice is to wait until you actually finish reading this section before getting up to do this, however, or you'll lose your train of thought...trust me on this, I have personal experience here.)* In the world of purebreds, a flaw in one breed is often a virtue in another, so it's hard to generalize, but Alphas in the purebred dog world are without exception exemplary examples of their respective breeds.

In humans, on the other hand, ideal conformation for the whole species was pretty well laid out by Leonardo DaVinci in the fifteenth century, and it's pretty much one size fits all. (*Michelangelo's David, you may notice, clearly does not have bowed legs, a receding chin, or a penis the size of a cocktail weenie...*)

What Alpha males of both the human and canine varieties do have in common is *physical soundness*, which dog breeders define as *fitness for function.* (Mutts, it should be noted, can be as sound, if not sounder, than their purebred cousins.) Same definition probably applies to men, and for the same reasons. These are the guys Mother Nature meant to reproduce themselves. They are generally reasonably tall, symmetrical, and muscular, and are naturally stronger than average whether or not they work out.

Now, obviously, an Alpha Male of Norwegian or Austrian descent is likely to be bigger than an Alpha Male whose ancestors hail from Southeast Asia (just as an Alpha Mastiff is likely to be bigger than an Alpha Chihuahua) but all of them will probably be on the high end of the curve for their particular ethnic group or breed. In this country, which is essentially an ethnic stew - what the dog world would call "mutts" - that would be over 5 foot 9. (In the Netherlands, with its more homogeneous "purebred" population, the *average* height of an adult male is an astounding 5 foot 11.)

In many species, however, a male of less-than average size with high intelligence, altruism, and good coalition-building skills (in other words an Alpha PSP) can achieve and maintain the Alpha position.

This no doubt explains the political success of James Madison, Father of the Constitution, author of the Bill of Rights, and 4th President of the fledgling and fractious United States, who was a veritable peanut, even for his era, but a hell of a coalition-builder.
From 1776-1816, when he retired from politics, the diminutive Madison ended up on the winning side of every single political argument without once changing his political views to do so - a claim damn few politicians can make even today, much less in the rowdy political arena of an emerging nation.
His political enemies claimed he was 5 foot 2; his friends claimed he was 5 foot 6. Both sides agreed Madison "wouldn't weigh 100 pounds if his hat was full of rocks." In spite of his diminutive stature, Madison was every bit as Alpha as his better-known contemporary, the extraordinary Jefferson, who towered over him at 6 foot 2 ½. And Madison's wife was a real pistol, which apparently bothered this quiet man not in the least - another mark of an Alpha.

Size notwithstanding, these guys are also generally well-proportioned which, in human male physiology, means the shoulders are wider then the pelvis, which is, by definition, narrow. Alphas do *not* have narrow shoulders and big butts. (After thirty-five or so they may have a gut, but *never* a big butt....) A classic V-shape will not positively identify an Alpha, if you've decided that's what you are looking for, but it will quickly exclude those who are not.

Alpha Males are *never* morbidly obese. Never. This is a biochemical result of their naturally high serotonin levels, not a result of careful dietary management.

As a group, Alpha Males don't suffer from excessive vanity. A guy who never has a hair out of place is most likely *not* an Alpha - they are always slightly more *relaxed* than that about their looks. *(In fact, the best thing that ever happened to these guys was the invention of perma-press...they've been wearing their clothes right out of the dryer for years, anyway.)*

As far as hair goes, unless they are in the military, it's often a little longer than the norm, and even Alphas in the military will push the regs on that issue. I personally suspect this is simply because they find getting a haircut annoying, rather than any sort of fashion statement, since these guys don't *make* fashion statements...Alphas consider "fashion" a foreign concept in the best of times, and they do not like to be "fussed over" or "groomed" in any sense of the word. (As any professional dog groomer can tell you, this is true of canine Alphas as well.)

Alphas go gray and/or bald with a lot more grace than most other men. They'd rather be drawn and quartered than wear a toupee or dye their hair. They'd never waste the time or money on hair plugs, either. And everybody can tell, anyway, so what's the point? Rogaine? A waste of money for a little fuzz. Besides, you gotta spend a lot of time looking for the fuzz in the mirror every morning, and the reason grayness sneaks up on them suddenly is that these guys only really use a mirror for shaving. Assuming they shave. (Lots of Alphas sport beards, whether they are in or out of fashion at any given time.)

Clothes? Easy. **Alphas are "conservative casual" dressers, with the emphasis on "conservative".** To the point of absurdity - when it comes to clothes, they are about as open-minded as your average three-year-old.

They pick out their own clothes. (Write that down somewhere.) NO woman has ever dressed an Alpha, to my knowledge, and if you try to buy him something that is not *him* (which generally means it's not identical to something he already owns, or has owned at some point in the past) he won't wear it. Period. These guys like catalogues, mainly because they *DO NOT SHOP* - they may *buy* things they need, but they don't shop.

Alphas wear their favorite clothes for years and years until they are literally falling apart, at which point they will replace them with *the exact same thing, honest to God.* (If you don't believe me, just ask L.L. Bean...) If, in the meantime (which could be a decade or more) the manufacturer has inconsiderately discontinued that item, they are Seriously Annoyed.

Shopping with an Alpha Male is an amazing experience for women. They will walk into a store, go directly to where what they are looking for should logically be, and if it's not there, *they will walk out.* (Don't even suggest they might want to consider some alternatives, because you will be wasting your breath. They are already out the door...)

These guys are not anal about taking care of their stuff, either. As far as they are concerned, clean is sufficient, and virtually anything can go in the washer with anything else, with no regard for color, even a leather bomber jacket. They come out just fine. If you choose to live with an Alpha male, *don't let him do laundry, even if he has a PhD and/or an IQ over 140.* (If you've lived with one for any amount of time, you've no doubt already figured this out the hard way....)

Alphas will not wear certain colors, even at gunpoint. You cannot convince one that it's OK for a heterosexual man to wear pink, for instance. Many will not even wear yellow or baby blue. Anything that is the color of an Easter egg they will not wear. These guys are very comfortable with khaki (a perennial favorite of Alphas), gray, brown, black, navy, dusty shades of blue, that nameless color that looks exactly like dirt, and dark olive green. Not dark green pants, though. They can only wear dark green on top. And plaid makes them uncomfortable. It's maybe OK on a shirt (flannel or cotton) but *never, never, never* on pants (every Alpha I've ever met would rather show up in public stark naked than in plaid pants)...and not on a sports jacket, either. **Houndstooth is viewed by Alphas as a form of plaid.**

Corduroy is OK, especially when it has started to wear out. (These guys *invented* suede elbow patches - it's one of their few historical contributions to fashion.) Tweed, unlike houndstooth, is *not* viewed as a form of plaid, so it's OK, too, if it's an acceptably muddy color.

Shoes? Just as bad. These guys would wear Docksiders to their own wedding if they could pull it off. They also like hiking boots. They will actually have shoes and boots resoled, which may cost more than actually replacing them. Remember what I said about Fashion Statements? The average Alpha Male will never make one with his footwear, either.

Let's take a minute and look at cowboy boots, which can be sexy in their own way, especially accompanied by a pair of well-worn levis and long legs. Like stiletto heels (and only marginally more comfortable) they throw the weight forward, which makes just about any guy's butt look tighter, and when it comes to actually roping a calf or something, they give new meaning to the term "digging your heels in", which is probably where that expression came from, come to think about it. In some parts of the country they are *de rigueur* as footwear for both men and women, although odds are you are probably not in one of those places right now. *Anywhere else, they are flat-out pretentious.*

As they are a singularly *unpretentious* group, there is one reason and one reason *only* for an Alpha to wear cowboy boots - and that is *because he is a Card-Carrying Cowboy.* **Cowboy boots are only found on Alphas who are from someplace where it is not all that unusual to see cows.**

In the Far North, say around Fargo or International Falls, and especially in the winter (that would be between October and May in a mild year) Alphas will often wear Sorel Boots, which, unfortunately, are not nearly as sexy as cowboy boots, anywhere they think they can get away with it. (If you've never seen a pair, there is simply no way I can describe them adequately.) But they are a whole lot warmer, especially if worn with a couple of pairs of gray wool socks, and they have way better traction than a pair of Tony Llamas on the ice, in the event you unexpectedly need to push a car out of a snow bank. (Pushing a car out of a snowbank in International Falls is only totally unexpected in July, just for the record.) In other words, for guys north of the 42nd parallel, Sorel boots are the arctic equivalent of cowboy boots in the west - a simple necessity, same as carrying a pocketknife. Guys who wear Italian loafers in Duluth in January are not Alphas.

Alphas do not generally own pajamas, nor do they own a bathrobe unless someone buys them one as a gift, in which case it hangs on a hook on the back of the bathroom door until it falls off from dry rot. Most Alphas sleep in the buff, and since they do *not* hang around the house undressed anyhow, so why would they need pajamas or a bathrobe?

Their idea of "undressed" is maybe sweats, preferably ragged and in a neutral color like gray...and some (usually those over forty) won't even wear *them*.

If an Alpha is wearing pajamas, odds are he's also got an IV drip taped to his arm. I have no idea why this is, but the Pajama Rule seems to be unassailable, and may be the *only* determining factor between a high-ranking Beta and a particularly organized Alpha in some cases.

Alphas rarely wear cologne. I suspect wearing cologne is a primitive instinct, like rolling in dead fish, and Alphas probably have no need to disguise their own scent. If their wives/daughters/girlfriends buy it for them, they will occasionally remember to wear it, but it better be English Leather or Old Spice, which are immediately recognizable as Guy Smells. It is almost an axiom that the lower on the food chain a guy is, the *stronger* his cologne will be. (Some of these guys would actually be better *off* rolling in dead fish, but that's just my opinion....and it's worse south of the Mason-Dixon line.)

Alphas generally don't go around wearing some other guy's name on the outside of their shirts, either. They are not all that impressed by Tommy or Ralph to begin with, and they have no problem with their *own* identity. Designer labels are a foreign concept to them, by and large. (For the same reason, Alphas don't plaster their favorite racer's NASCAR number on their cars, either...)

If being seen with a snappy dresser is important to you, these are *not* your boys...left to their own devices, their idea of *really* dressed up is an oxford shirt, a blazer, and a pair of khakis, tie optional. If you expect more, you will be disappointed, trust me...

Alphas are typically the most underdressed guys at any function, and it works for them.

Habitat

There are no Alpha male interior designers. Not even gay ones, although there are most certainly gay Alphas. (I know, I know - this flies in the face of conventional evolutionary biology, but it is a fact nonetheless.) The *reason* there are no Alpha interior designers is simple - Alphas, as a rule, don't have much in the way of what we might call "nesting" instincts. Alphas are uniformly low in *prolactin*, the hormone responsible for nest-building and caring for young. This can be a problem in the "home-improvement" department. (But the payback is that the prolactin deficit also gives them a shorter-than-average sexual refractory period, which some women would consider a fair tradeoff ...)

For your average garden-variety Alpha, a basic minimum of domestic comfort and cleanliness will suffice, and some semblance of organization, if that's personally important to them (and that's a different gene entirely), but that's really about it. "Cozy" is not a concept they are particularly in tune with, unless maybe referring to a warm, dry tent as opposed to a cold, damp one. In any case, neither requires the addition of knickknacks. Every Alpha I have ever met loathes knickknacks.

Nor are Alpha males particularly sensitive to color. After moving into new digs, an Alpha is perfectly capable of living with the wall color choices of the previous inhabitant indefinitely, unless those colors happen to be pink or lavender, in which case he will probably paint over them in white.

In the home décor department, Alphas are definitely minimalists, and their personal "stuff" (while it may be high quality and even occasionally beautiful) is generally functional rather than decorative - if it doesn't serve a purpose, it simply doesn't occur to them to own it. Many single Alphas, especially younger ones, mostly live with furniture donated by older female relatives until they get married. An amazing number have never set foot in a furniture store.

About the only thing an Alpha has any really strong feelings about in the home-decorating department is recliners.

Alphas, to a man, *loathe* recliners. Now, there are many guys who honestly feel the recliner is the greatest invention of mankind to date right after the remote-control (I have a Retriever friend who owns three) but Alphas hate 'em. This has nothing to do with refinement of taste or snobbery, since these guys don't have an abundance of either. No matter what their age or socioeconomic status, these guys are *seriously uncomfortable* in recliners, and rarely if ever will sit on one, much less go out and actually *purchase* one for their own use.

If an Alpha finds himself in a situation (like in someone else's home) where he must actually sit in a recliner, he will sit gingerly on the edge of the seat, being very careful not to allow it to actually *recline,* which can be pretty entertaining to watch. There is a logical reason for this, and it speaks directly to pack status - a recliner, by its very engineering, forces one into the most vulnerable of all positions - lying on one's back with one's throat exposed. *This is not a position of relaxation to an Alpha,* unless he is either alone or post-coital.

Alphas tend to be packrats as well, which certainly adds nothing to their housekeeping skills. They will, to a man, justify this by saying that you never know when you are going to need something again, but it's a lame argument for the most part. The truth is, they are simply emotionally incapable of getting rid of something they've had for any length of time simply to replace it with something new. (Alphas generally have an appreciation of antiques that I think is a direct reflection of this philosophy. If something is old but well-made and still useful, they respect it.)

As this applies to women as well (these guys will NEVER trade in an older model for a young trophy wife) it's a failing worth living with in the long run...even if it means you have to put up with his collection of old coffee cans.

Alphas are simply not conspicuous consumers. Their personal confidence level is such that they have no need to buy anything simply to impress anyone else. *A guy with a six-figure income who wears a Timex and drives a Ford Explorer (these guys view cars purely as transportation) is probably an Alpha.*

The other half of habitat, of course, is the workplace - outside of his den (or a trout stream), where is one most likely to encounter an Alpha?

More and more often, an Alpha is likely to be working for himself. The days of Alphas running large corporations is more or less over, unless said corporation was actually founded by the Alpha in question. The amount of bullshit one has to put up with in order to climb the modern corporate ladder far exceeds the Alpha's bullshit-tolerance level. (Because of his high serotonin levels, the average Alpha is pretty self-directed, and not good at taking orders he knows damn well are stupid.)

Your garden-variety Alpha would rather work for himself, even if it means earning less. Alphas are not particularly motivated by money, or the material trappings of success, although some of them are roaringly successful. If one had to choose a single word that describes what *does* motivate them, that word would be "excellence."

Whatever Alphas do, they generally want to do it well. If that brings them material success, that's OK, but if it does not, that's equally OK, as long as it pays the bills. These guys will quit a high-paying, but unsatisfying, corporate job to own a vineyard, or a fly-fishing shop in a heartbeat, if the opportunity presents itself, and his family won't starve as a result.

Even the military, long a stronghold for Alphas, has reached a situation where its top positions are more often than not held by Betas, who have a greater tolerance for the administrative and political bullshit that determines to a large degree success in the modern military. Young, tough, and idealistic Alphas may still be found in the military (mostly in Special Forces) but odds are they are going to walk away long before they are old enough to wears stars on their shoulders.

Politically, Alphas are generally practical moderates, more likely to lean to the left than the right (it's that altruism thing) but in both cases they view politics as an opportunity for public service rather than power.

There are no Alphas on the Extreme Right.
Zip.
Zero.
Nada.
(If you feel immediately inclined to disagree with this blanket statement, just try to name one. *Go ahead, give it a shot...* absolutely *everyone* comes up blank.)

Politics, in case you haven't figured it out yet, is simply about pack order, and pack order is about brain chemistry. The current Political Right is literally awash in excess cortisol, noradrenaline, and testosterone, with serotonin and altruism nowhere in evidence. Hey, if you don't believe me, just turn on Fox News.

Unfortunately, because of the professional "political handling" required of candidates in a political system designed for the mass media, and their innate irritation with being "handled", fewer and fewer Alphas are willing to run for office at anything other than the local level. Unless there is a major change in that regard (which seems highly unlikely, unless maybe this book sells a whole lot more copies than I actually expect it to) I suspect the odds of finding an Alpha in the White House in the future will be as unlikely as finding one wearing a General's stars. The political arena seems to be more and more the province of Perpetual Puppies, Leglifters and Fearbiters...which, frankly, doesn't speak well for the survival of the species.

Mating Habits

As husband material, Alphas are not every woman's cup of tea. They won't tell you how they're feeling - in fact, they won't even tell you when they need to go to the *emergency room*. They are not particularly easy to housebreak, they are bad shoppers, and they'll step over a pile of something 57 times without ever thinking about picking it up. They possess no nesting instincts whatsoever. If home-improvement projects are your idea of a fun weekend, this guys will be a sore disappointment.

On the plus side - *and this one is a big plus* - Alphas are monogamous. One of the flat-out funniest things I have ever seen is a book I ran into recently entitled - honest to God - How To Become an Alpha Male, *whose author promises that if you buy this book (for only $49.97) you too will have sex with 20 women a month...he should have called it How To Become a Leglifter. What an idiot.*

Alphas do not have casual sex - they're not capable of it. Once married, Alphas are less likely to cheat than most other PSPs - oddly, a trait they share with Omegas. They are among the least likely to end up divorced. In fact, virtually all of them will stay married to the same woman for their entire lives, unless she either leaves, which is unlikely, or actually drops dead. Alphas probably have very long repeats on their vasopressin receptor genes.

Alphas tend not to be sexist, are never sexually crude, and I've never yet heard one tell an off-color joke at a woman's expense. In fact, Alphas actually hold women, as a group, in higher regard than many other PSPs. They put up with a lot of annoying crap from their mothers and sisters and daughters, with reasonably good humor, and are fairly protective of them, as is any Alpha of any species. It's part of who they are in the pack.

But an Alpha also tends to be what my mother used to call "a *man's* man", rather than "a ladies' man". Because most of their interests are pretty traditionally male interests, and they are not great communicators of their feelings (which is about as great an understatement as one can make), they rarely have a large circle of close female friends. *(Those would be Retrievers for the most part...)*

Alphas are actually a lot less preoccupied with sex than most PSPs. They never visit pornography websites. Most have never had a subscription to Playboy or Penthouse, and they spend less time talking about sex than most guys. They rarely, if ever, try to pick up women and don't hang around bars much.

Once they are actually *in* bed, though, Alphas will blow every other PSP out of the water. These guys do not suffer erectile dysfunction, and they have the stamina of an 18 year old well past the age when most other guys need Viagra to function at all.

The sexual superiority of an Alpha is primarily biochemical - high serotonin coupled with adequate testosterone and their lamentably low prolactin levels are probably more responsible for it than any conscious effort on their part. Since these are the guys Mother Nature *intended* to do most of the breeding, sex, like leadership, is as natural to an Alpha as breathing. They don't waste a lot of time thinking about it, or (God forbid!) *talking* about it, they just *do* it. And like most things they do, they do it well. Don't expect sex in an elevator or anything... well...*weird*...from an Alpha, though, because they'll look at you like you're insane. They are proficient, but reasonably conventional.

On the other hand, their altruism and natural respect for women makes them extremely *considerate* lovers - they derive pleasure from giving pleasure. And since high serotonin levels in the male brain delay orgasm, they're actually in a position to pull it off.

Alphas never suffer from premature ejaculation, even in their twenties. Women who are not crazy about frequent sex will want to stay away from these guys, though…it's not something they outgrow after a couple years of marriage, and lack of it makes them irritable.

Alphas have no patience at all with weak or silly women and if you hope to attract the attentions of one, he'll have to find you intelligent and interesting, as well as sexy. (Oddly, Alphas, to a man, prefer conventionally sexy women. They are never attracted to boyishly thin or pubescent women, which probably has something to do with evolutionary biology.)

They are pretty good dinner dates, if you can get one to *make* a date. Their manners are good, they leave generous but not outrageous tips, and never send food back or harass service personnel.

Gossip is beyond them, so talking about people they don't personally know (these include most "pop culture" icons, by the way) will probably bore them senseless. Politics, history, and whatever their particular hobbies or interests are will get you farther conversationally. Alphas read a lot compared to a lot of other PSPs.

Assuming you have attracted the attention of an Alpha sufficiently to find yourself actually *married* to one (and Alphas have no real fear of commitment once they think they've met the right woman) they make pretty fair husbands, housebreaking issues aside.

As a group, they are not threatened by confident, intelligent women, they are not particularly *controlling*, and don't need constant contact with their mates to be comfortable, because they are neither particularly jealous or emotionally needy. Women with high-powered jobs will often do well with an Alpha mate. They are one of very few PSPs who will not be threatened if their wife makes more money than they do.

Alphas make good fathers as well although if you expect them to be disciplinarians, you're going to be disappointed. In most any species, Alphas will leave the day-to-day disciplining of the young to females. They are remarkably tolerant parents, but they have high expectations for their offspring, and their kids know this instinctively, rarely challenging their authority. In fact, like dogs and horses, children in general seem to viscerally recognize an adult who's an Alpha, and tend to respond accordingly.

Oddly, Alphas, who are usually animal lovers and often own a dog or two, are more tolerant of cats than many other PSPs, and they'll often share their space with one, especially if they are single and in a situation where dog ownership is not practical. Unlike a lot of men, they don't find independence in either women or cats particularly threatening.

4

Betas

In a wild canine pack, the Beta is the second-in-command position. The Beta will never challenge the Alpha for his leadership position (mostly because he doesn't really want the job), but should the Alpha be killed, the Beta will immediately assume his duties, after the rest of the pack dispatches the challenger, which is a nice way of saying they all gang up, turn on him, and tear him to shreds. (I'm not making this up; it's actually another fact from the wolf-researchers.)

Now humans, of course, are far more complex, and so we have developed a far more complex system to take care of that particular possibility. We call this system..........

The Vice-Presidency.

And Betas make wonderful Vice-presidents. So much so, in fact, that if there were ever a conference of Betas, it would be populated with the vice-presidents of almost every organization on the planet. These guys are better at being second-in-command than any other group.

Intelligent, caring, and endowed with a tremendous sense of responsibility, Betas are fully capable of leading at any level if need be, but they do not necessarily seek it out, nor is it a particularly *comfortable* position for them, either physically or psychologically.

The pharmaceutical industry would be bankrupt without Betas. They are by far the greatest consumers of Tagamet, Maalox, blood-pressure drugs and Viagra, all brought on by the stress of leadership.

The Viagra-thing, amazingly, has been also found to be true in wild packs - upon assuming Alpha status but lacking an Alpha personality, some Betas become incapable of fulfilling their breeding duties...as far as we know, canines don't have heart attacks or develop ulcers, but if they did, these are the dogs who would no doubt have them.

Betas will take excellent care of those whose welfare is entrusted to them, both in their personal and professional lives, it's just that they *worry* about it more.

Betas are not lacking in courage but they have a decided distaste for conflict and, because of that, they are negotiators by definition. Sometimes by profession. Betas will always try to find a solution that both accomplishes the necessary goals and involves the least amount of conflict. They are excellent problem-solvers.

Fairness is a big deal to Betas, whereas Alphas will simply shrug and tell you life is not fair. Likewise, kindness figures into many decisions Betas make in life. A good deal of what defines the Beta is *prolactin* - they carry higher levels of it than most PSPs, which why they are so damn *nice*.

A Beta will intentionally *let* his kids win Board games occasionally - an Alpha will not. It's not that Alphas have a personal *need* to win at Chess, Monopoly, or even Candyland (*those are Leg-Lifters; they are so pathologically competitive they'll cheat a five-year-old at jacks if that's what it takes to win*) but they are incapable of dishonesty of any sort - Betas, on the other hand, are perfectly capable of harmless dishonesty for the purposes of kindness. For this reason, Betas make some of the best fathers. In the world of dogs, both wild and domestic, Beta males interact more with the pack's puppies than will the Alphas, who are tolerant but not particularly playful.

Betas are far more detail-oriented than Alphas. Show me a guy whose financial and personal affairs are absolutely in order, whose will is constantly updated, and whose checkbook is balanced to the last penny, and I'll lay you money he is a Beta. These guys are an insurance man's dream - in fact, many are actually *in* the insurance business, because they *believe* in insurance, and lots of it. The thought of their family going hungry should something untoward happen to them is one of the many things they worry about.

Betas are often better communicators of their feelings than Alphas, although they are not in a league with, say, Retrievers in that regard. (But, then, almost *no one* is...including many women I know.) Betas do, however, share with Alphas a deep and overriding need to never appear foolish. They are endowed with a fair amount of personal dignity and old-fashioned modesty. (These are *not* guys who leave the bathroom door open....)

Again, like Alphas, the Beta has a well-developed sense of ethics. Morality is rarely a gray area for them, although they probably worry more about the practical ramifications of a moral decision than Alphas, who have a decided "let the chips fall where they may" attitude in that regard, which explains why Alphas are rarely found in the upper levels of corporate management any more.

In general, Betas have more patience than many other PSPs, and often more tact. They instinctively know the correct answer to a question like "Does this skirt make my butt look too big?" which is probably why so many women think they make the best husbands. (This is a question you never want to ask an Alpha, by the way...)

113

In the world of dogs, Betas are considered to be very trainable and easy to housebreak, and the same is true in the world of men. Betas are invariably the most housebroken of men - generally tidy and capable of actually cleaning a bathroom once in a while. Odds are they even know where the vacuum cleaner is kept.

For some unfathomable reason, the greatest glorification of the Beta male in history occurred on television in the fifties and early sixties. Remember Ward Cleaver sitting on the edge of the bed, talking to the Beav? Ozzie Nelson? Betas, both of them. Maybe there was something about the *orderliness* of that era that made it the perfect venue for the Beta male...

Sometimes it is almost impossible to distinguish between a high-level Beta and an Alpha, since there is so much crossover in terms of personality and general demeanor. And this makes sense, since the Beta will more often than not find himself in a leadership position, responsible for the welfare of an entire pack. So how can you tell?

You have to look at Plumage and Habitat, mostly. And sex...

In general, a guy who gets a substantial paycheck signed by someone else his entire adult life is more likely to be a high-ranking Beta.

An Alpha is more comfortable working for himself, and will attempt to do so if he can manage it without placing his family in jeopardy, even if it results in less money. Betas tend to be more concerned with job security, and will put up with a fair amount of crap within the organization to secure it. If an Alpha (or a Junkyard Dog) works for someone else much past the age of thirty-five (which often happens in fields like academia, where starting one's own University makes little practical sense), he likely operates in an environment where he is pretty much running his own show, with little direct supervision and a great deal of autonomy. Betas virtually *never* work for themselves, although they may form a corporation which pays them a salary on a particular date each month, even if it's a very small business and they sign the check themselves. For some reason this makes them feel more secure.

Plumage

Physically, Betas are a fairly attractive group, although not always as tall as Alphas. In fact, a short guy *without* an attitude is usually a Beta. They are never flashy men, nor roaringly sexy at first impression, but they *are* solidly attractive. And they're generally well-groomed, if that's important to you. (I personally know a couple who are actually gorgeous by anyone's standards, although that's probably not the norm for this PSP.)

Betas take pretty good care of themselves as a rule, and are usually in good shape, because they take pretty good care of *everything* they are responsible for - it's part of their nature.

Rarely, if ever, obese, these guys are very likely to belong to a gym - not because they are particularly vain, or want to be brawny or muscular, which most of them are not, but because they are the group of males most concerned with cardiovascular fitness. (As well they should be - heart attacks are almost singularly the province of Betas, which is probably related to their cortisol levels - they are pretty vulnerable to the effects of stress.) They are often marathon runners, or cyclists. Betas probably make up the bulk of the golfing population as well, and they usually play a fair game of tennis. This is probably because the average Beta prefers sports that don't involve actual violent physical contact, or killing anything. Although they are not cowards by a long shot, Betas generally don't like to *hurt* themselves, nor do they derive any visceral pleasure from slamming their body with any amount of force into someone else's. (Those would be Junkyard dogs and Leglifters...)

In fact, some (though not all) Betas run to hypochondria, and spend way more time in doctor's offices than do Alphas, Junkyard dogs, or Leglifters, all of whom generally will only see a doctor if they can't stop the bleeding themselves with direct pressure and a greasy rag...Betas tend to be worriers, and one of the things they worry about is their health.

They don't worry about their health because they are self-absorbed or narcissistic, mind you - what they are *really* concerned about is what will happen to their families, or their company, or whoever else is depending on them, should they end up incapacitated, or (God forbid) actually *dead* because they failed to take care of themselves. The upside of this is that when they actually *are* in need of medical treatment, they make co-operative and non-demanding patients, and they tend to be nurses' pets. (On the other hand, the entire medical profession finds Alphas, Junkyard Dogs and Leg Lifters exasperating, and with good reason....)

If a guy knows his own blood pressure, HDL, LDL, and total serum cholesterol levels, odds are he's a Beta. Betas also eat less red meat than most guys, not because they don't like it, but because they are watching their cholesterol and saturated fat intake. (The other high-ranking PSPs are all die-hard red-meat eaters, and have no apparent fear of French fries, which many of them consider to be an actual Food Group, along with meat, cheese, and beer.) Since this is a group prone to heart attacks, it's probably wise.

Beta males are, by and large, a *tidier* group than many other PSPs. They are more detail-oriented, and getting a haircut is not a detail they are likely to overlook. Unless they are engaged in the political arena, Betas have their hair *cut* rather than *styled*, but at least they do it regularly. They also tend not to consider the iron a foreign object. In fact, guys who actually know *how* to iron are often Betas. Betas are not nearly as rumpled as Alphas, and their clothes are generally pressed.

And they are among the few male humans to have mastered the art of doing laundry without ruining most of it. Unlike an Alpha, you can actually *trust* a Beta with laundry - but, then, you can trust a Beta with almost anything, including the care of small children - that's the beauty of them.

Like the Alpha, Betas are conservative dressers for the most part, but unlike Alphas, they *will* wear clothes purchased for them by a spouse or other close female relative, provided that person has reasonably good taste, and they will wear a suit with less obvious discomfort.

I have it on good authority that a Beta male will wear something that *does* makes him look a little...well...*silly*, if it was given to him by a small child or elderly relative of whom he is inordinately fond, and he doesn't have to actually go out in *public* in it.

These guys actually *shop,* choosing their clothes for mainly practical considerations, but with the same care and attention to detail that they give everything else...and they will accompany women on shopping expeditions with fairly good humor, whereas a Leglifter would rather chew off his own arm (unless, of course, the woman is planning to shop at Advance Auto.)

Betas are *appropriate* dressers, and, because of this, they tend to have much more extensive wardrobes than most guys, although they really are not "clothes-horses" in the classic sense. What I mean by this is that they have actual *categories* of clothes - dress clothes, work clothes, casual (weekend) clothes, and clothes appropriate to whatever hobbies they pursue. Because of this inborn sense of the appropriate (which is no more or less than their inborn and unerring understanding of protocol) a Beta will never, for example, show up at a Bar Mitzvah dressed for duck-hunting. Betas will have their shoes shined, or even shine their shoes themselves if need be. These guys own *shoe trees*, and actually use them. (This is part of their general philosophy of taking care of things.)

Like Alphas, the only Betas who will wear cowboy boots are involved in the Livestock Industry (unless of course they live in Wyoming, Montana, and parts of Texas and Colorado, where it is an actual State Law that anyone over the age of three must wear them at all times, and they actually bronze little baby cowboy boots and use them as bookends.) Betas are generally not pretentious.

They can sew on a button if they need to. They actually know how to negotiate the perils of drycleaners, since a lot of them wear suits to work.

In fact, Betas are more *likely* to wear suits to work than Alphas, since they form the backbone of Modern Corporate America for the most part. And as such, they are more vulnerable than most PSP groups to age discrimination - these are the guys that have 28-year-old MBAs breathing down their necks, which affects several aspects of their toilette, as it were....*Like their hair.*

Betas are *not* above The Comb Over. For the uninitiated (and I honestly cannot imagine who that might be, but I'll explain it anyhow) the Comb Over represents an attempt to disguise thinning hair by allowing the hair in the thick places to grow long enough to comb it over the thin places, and I'm being kind here, because "the thin places" are usually pretty bald. It's relatively ineffective, but I guess it makes the Comb Overer feel like he is at least doing *some*thing about it. In fact, your typical Beta is often a Rogaine consumer as well, and will certainly take the Grecian Formula route, more to avoid looking like The Old Guy in his department than out of any real personal vanity.

In short, a Beta Male *worries* about his hair. If he's lucky enough to still have the same crop he started with, he'll keep it carefully cut and in place. If not, he'll attempt to make the most of what he's got. Once that looks fruitless, he'll give up. (This is not a group that's generally comfortable wearing a rug, either.) If there is ever a sure-fire cure for male-pattern baldness, however, he'll be first in line.

Around the house, Betas own bathrobes, and they actually wear them. *Over their pajamas.*

Betas do *not* sleep in the buff, even when they are sleeping alone. They find it uncomfortable. These are not silk pajamas, either, unless they have received a pair as a gift from a female of whom they are fond, in which case they will wear them to please her, and then generally only in her company. No, Beta Pajamas are cotton in the summer and flannel in the winter, and they are usually a nice muted plaid or foulard.

Older Betas tend to wear classic button-front PJs, while the younger ones usually wear those boxer/tshirt combos. (This is probably because Betas find boxers comfortable attire in the underwear department as well...rarely will you find a Beta in bikini briefs, or even standard white cotton ones - these are boxer guys.) When they are any farther from bed than the bathroom, and in the event the bathroom is down the hall, the pajamas are covered by a well-tailored bathrobe. They are fully capable of sitting around on a Sunday morning reading the paper in their bathrobe and slippers, as long as they don't have company over.

Betas are essentially modest guys, but they don't seem to share the Alpha's somewhat obsessive need to be fully dressed under all circumstances except when sleeping or engaging in sex, both of which acts are performed by Alphas only when totally naked. **In fact, except for when actually taking a shower or undergoing an autopsy, Beta males are almost *never* totally naked.**

Betas are not nearly as conservative about colors as Alphas, either. They *will* wear pink dress shirts, and their casual clothes may actually include pink, yellow, and madras plaid items, patterned sweaters (argyle is a perennial favorite of Betas), and sometimes even green corduroy slacks with little ducks embroidered all over them. And I might point out, none of these articles of clothing make them resemble Elton John in the least.

They will wear jewelry, although never anything gaudy. Betas wear rings, for instance - wedding rings, and school rings, mostly. (In some parts of the county, the ubiquitous Mason's ring is as much a part of a Beta's jewelry wardrobe as his wristwatch. In other parts of the country - mostly those parts south of the Sweet Tea Line - it's equally as likely to be a VMI or Citadel ring.)

Betas are more apt to wear cologne than Alphas, but they won't drive you out of a room with it. Betas can wear ties without obvious discomfort, and are the PSP most likely to wear actual bowties with a straight face.

Betas will carry an umbrella when it's raining. They will have one in their car even when rain is not forecast, because you just never know.

Habitat

In the dog world, Betas are notoriously easy to housebreak, and the same is generally true of human Betas as well.

Betas are, as previously mentioned, a reasonably tidy bunch and, even when single, maintain a level of housekeeping generally above the norm for human beings carrying the Y chromosome. (The pleasant tidiness of a Beta should never be confused with the obsessive neatness of a FearBiter, however, which is a different level entirely.) The domain of a single Beta won't look like Martha lives there (unless he's had a decorator come in) but it probably will be somewhat better than an Alpha's efforts, and a *lot* less disgusting than the digs of a young Leglifter, at least from a female standpoint.

Betas have reasonably good and entirely conventional taste, although they are not extravagant by nature. Because they are fairly frugal, not overly insecure, and don't mind shopping as a concept, these are the guys most likely to frequent garage sales, which is why they often actually own more furniture early in their single life than Alphas, who, through sheer lack of interest, tend to mostly wait until they inherit it or marry a woman who already owns some.

In addition to furniture, Betas often own actual cleaning products besides laundry detergent and Turtle Wax, and use them with some regularity. This endearing trait translates to bathrooms a woman is not entirely uncomfortable showering in, should she find herself in that situation.

Betas are not particularly handy in terms of frame-up construction, (one is unlikely to find a Beta in the contracting business unless he's the accountant) but they generally enjoy home improvement projects requiring slightly more finesse, and when they undertake a project, they will buy all the necessary equipment to do it right and generally finish a project once they've started it.

On the other hand, if a home-improvement project is beyond them, Betas have absolutely no problem hiring someone who actually knows what they are doing. (This separates them from several other higher PSPs.) A Beta will hire someone to tear apart his bathroom or build a garage so he can spend his spare time carefully restoring the mahogany woodwork on his sailboat, which is probably a classic.

Betas, for some reason I have never figured out, are often good sailors, and are at home on the water. And of all the branches of the military, the one they are most apt to join is the Navy. Weird, but true...

Betas like classics of every sort, and probably make up the bulk of the classic car owners on the planet.

They have a particular affinity for little ragtop English classics - MGs and Triumphs, especially - which are sporty and fun to drive, but not overly testosterone-laden. (Betas do *not* own classic 60s muscle cars, like Cobras, Camaros, and GTOs - all vehicles which - although many people do not know this - actually will run on pure testosterone as well as premium unleaded.)

Betas enjoy tinkering with their classic cars on Saturday afternoons, and will do a lot of the work themselves, although they'll probably pay someone else to replace the transmission - unlike a lot of other guys, Betas seem to know their mechanical limitations. Some Betas actually collect classic cars, and will have two or three. They also have far too much sense to actually drive one to work. A Beta's "daily driver" will generally be a sedan, a high-end Japanese car usually (if they can afford it, a Lexus is the Beta's car of choice) - never flashy, never red, and always well-maintained, with the oil changed on schedule and a noticeable lack of crunched-up Burger King bags on the floor of the front seat. These guys wash and wax their cars regularly.

"Work", for a Beta, will nine times out of ten involve a paycheck. Although some actually own their own businesses (which are invariably set up as corporations so that they still get a paycheck) they are more likely to work for someone else, as Betas are not notorious risk-takers.

And Betas make great employees - honest, responsible, and hard-working, these are the guys who used to get a gold watch after thirty years of loyal service to a company back when employee loyalty still had value. Even in today's corporate environment, they tend to change jobs with less frequency than most, as Betas are most comfortable with familiarity.

Like Alphas, Betas are intrinsically honest, and will leave a corporation before they'll get personally involved in what they consider to be unethical or potentially illegal behavior. They'll usually hang in there in a hostile work environment a lot longer than an Alpha will, however, since they will worry about the consequences quitting will have on their finances. This sort of stress is part of why these guys get ulcers.

Politically, Betas are *always* moderate conservatives, as they are moderate conservative men by definition, and not really political animals by temperament. Back in the Good Old Days when the GOP was defined by 'Main Street Republicans' - those sober, socially and fiscally responsible businessmen of the Eisenhower era - Betas of the Protestant persuasion invariably voted a straight Republican ticket, and expected their wives to do likewise. (Betas of the Jewish persuasion, on the other hand, invariably voted a straight Democratic ticket, and hoped their wives would too. Jewish Betas do not tell their wives how to vote.)

Today's Beta generally describes himself as an Independent, and is disgusted by politics in general. A few of the older ones are still to be found in the national and local political arena, where they make up the moderate wing of their particular party of choice, but they are dying out fast and not being replaced, which is too bad.

Anyhow, it should be pretty clear by now why Betas are considered by many women to be ideal husband material...they are honest, financially responsible, more or less born housebroken, and easily trainable in the areas where they may be deficient. But what about actual sex?

Mating Habits

Physically, Betas are not usually over-endowed with testosterone, or the resulting body hair, or sexual aggression that so often accompanies it. In fact, next to Omegas, Betas are the least sexually aggressive males you'll run into. Not the least *sexual,* just the least sexually aggressive, which is an important distinction.

Like Alphas, Betas harbor an innate respect for the female gender. Unlike Alphas, they are usually capable of actually *communicating* with people of the female gender to a fair degree on an emotional level. And, like Alphas, they are never sexually crude or blatantly chauvinistic. They are pretty Sensitive Guys.

Betas are worriers, though, and one of the many things they worry about is pleasing women sexually. Mens' magazines (you know - the ones that have articles on flattening your abs, lowering your stress level, and pleasing women - not the ones with centerfolds depicting naked and airbrushed co-eds) are really *geared* toward Betas, who make up a large percentage of their readership and Betas, in turn, get a lot of "women-pleasing" tips from them. (Your average Alpha, or even your average Leglifter for that matter, would no sooner buy one of these magazines than he'd buy an issue of Creative Embroidery...not that they're *opposed* to them - it's more like it just doesn't *occur* to them.) But Betas love 'em.

This is because, as a group, they are not overly secure in their sexual attractiveness, and they worry a lot about their actual sexual performance. (In fact, the first worry often has an unfortunately negative impact on the second, but there doesn't seem to be much they can do about that...and their higher-than-average prolactin levels don't help, either.) As a result, Betas tend to be attentive and considerate, if not always athletically spectacular, in bed - and let's face it, from a woman's viewpoint, attentive and considerate counts for a lot, which is something Leglifters haven't figured out yet.

With Betas, it's initially *getting* them into bed that can be the problem. Women attracted to a Beta may need to take the initiative, as these guys don't like to look foolish, and won't set themselves up for rejection, or even the *possibility* for rejection, which may leave the woman (especially after they've been dating for a while) thinking he isn't interested when in fact he's obsessing about how to approach the subject. But women need to be careful not to appear sexually aggressive around Betas, either, because this can backfire.

Betas are generally put off by flashy women with a lot more sexual experience than they have. Remember, these are pretty conservative guys, and tend to be attracted to women who are more "ladylike" all the way around...and besides, Betas generally see sex as part of a long-term relationship, rather than a pleasant way to spend an evening with a woman they barely know. (When you worry about your ability to perform in the first place, the concept of bed-hopping is a nightmare...) Betas generally prefer pretty, reasonably demure women over flashy ones.

The upside of this, of course, is that assuming she finally gets him into bed, a woman doesn't need to worry unduly about her Beta mate running around on her. Like Alphas, Betas are pretty monogamous, although probably not to the same degree, nor for the same biochemical reasons.

A Beta trapped in a miserable marriage is more likely to find a more emotionally fulfilling relationship outside his marriage (with or without sex) than he is to file for divorce, especially if there are still kids at home. This most likely has something to do with prolactin and nesting instincts. Betas are highly unlikely to engage in casual sex - if there is another woman, odds are it's a serious long-term relationship and he's in love with her. It's positively amazing how many "other women" are involved in a long-term relationship with a Beta. Amazing and *stupid*, because these guys are not gonna leave their wives - they *can't*.

It's a rare Beta who will actually file for divorce - even if the marriage is awful and their wife is a shrew, these guys will stick it out for decades, all the while secretly hoping that she will make the move. If they do end up divorced, they will inevitably remarry. By and large Betas *like* to be married. They enjoy having a home and a wife to come home to. They are pretty easily satisfied, and therefore not hard to keep happy. I suspect the main reason women leave them is simply *lack of excitement* - these guys, in truth, can be a little...well...boring, and if you crave adventure and excitement in your life, you won't do yourself (or the Beta) any favors by marrying one.

If financial stability and domesticity, however, are more important to you than excitement, adventure, and hot sex every morning, these are definitely your boys.

Betas want to take care of their wives, because they are nurturers by definition. That's either your cup of tea or it's not.

Betas make wonderful fathers. Even unhappily married, or divorced, they make great fathers, and never shirk their parental responsibilities, emotionally or financially. (I seriously doubt there is a Beta anywhere who is behind in his child-support payments.) Betas, like Retrievers and Perpetual Puppies, are naturally good with children, and will take as active a role in raising their kids as their career permits. (They probably carry higher than average levels of both prolactin and oxytocin than most of the other high-status PSPs do, which is what makes them more nurturing.)

Betas actually spend time *talking* with their kids when they are little, and will take their 10 year-old daughter out to dinner. They take more of an interest in domestic life than most PSPs, and genuinely enjoy spending their weekends playing with the kids, working around the house, and maintaining the lawn.

Providing the best life they can for their family is very important to Betas, and they generally invest wisely for their children's education, as well as carrying more insurance than the average human being deems necessary, in the event something untoward should happen to them.

Ward Cleaver was definitely a Beta.

5

Junkyard Dogs

"At this instant, the whole of my life seems to be condensed into one wonderful moment."
-*Yuri Gagarin, Soviet cosmonaut and the first man in space, just before liftoff in April, 1961*

"Dear Lord...please don't let me fuck this up."
-*Alan Shepard, US astronaut and the second man in space, just before liftoff in May, 1961.*

Now *this* is an interesting group! Probably the most complex of men, the Junkyard Dog is a puzzle to many and, like Alphas, highly misunderstood. But they are fascinating characters, whether you personally happen to like them or not.

Nine times out of ten, when a man figures out he is probably *not* an Alpha (usually due to the monogamy issue), his second choice is Junkyard Dog. In fact, next to the Alpha, the Junkyard Dog is the PSP a lot of people (especially men) seem to understand *viscerally*, even if they understand little or nothing about the phenomenon of pack order. The term is often used with fair accuracy and often, I suspect, with less insult than one would initially assume, even by one's sworn enemies.

The quintessential Junkyard Dog of our era, James Carville, has actually been referred to as such, both in print and on national television, by people who probably who have little or no experience with dogs. There's almost a grudging sort of admiration that goes along with calling someone you detest a junkyard dog, especially if you are a guy. Go figure...

And these guys often have more than their fair share of sworn enemies, which doesn't seem to bother them a bit. (On the other hand, the very *thought* of having made an enemy sends a Retriever into a frenzy of anxiety...)

Junkyard Dogs don't need to have everyone like them - it's just not that critical to their self-esteem. And unlike Alphas, they generally don't feel the need to be respected by everyone, either. In fact, the Junkyard dog is usually not so much respected, admired, or liked, as flat-out *feared*, which is perfectly OK with them. There is something slightly *dangerous* about these men, and they know it. *And* they enjoy it.

So, what exactly makes one a Junkyard Dog?

On the plus side, they are intelligent, physically and mentally tough, and have courage to spare. When it comes right down to it, they probably have all the qualities needed to be an Alpha, *except* the automatic instinct to put the survival of the entire pack ahead of their own.

A Junkyard Dog is unlikely to receive a Medal of Honor posthumously. Although pretty fearless, the considerable self-interest of a Junkyard Dog makes him disinclined to "take one for the team", so to speak. In the words of one very famous, and highly quotable, Junkyard Dog (clearly a perennial favorite of this PSP - no fewer than three of whom *actually quoted this line to me*):

"The purpose of war is not to die for your country; it's to make the other poor bastard die for his." - General George S. Patton

It's not so much that they are without loyalty or ethics - these guys can be *the* most loyal of friends, and certainly they are the #1 one guy you'd want to have behind you in a bar fight. (In fact, most Junkyard Dogs actually *enjoy* a good bar fight on occasion...) Nor are they unethical or completely self-serving.

It's more that their loyalties are more narrowly defined than are a lot of other pack animals, and their sense of ethics is very much defined by their own personal code, rather than one imposed on them by religion or philosophy, two subjects on which they are often surprisingly well-read.

And it's not that a Junkyard dog *wouldn't* save someone else's life if the situation arose, but if it's someone he dislikes, he certainly is not going to put his own life at risk to do it. (This is the same guy who, especially when he's young and loaded with testosterone, will risk his life for no reason other than for the adrenaline rush that accompanies it. Go figure.) And if it's someone he truly detests, he can probably watch them self-destruct without lifting a finger and with no particular feelings of guilt whatsoever. (It should not come as much of a surprise that most good fighter pilots are Junkyard dogs - these guys are only team players to a point.)

I suspect that, unlike Alphas and Betas, the Junkyard Dog doesn't have two copies of that short repeat on the DA receptor gene on chromosome 11. Rather, he's what geneticists call a *heterozygote* - he's carrying one copy of the 'altruism' variant, and one copy of the 'novelty-seeking' variant.

Because of the altruism variant, the Junkyard Dog is pro-social; he's a pack animal through and through, and generally represents a fairly high pack status position. In fact, many famous heroes were pretty clearly Junkyard dogs, which is not surprising as this group tends to be courageous to the point of rashness. But it's rarely, if ever, heroism born of an overriding love of, or even a sense of responsibility toward, his "fellow man", because that's not what makes them tick. The heroism of a JD is more the result of high-testosterone, rather than high-oxytocin, or even high-serotonin, altruism.

What makes a Junkyard dog tick is the *kick*. (This was actually explained to me by a Junkyard Dog, by the way...) Whatever they do, they do to excess, especially when they are young and when their testosterone levels are highest. (Even on a slow day, these guys carry pretty high baseline T levels, probably a couple points above any of the other high-ranking PSPs.) And they do it for the kick, which is, as far as I can tell, a state of mind they achieve by pushing the limits on anything.

As Yuri Gagarin put it so eloquently, that kick is the condensation of life into one wonderful moment. And, as Alan Shepard revealed so succinctly, albeit somewhat less eloquently, the kick is in no small measure actually *enhanced* by the possibility that one may indeed screw it up. Without that measure of danger, it's no fun at all.

These guys are risk-takers, and the release of dopamine is the kick. Without a love of risk (and high testosterone levels) you simply cannot be a Junkyard dog. Which is why, incidentally, this is one of the PSPs most likely to use drugs and alcohol, especially when they're young. Their tolerance for alcohol is usually higher than average - a lot of these guys display the characteristics of having been genetically short-changed in the HT1B receptor department; as soon as their serotonin levels (which although variable are usually reasonably high on a good day) drop, they are inclined to get irritable and drink too much. When you combine alcohol's ability to further raise testosterone and lower impulse control with an innate love of risk, you've got the potential for some serious trouble. Not to mention the ability of alcohol to block *vasopressin*.

In fact, a female friend of mine suggested that if one is in the market for a Junkyard dog much over the age of 30, an AA meeting might be as good a place as any to look. The ones you'd still find hanging out in bars at that age usually aren't worth having...

Now, one might intelligently wonder why (and how) a gene which inclines its owner toward personal risk-taking would survive to this day in any species with pack instincts like ours, especially since the mortality rate on this group is higher than average. The truth is, in the long run, the risk-taking gene often benefits the pack as a whole - think about guys like Marco Polo, Christopher Columbus, Lewis and Clark or more recently, Yuri Gagarin, Alan Shepard, and Neil Armstrong. I know, I know - the last three had The Right Stuff, and for some reason most people think astronauts are by definition "Alphas"...*but they are NOT.*

Alphas are not likely to take stupid risks just for the hell of it, not because they lack courage so much as they know instinctively it's probably not in the best interest of their particular pack to do so. (Alphas have two copies of the altruism variant - they are not novelty-seekers by a long shot.)

Do you honestly think a guy who actually volunteers to be *shot into space in a rocket* without any real guarantee that the Omega nerds biting their nails back in Houston can actually get him back in one piece is gonna be an Alpha? *As IF.*

If you think about it for more than thirty seconds, it's a really, really, really dangerous and *stupid* thing to do from a self-preservation standpoint. And most astronauts have traditionally been married men with young children - one guy was actually *up in space,* doing no doubt Really Important NASA Stuff, while his wife (I am not making this up, it's actually on NASA's website) *was in the delivery room bearing their child.*

Nope, most astronauts, like most fighter pilots, are Junkyard Dogs - dyed-in-the-wool *risk-takers*. In fact, in the early days of US space exploration, most astronauts *were* former combat fighter pilots - guys who'd actually shot down a Soviet MIG or two.

Although explorers are, by nature, not motivated purely by altruism (I'm pretty sure Lewis did *not* tell Clark, "Man, if we risk our lives for a couple years traipsing around in hostile Indian and grizzly bear country and actually manage to find the Northwest Passage, we'd really be helping a lot of people...") their actions often do, historically, wind up benefiting the pack as a whole, resulting in the discovery of new food sources, critical natural resources, and, in the case of Lewis and Clark, a future corporate home for Microsoft and a lot of previously undiscovered salmon.

In fact, this gene variant enjoys a far higher incidence in the US than it does in many other countries, which really isn't surprising if you think about it. Most Americans, after all, are the descendents of immigrants - the people who didn't stay home.

Exactly how this gene has managed to survive for thousands of years, when it is found primarily in men who are less likely to see their fortieth birthday than many other PSPs, is a simple and elegant piece of work on Mother Nature's part:

Junkyard Dogs are extremely attractive to women. Historically, Junkyard dogs have managed to pass the genes responsible for their PSP on to the next generation by procreating early, for the most part. (This is probably less true today than in times past, since procreation is no longer an inevitable result of mating, but the instinct is still there.) Junkyard dogs, from an extremely early age and until they ultimately fall apart, are devastating males. They can be tough and mean in the world of men, yet sensitive and utterly romantic around women. (This distinguishes them fairly easily from Leg Lifters, who generally possess the first two qualities in spades while lacking the last two entirely.)

Junkyard Dogs are the guys your mother warned you about. They have such a contrary romantic appeal in fact, that the romance-novel crowd now actually considers them a specific group, dubbing them "Gamma males", which is a move in the right direction, if not an exactly accurate name, implying as it does that they are automatically third in line in the pack-hierarchy behind Alphas and Betas, which they are not.

In any pack, the Junkyard dog tends to be found precisely where he wishes to be at that particular moment. And where he *wishes* to be is just as often determined by what is in *his* best interest as what may be in the best interest of his pack. This is a major difference between the Alpha personality and the Junkyard dog personality.

If Harry Truman had been a Junkyard Dog instead of an Alpha, he'd have simply told FDR and the Democratic Party bosses to stuff it.

Because he is both intelligent and charismatic, the Junkyard Dog can make a good leader of men - assuming he wants to, and sometimes even when he doesn't. Leadership, in their case, is as often born of a unique form of exasperated altruism, and there's often a grudging quality to it, a sort of "OK, I'll do this but only until you can find someone else, because I've really got better things to do…" attitude toward it.

Much of what makes these guys so conflicted as a group is a constant inner battle between what they know they should do and their considerable self-interest. This constant inner conflict literally defines the PSP.

Plumage

Junkyard dogs are pretty physically attractive guys, though not always in the most traditional sense. They can be tall or short, fair or dark - about the only physical common denominator is toughness. What they *all* share is *coolness*, in a Joe Camel "sets your father's teeth on edge when he comes to pick you up" sort of way. These guys intrinsically understand "cool" as a concept from an early age, like maybe when they start kindergarten, or thereabouts. Their unerring sense of what is cool and what is not is inborn, and relies on no one else's judgment. (In fact, Junkyard Dogs rarely rely on anyone else's judgment for anything.)

Junkyard Dogs *define* coolness, and set the "cool" standard for all other males. (If this was not true, nobody but actual *bomber·pilots* would wear bomber jackets, would they? When they returned to civilian life after WW II, Junkyard Dogs made that particular garment cool for millions of other men, just by wearing old jackets designed and issued *by the government*, not an institution generally known for its fashion sense.) They are also sexy (probably the flat-out sexiest PSP when they're young) and that comes through in the clothes they wear. No matter what their personal style, these guys *have* style, and better taste than a lot of males with high testosterone levels. There's always something a little bit *swashbuckling* about them (which is not surprising when you consider that most successful pirates were probably Junkyard dogs) but inherently masculine - there is nothing *androgynous* about a Junkyard Dog, although they are not without vanity.

Junkyard Dogs don't wear pink, either. They are for the most part pretty conservative about color. But they *do* wear black - not surprisingly, black is a perennial favorite of this group. (I think it's that pirate thing again...)

Junkyard dogs will often spend a lot of money on their clothes as soon as they can afford to - not so much because they care about impressing anyone so much as because they are self-indulgent. But unlike Specials, they'll also show up at their cousin's wedding sans socks and in old jeans and a (black) t-shirt, *maybe* with a blazer, if they happen to feel like it. (They do not share the Beta's sense of protocol *at all*.)

I suspect that the fashion genre known as "throwaway chic" was pretty much invented by Junkyard Dogs, and copied by zillions of "JD wannabes".

When they do have to get dressed up, Junkyard dogs of a certain age and socioeconomic group will more likely wear Brooks Brothers. (Armani, several JDs explained to me, was for Leglifters - looks like you're trying too hard.) These same guys are also comfortable in a pair of well-worn jeans, and can actually make a flannel shirt look good, especially with the sleeves rolled up.

Even a *preppie* JD can somehow lend that notoriously unsexy genre a certain amount of casual panache that no other prep can manage. (JFK being the quintessential example here - he could turn even the hopelessly dull prep look of the 50s into something cool just by unbuttoning his collar, rolling back the cuffs, and donning a pair of sunglasses...)

Junkyard dogs *all* wear sunglasses. But Junkyard dogs will not carry an umbrella. Go figure.

In short, it's not so much *what* a Junkyard dog wears so much as the careless ease with which he wears it that matters. These are high-testosterone guys, confident in their masculinity.

Habitat

Mahatma Gandhi (the guy who said "Live simply that others may simply live") most likely was NOT a Junkyard dog.

Junkyard dogs are notoriously self-indulgent, and generally surround themselves with the finest of whatever it is that floats their particular boat. They don't do it to impress anyone, as these guys have little, if any, personal need to impress anyone - they do it simply because both buying and owning things they want brings them personal pleasure.

(This likely has something to do with dopamine.) Because they have surprisingly good taste for high-testosterone men (a combination they share with Specials, interestingly enough - there's gotta be a gene for good taste yet to be discovered) Junkyard dogs usually have pretty interesting digs, and tend to surround themselves with both quality and comfort.

They often collect some pretty decent art, generally have very eclectic taste in music, as well as a penchant for ethnic foods and high-quality spirits - these are not really "hot dog and a Budweiser" guys, although they'll cheerfully consume both at a ball game. In fact, the best word for a Junkyard Dog's taste overall may well be 'eclectic'. This is the result of the novelty - seeking gene, of course - they are eclectic men by definition.

This innate good taste is offset by a complete lack of domesticity - this is a pretty low-prolactin group, especially when they're young. For example, a Junkyard Dog may well be a proficient gourmet cook, but don't expect him to do the dishes...that's a boring detail they have no patience with.

Junkyard dogs are not particularly easy to housebreak. This is actually a nice way of saying that around the house most are pretty much pigs and really need somebody to pick up after them from childhood through old age, which is important to know from a female standpoint, unless they have paid domestic help. Testosterone generally does not make for good housekeeping skills.

Junkyard dogs are "equipment freaks", to a man. Whatever their particular interest, they will inevitably own all the very latest equipment available for it, and will replace it frequently with whatever is newer and better. This principle applies to everything from audio equipment to guns, and no doubt is also caused by the novelty-seeking gene. (I've never yet met a Junkyard dog who didn't own at *least* one gun, so if firearms make you nervous, these are probably not your guys...in fairness, though, this whole PSP is knowledgeable and proficient around guns and rarely own a weapon they can't break down and put back together in the dark - unlike the dangerous idiot who keeps a single loaded pistol he can barely fire in a drawer.)

Junkyard dogs *do not* drive minivans under any conditions. Junkyard dogs drive pretty cool cars, one of which is generally 4-wheel-drive. Nor will they drive a French car, simply because Junkyard Dogs do not like anything French. (I have no idea what *French* Junkyard Dogs drive, but it was suggested to me that it was a moot point, since there *aren't* any French Junkyard Dogs...did I mention these guys can be *mean*?)

Again, they don't choose their cars to impress - they choose them for performance, speed, and/or toughness. And style. These guys often have a special affinity for German cars - BMW, Mercedes, and Porsche are all favored for their engineering. *(If there breathes a Junkyard Dog who has not actually driven on the Autobahn, I haven't met him yet... it's one of the hallmarks of the PSP.)*

Jeeps, Land Rovers, and 4WD pickups are also favorites of this PSP - these are eclectic guys, after all, and if you can't go 100 mph on a well-engineered piece of asphalt, you might as well be off-road in some Godforsaken place, dodging irate water buffalo or well-armed revolutionaries of some sort...and most Junkyard Dogs, by the age of thirty, have been to a lot more Godforsaken places than most people.

A man who's reached the age of thirty without having his passport stamped is probably *not* a Junkyard Dog. So what do Junkyard Dogs do for a living?

A fair number have military experience, but rarely of the ordinary sort - they're usually Special Forces, fighter pilots, or Military Intelligence, all areas where brains as well as testosterone are a prerequisite. (This is how most of them got to visit all those Godforsaken places, of course...)

In truth, Junkyard Dogs are attracted to the military as much for the adventure and the travel as for any real overriding urge to serve their country. These guys are rarely knee-jerk "my country right or wrong" sort of patriots (those would be Leglifters) unless, of course, their country is actually *attacked*, in which case you probably want to get out of their way...they have a strong noradrenaline response and, when provoked, they can be pretty aggressive. (Like a good protection-trained Doberman, a Junkyard Dog will never choose flight over fight in the face of a threat.)

Once they outgrow that (rarely are Junkyard Dogs career military any more - they're as temperamentally unsuited for the New Military as Alphas) they are found in lots of various professions - it's that eclectic thing again.

The most physical of them (and nearly all of them were competitive athletes as kids) are often firefighters and search-and-rescue guys, risking their lives on a daily basis for a paycheck.

The ones with military backgrounds (and security clearances) often work for one of those government intelligence agencies with three-letter names, although the CIA probably gets a bigger chunk than the FBI, which is perceived by Junkyard Dogs as populated primarily by Boy Scouts.

Spycraft is highly appealing to their sense of adventure, which is reflected in their reading tastes - Nelson De Mille, Tom Clancy, and Jack Higgins are perennial favorites of this PSP.

In the world of medicine, they are transplant surgeons and emergency and trauma guys, where the adrenaline flows on a daily basis. Junkyard Dogs do not become dermatologists.

In the legal profession, Junkyard Dogs are almost always defense attorneys, where brains, high testosterone, and the ability to narrowly define one's ethics and loyalties as the situation warrants are all advantages.

In science, they are most apt to be found in physics and molecular genetics, the two fields that attract high-testosterone types. (I have no idea why, frankly - I just read that somewhere...I actually have no idea what physicists even *do*.)

Because they are not (outside of an actual combat situation) particularly self-directed like Alphas, or self-disciplined like Betas, Junkyard Dogs are more apt to work for someone else than themselves. (Think about it - in the world of dogs, the junkyard dog works for the owner of the junkyard, not himself.) But they almost always have a particular skill that allows them a degree of autonomy - in any job situation, these guys are not classic team players; they're actually more like "hired guns." (This is obviously very true of canine junkyard dogs as well....)

Impatient and incapable of suffering fools gladly, they are not temperamentally suited to climbing the corporate ladder, nor are they particularly driven to do so. In fact, they are probably *least* likely to be found in traditional "business" fields. Nor are they likely to pursue a career in education - these guys generally are only found teaching at the University level, in no small part due to their deficiency of patience.

They usually seek (and train for) reasonably high-paying jobs, not because they are ambitious in the traditional sense, but because for most of them, the real purpose of a job is simply to provide the expendable income to buy the toys they need to play the games they play when they are not working. And they like expensive toys.

The exception here is the situation in which the job itself is the game and provides the toys - for example, if you fly a 747 out of Dulles for United during the week and an F-16 out of Andrews for the Air Force on weekends, you probably don't need to make payments on a plane of your own....

Probably for this reason, one business Junkyard Dogs will own is an auto-repair shop; more often than not import auto repair. If your mechanic has an MBA and an attitude, odds are he's a Junkyard Dog. (It's absolutely amazing how many of them are out there...something you learn if you are cursed with the particular gene mutation that causes you to own vintage Jaguars...) And maybe guys who own junkyards are Junkyard Dogs as well...I've honestly never checked.

In short, Junkyard Dogs never have jobs they find boring. The minute they're bored, they move on.

Like Alphas, most Junkyard dogs are pretty well-read in history, politics, world religion, and philosophy. They are particularly fond of military history, which is probably why so many of them can quote Patton, universal hero to them all. (In contrast, most Alphas think Patton was an insufferable hot dog, and are more likely to hold up Omar Bradley or even Germany's Rommel as better leaders of men. Unless you have a particular interest in military history, this is an insufferably boring argument, by the way...)

Junkyard Dogs, not surprisingly, are for the most part politically eclectic as well, and very hard to categorize. Assuming they will admit to a political affiliation, they are as likely to be Democrats as Republicans. They tend to be social liberals, as this is not a PSP that feels the need to tell other people how to behave. (They're never hypocrites; most of them are not choirboys, either.) These same guys, because of their testosterone levels and military training, tend to be pretty hawkish in the foreign affairs department.

Although a few of them (JFK was a classic) find their way into the political arena, they generally find most politicians insufferably stupid. (This seems to be true even of the ones who do end up in politics, come to think about it.)

And, like Alphas, the possibility of another Junkyard Dog ever making it to the Oval Office anytime in the foreseeable future is severely hampered by their refusal to be handled and groomed, or to read from a prepared script. (It is entirely possible that John McCain could prove me wrong, here....) They are far more likely to be the political consultants masterminding campaigns, where brains and the love of a good fight count for more than a slightly checkered past, which most of them have.

Mating Habits

This PSP is arrogant, moody, impatient, restless, adventurous, easily bored, and self-indulgent, which is certainly not every woman's description of the ideal mate. On the plus side, they are interesting, highly intelligent, sexy, and can be very romantic and charming when they feel so inclined.

They are also notoriously good in bed. As most women are well-aware, the combination of adventurous and romantic is pretty hard to beat when it comes to sex. Throw in the Junkyard Dog's affinity for danger, and you've got the recipe for a sexual experience that women are apt to remember well into old age, even if the relationship itself didn't work out.

It was suggested to me (by a woman, not a Junkyard Dog!) that every woman should have at least one relationship with a JD at some point in her life...I'm not at all sure if that's true, since these guys can be emotionally devastating if you're not pretty tough yourself, but I'm putting it in here anyway. There is no doubt you can learn a whole lot from them sexually, which can come in handy and which is what I suspect she was referring to.

Unfortunately, Junkyard Dogs don't always wear as well as Alphas as they age, a downside of the risk-taking personality's effects on the body. The ones who continue their hard-drinking ways much past thirty usually fall off considerably in the sex department as they age and their libido is no longer supported by the testosterone levels of youth. And because they're not particularly self-disciplined, once they give up competitive sports they tend to lose the hard-muscled toughness that they all display when young, although they are rarely obese. (These guys are not without vanity, which can be a saving grace.)

And this is important - the Junkyard Dog's high baseline testosterone levels puts him at higher risk for prostate cancer as he ages as well, which is something to keep in mind if you happen to be married to one. (Like the Alpha, this is a PSP unlikely to see a doctor unless he's actually bleeding profusely...and an annual checkup is not a bad idea for these guys.)

Women who are successfully married to Junkyard Dogs for any length of time are a special breed. Intelligence and a quick wit are essential, or they'll be bored by the end of the first date. A smart mouth is also not a bad idea if you really want to keep up. Women who appeal to Junkyard dogs are usually attractive and sexy (these guys have good taste) but essentially tough, which are two qualities they both admire and require in a woman.

If you should find yourself enamored with one, there are a few things to keep in mind:

1. Monogamy is *not* a prerequisite of this PSP - they come in both flavors. Until such time as gene-testing is available, you might want to check out his ability to concentrate urine... these guys have the *novelty-seeking* gene, remember? They are easily bored. Unless he inherited a boatload of vasopressin receptors (a Junkyard dog whose father is still married to his first wife might be a better risk than most) the odds of keeping him at home are gonna be pretty slim.

2. Junkyard Dogs are pretty moody and don't have the best of dispositions. Living with one is a lot like living with a Doberman pinscher - women who have no ability to comfortably deal with potentially aggressive dogs are gonna be in trouble early on. (This is not a skill one can easily learn, by the way - you either have a natural aptitude for it or you don't.) Nagging, bitching, whining, and out-and-out confrontations are rarely successful techniques for dealing with Junkyard Dogs. Good timing, a sense of humor, and the ability to stand your ground when necessary are prerequisites.

3. Junkyard dogs are more independent and need more personal space than most PSPs. If you need to know where your mate is at all times, it's simply not going to work out. (I know women married to Junkyard Dogs who sometimes don't know exactly which *continent* their husbands are on, much less exactly when they'll be back…)

Frankly, in spite of their considerable attractiveness, a Junkyard Dog is *not* the right guy for most women, but if think you're up to the job, they actually don't make bad husbands. They can be extraordinarily sensitive and supportive partners, and they are pretty self-aware and comfortable with who they are - more than many other PSPs, which is how I found out a lot of this stuff.

For example, I asked a ton of Junkyard Dogs what they wore to bed, and they all answered promptly (they all sleep naked, by the way) without any embarrassment at all. In fact, most of them never even asked why I wanted to know. On the other hand, Alphas, who also sleep naked, found that to be an uncomfortable question. Junkyard Dogs are better communicators than Alphas.

They're also never threatened by tough, intelligent, or independent women. But as a group they're not easily threatened, anyway. And no woman ever leaves a Junkyard Dog because she's bored.

They make good fathers for the most part, and a lot of them are surprisingly comfortable around babies, which implies reasonably high prolactin levels at least on occasion, and which might also explain their better-than-average decorating skills for high-T guys.

Also surprising for guys who are notoriously sexy is the fact that Junkyard Dogs can also go without sex for fairly extended periods without getting cranky if they are doing something interesting, like maybe when they're in combat or exploring the surface of the moon. This is a major difference between Junkyard Dogs and Alphas, who require a steadier, if less varied, sexual diet.

Once the kids get older, though, they're more like Alphas in the day-to-day discipline department, involved but perfectly content to leave the more mundane aspects of child-rearing to their wives. Since they often have jobs that involve travel, this works out pretty well.

Bottom line is this:

If you want a stay-at-home sort of guy who will be wherever you need him to be whenever you need him to be there, you're gonna be *really* disappointed with a Junkyard Dog.

If, on the other hand, you honestly *don't mind* driving yourself to the hospital while you're in labor and delivering a child while its father is at a conference somewhere, out of the country, or in actual *outer space*, these are your boys. It maybe helps to have a copy of the novelty-seeking gene and a fairly high testosterone level yourself.

6

Retrievers

There are few dogs as universally attractive, charming, and well-liked as the group of sporting dogs known as Retrievers, which accounts, in no small part, for their popularity - over the last several years, the Labrador and Golden Retriever breeds (the best-known of the bunch) have ranked #1 and #2 respectively in registration numbers out of over 150 AKC breeds.

The same is true for the PSP of the same name, truly one of my favorite groups. Retrievers are pretty hard to dislike.

This is probably not a coincidence. When evaluating puppies, the inclination to retrieve has long been associated with social attraction and pack-dependence.

They love people, which is why they are one of the few PSPs who are naturally attracted to politics as a career. Retrievers are, by nature, kind. They *care* about people, especially those less fortunate than themselves, and they are attracted to politics because they honestly think they can make a difference.

For this reason, they are way more likely to be Democrats than Republicans...I mean, think about this - in the canine world, in addition to retrieving ducks and/or tennis balls, Retrievers are seeing-eye dogs, therapy dogs, and service dogs, carrying little packs on their back and pushing elevator buttons for quadriple-

gic owners. It's astonishing how many Retrievers get awards each year for saving lives through feats of sheer bravery, putting their own lives at risk to do so - if these dogs could vote, do you honestly think they'd vote Republican?? No, they would not. Wirehaired Dachshunds would vote Republican.

Retrievers almost always start out early in life as "golden boys" in the eyes of adults. They're student body presidents, Eagle Scouts, camp counselors, youth leaders in their church; a lot of them have actual *resumes* before they even hit the adult world running. They *need* them at an early age, of course, because probably 99% of the college scholarships awarded by prestigious universities every year go to Retrievers, and the competition for them is fierce.

With testosterone levels usually on the high side of average, Retrievers can be pretty competitive, whether in sports, politics, or within whatever career they choose, but they are *nice* about it - they believe in teamwork and good sportsmanship, and they don't cheat (except sometimes on their girlfriends and wives, but we'll discuss that later) because they believe in fair play, and they are gracious losers if they don't win, giving their victors due honors with more generosity than most.

Any man who can say "You're really a great player - I sure wish I had your forehand shot!" (and mean it), rather than grousing about how he got beat, is probably a Retriever...

Retrievers are rarely judgmental. The guy who said "Harsh judgments make hypocrites of us all" was most assuredly a Retriever.

Nor are they particularly good at bearing a grudge, being remarkably more forgiving of the weaknesses of others than the male population at large. They are also capable of producing an apology easily when the situation warrants one, and *meaning* it.

Part of the reason for this is that Retrievers, unlike most males, have little difficulty communicating their own feelings, thoughts, and fears, even in public. If they've just acted like a roaring jerk, not only are they capable of *admitting* it, they are also often actually capable of explaining *why* they were acting like that, which sets them apart from nearly all other PSPs.

As well as being tuned in to the feelings of others to an astonishing degree, these guys are pretty self-aware compared to the male population in general and are, by and large, good *communicators*. This makes a lot of other guys wince, but women appreciate it. Retrievers are friendly, outgoing, generous, and loving.

The biochemical reason for the "soft side" of the Retriever is oxytocin - the "tend and befriend" hormone. *Although women generally produce more oxytocin than men do, there is certainly the same variation among individuals of both genders as there is with any of the hormones we refer to as either "male" or "female" - in fact, the whole idea of assigning specific genders to hormones that both sexes produce is probably stupid if you think about it.* Anyway, Retrievers have all the earmarks of high-oxytocin males - they are empathetic and sensitive to the feelings of others to an astonishing degree. Toss in a couple of copies of the 'altruism gene' variant on chromosome 11 and higher-than-average male estrogen levels and you have the recipe for a man whose 'interpersonal relationship skills' can surpass that of all other male PSPs. In fact, the Retriever is really the *only* PSP that understands the concept of nurturing and tending friendships in the same way that women do.

Show me a guy who still has friends from grade school, and I'll show you a Retriever. *Bill Clinton (and unless you're really slow on the uptake you've probably figured out he's the QUINTESSENTIAL Retriever of our era), actually counted among his White House Cabinet two men he'd first met back at Miss Marie Purkins' School for Little Folks in Hope, Arkan-*

sas when they were all five years old! I mean, seriously - how many middle-aged men do you know who can still count as personal friends guys with whom they went to NURSERY SCHOOL? Face it, even most women (who are usually far better at maintaining friendships over long periods of time) can't make that claim. It's absolutely astonishing.

Retrievers make pretty good leaders for the most part.

They surely have many of the qualities needed to assume a leadership position, and most of the qualities needed to maintain it. They generally make understanding and innately fair bosses, and inspire strong loyalty in those who work for them.

Retrievers have the "altruism gene" in spades, and it's as likely to be displayed as the high-oxytocin "kind and compassionate" (rather than the high-testosterone "physically heroic") variety.

They are terrific coalition-builders, which is how they get into leadership positions in the first place. And Retrievers build coalitions in a fairly unique and totally fascinating way. While most coalitions are frankly the result of shared self-interest among disparate groups, appealing to what is, in all honesty, not the best side of human nature unless you happen to be a die-hard fan of Ayn Rand, Retrievers have this weird ability to build coalitions by making everyone feel like an integral part of the process. And the reason they can pull this off is because they honestly believe everyone *should* be part of the process - it's part of being an extremely pro-social animal.

What sets Retrievers apart from Alphas (and what trips them up throughout life, both as leaders and with women) is the *other* personality trait they share with their canine counterparts:

Retrievers have an overwhelming, totally irrepressible, need to be loved....*by absolutely everyone.* Any dog person knows it's no real *compliment* to be loved by a Retriever, because they love absolutely everyone with an appalling lack of discrimination.

This is why, for the most part, the whole group (with the notable exception of the Chesapeake Bay Retriever, the toughest of the bunch) is particularly useless as guard dogs - everyone who's ever owned one knows they would gladly welcome a burglar into the house, and then helpfully lead him right to the family silver, tail wagging the whole time. (I've always suspected that this is because they really hate to be alone, and they figure that even a burglar is better than no company at all...)

Because they're among the most social of animals, Retrievers of both species are people-pleasers by definition; they are truly unhappy if they know somebody's mad at them, and they will honestly try to amend the situation if they can. This causes problems in elected office, where by definition you've probably pissed off at least half your constituency on any given day. The fact that these are mostly the people who didn't vote for you in the first place doesn't make it any less awful for a Retriever. (They're all compulsive poll-checkers primarily for this reason.) But in spite of that, they are as a group more attracted to political life than any other PSP I can think of besides Leglifters and Lone Wolves.

The major difference is that Leglifters and Lone Wolves (both of whom are pretty much totally lacking in altruism) see political office primarily as an opportunity for dominance and power, which is mostly what politics has been about since well before the time of Machiavelli.

It's hardly a coincidence that men, who have a far stronger biological imperative for attaining and maintaining pack status than females, have completely dominated politics throughout most of history. And most of these males have traditionally been pretty high-testosterone guys.

On the other hand Retrievers, who have bucket-loads of altruism and enough oxytocin and estrogen to help offset the testosterone, view politics primarily as an opportunity for helping those less fortunate than themselves. **This essential difference is largely responsible for the current two-party system as we know it.**

Besides high baseline levels of oxytocin and a couple of copies of the altruism gene, Retrievers generally also display the characteristics of fairly high serotonin levels - a generally calm demeanor, reasonable impulse control, and a fair amount of self-confidence. They rarely suffer from clinical depression; Retrievers are by definition optimists with a fairly positive view of the world and although (like anyone else) they can certainly feel depressed at times, it's rarely a long-term chronic problem with them.

Retrievers rarely suffer from chronic stress, either; their "flight-or-fight" response is certainly adequate for survival, but generally not over-developed like a Sentinel's. And like women, they tend to respond to stress by *talking,* which is probably good for their overall health.

Like their canine counterparts, Retrievers are also remarkably adaptable and resilient - probably the most adaptable and resilient of all PSPs. These guys can "take a licking and keep on ticking" like no other guys on the *planet.* This is because they are among those rare males who carry both high testosterone *and* estrogen levels, which would account for this resiliency and stamina, both of which are associated with estrogen. (It would also explain why they often have bigger butts than Alphas, and are heavier through the thighs.)

The stamina comes in pretty handy during a campaign, too, and these guys *love* to campaign. It gets them out where there are literally *thousands* of people to talk to and meet and hug and shake hands with *all at once,* which is akin to plunking their four-legged counterparts in a room full of tennis balls.

Plumage

Retrievers are, as previously noted, an attractive bunch for the most part. They are generally blessed with fairly regular facial features, and some are gorgeous by any standards. They are usually taller than average, broad-shouldered, with a body built more for endurance than speed. (In other words, they tend to be built more like Retrievers than greyhounds.)

Retrievers usually carry a full head of hair well into middle age and beyond. *In fact, I've yet to meet a Retriever with male-pattern baldness, now that I think about it...somebody really ought to fund a study on that. Maybe, like women, even the ones carrying the gene for it are protected from MPB by their higher estrogen levels?*

What really sets a Retriever apart physically, though, is an almost indefinable *softness*, even when they are big men in good physical shape. There is just somehow less of a "hard-edge" to them than one would find in Alphas or Junkyard dogs, both of whom carry more lean muscle, at least when young. Retrievers have a sort of "teddy bear" quality, and are often described as such.

Women who are attracted to "teddy bear men" are really attracted to Retrievers. A great big guy who is huggable is probably a Retriever - a great big guy who is *not* huggable is probably a Leglifter...and is more likely to be described as "a bull of a man" rather than "a bear of a man", anyway. *And which is probably why stuffed bulls have never had the universal appeal of stuffed bears, come to think about it...bulls are just not huggable, unless maybe you're a cow.*

Retrievers often fight a weight problem most of their lives, mostly because they are comfort-seekers by temperament, and food is, as every woman knows, one of life's greatest sources of comfort. (Or maybe it's because he carries higher levels of oxytocin and estrogen.) They may work out, but they really don't like to, so they are usually in the best shape of their lives sometime between 16 and 30, and it's a constant battle from then on. The general difficulty that all Retrievers have saying "no" certainly doesn't help their weight problem either.

Retrievers *love* food, every last one of them. And being innately sensitive, they would never hurt a hostess's feelings by turning down seconds, even if it was something they didn't really like - as is also true with Betas (the other innately kind PSP). Retrievers are easily capable of dishonesty in the name of kindness. At a potluck picnic, a Retriever will actually take a big helping of whatever dish looks *least popular*, just so the person who brought it won't feel bad. (How can you not love these guys?)

A lot of Retrievers actually know how to cook, and they like to feed people. They can't *stand* the thought of anyone going hungry, and would feed the world if they could.

A Retriever friend of mine once realized he couldn't possibly marry a girl he'd been dating when he discovered that she was sort of...well...maybe a little STINGY?...about food, and that her mother had precisely the same failing. He suspected it was a family trait. And one that bothered him a lot.

As far as clothes go, Retrievers are rarely if ever "cool" like Junkyard dogs - they weren't the coolest guys, by far, in high school and they are not particularly cool as adults. They're not geeky, though, because they usually have reasonably good taste and sufficient testosterone levels to preclude geekiness, which is a pretty low-T trait.

They're basically altruists by nature, and I've never yet met an altruist who was a clotheshorse. I suspect they view being overly obsessed about clothes as a little bit selfish and maybe...well... *shallow* when there are people going to bed hungry in the world.

It's not that they don't *like* nice clothes; it's just that they rarely go out and *buy* them. If a wife or girlfriend buys him something gorgeous, he'll be pleased (in truth probably more with the thought behind it than the gift itself), and he'll cheerfully wear it, but it is just not that *important* to them, and "style" is not a concept they are particularly familiar with.

Comfort, on the other hand, *is* important to a Retriever, and they lean toward comfortable clothes. If they are not wearing a suit to work, they often favor worn blue chambray work shirts, or flannel (plaid flannel usually). These guys are real fans of corduroy - more so than any other PSP. Maybe because it's soft. (They especially like that caramel brown color that corduroy so often comes in.) Probably for the same reason, they are more likely to wear suede than leather. And they like sweaters. And sweatshirts. In fact, they often consider sweats to be the perfect attire for almost any occasion, and use them the way Betas use a bathrobe. On weekends, even if he's not going anywhere or doing anything that remotely resembles exercise, a Retriever will invariably be found in sweats and running shoes.

You'll *never* find a Retriever in skin-tight jeans...their jeans are almost always "relaxed fit, cut a little fuller through the seat and thighs". (This is probably because Retrievers themselves are often cut a little fuller through the seat and thighs.) They wear jeans a lot, even when they're 75 years old. Unpressed Dockers are their stock in trade for "dress wear." Designer labels are entirely foreign to them. Most Retrievers don't even know who those guys *are.*

In a crowd, a Retriever is pretty easy to spot by his shoes. Unless forced to wear them as part of his job, he'll often not even *own* a pair of dress shoes. They wear running shoes and sneakers a lot, although these are guys who really aren't "runners" by definition - they just like the fact that they are soft and comfortable, I think. They like shoes with squishy thick crepe soles, too, and favor suede and nubuck over leather that needs to be polished. You are unlikely to find a Retriever in a pair of Italian loafers under any circumstances.

They do wear boots. Retrievers from the West wear cowboy boots, of course. (But then, so does everyone else from the West.) And chukka boots were a real favorite a while back. Now they wear hiking boots, mostly. This is probably because Retrievers enjoy hiking - lots of nature-lovers in this PSP.

All in all, Retrievers tend to look a little bit *rumpled,* even in evening wear. It's part of their charm. They usually have good thick hair, but it's always a little tousled, and rarely styled. Like Alphas, a fair number of them sport a beard at some point in their lives. If a crisply-pressed man is important to you, these guys will be a constant source of frustration. Besides, if you are overly concerned about clothes, you probably aren't going to have a lot of other things in common with them, anyway.

Habitat

Retrievers have pretty good nesting instincts, and generally live in comfortable, although rarely ostentatious, surroundings even when they're single - assuming they don't still live at home, which a fair number of single Retrievers do. They usually have pretty complete kitchens, because they like to cook (and eat.) *This is frankly why a lot of single Retrievers still live at home. As a group, they are usually pretty fond of their Mamas (especially in the south) and odds are Mama is a great cook. So don't try reading a lot more into it than that, because it's probably not there.*

Retrievers who do live on their own choose their furnishings based entirely on comfort, and this means they own *at least* one recliner, and sometimes two, even when they live alone, which I've frankly never understood.

If Alphas can be identified by their universal aversion to recliners, Retrievers can just as easily be identified by their universal *love* of them.

The recliner is invariably the Retriever's absolutely favorite piece of furniture. Like their canine counterpart, Retrievers find lying sprawled on their backs with their throats exposed *a perfectly comfortable position* - in fact, come to think about it, the recliner is a lot like the human version of the L.L. Bean dog bed. The Retriever's idea of relaxation after a hard day is to kick back in the recliner with a cold beer and a bag of chips (or a pizza) to watch a little football.

For some reason I haven't yet figured out, most Retrievers really like football, especially college ball. A fair number of them play (or played) it, and the rest watch it. They maintain strong lifelong loyalties to their Alma Mater in this regard. If they went to LSU (even if they majored in anthropology there and never played any actual college ball themselves) and LSU is in the playoffs, they are gonna arrange their schedule so they can watch LSU play. Retrievers are very loyal. Their canine counterparts feel the same way about Frisbee.

Next to the recliner, the Retriever's *second-favorite* article of furniture would unfortunately appear to be the TV tray, and he usually will own several. Since these guys are completely devoid of elitism, any suggestion that they may perhaps be... well...*tacky?*...will be met by the Retriever in question with surprised hurt. They *belonged to his grandma.* (The fact that he got them because no one else in the family *wanted* the damn things simply never occurs to him.) Besides, what could possibly be handier next to a recliner? If you choose to cohabitate with a Retriever, don't even *think* about trying to talk him out of the recliner. You may or may not have better luck with the TV trays.

Retrievers have a pretty wide range of interests as a general rule, although most of them lean toward what women refer to as "outdoorsy" interests. Lots of fishermen in this group. They generally like camping, gardening, hiking, boating, and water sports. Retrievers all seem to like water, and are usually good swimmers and sailors. (Often their first real paying job is being a lifeguard.) Among the older ones there are a fair number of duck hunters.

Hunting, although less popular than in years past as we've become a more urbanized society, is a sport that strongly reflects our hunter-gatherer roots, and is generally limited to the higher-testosterone PSPs. Even between these guys, there is a difference; for Leglifters, the killing itself is the sport - what Steinbeck called "creative destruction". Retrievers, like Alphas and Betas, see hunting as a source of (usually very expensive) food, and will only kill that which they will eat. They are responsible and ethical hunters, and have little or no regard for the other kind. For a Retriever, cooking and serving fish or game he has bagged himself to people he cares about is a great source of visceral pleasure. It's no doubt the exact same sort pleasure and satisfaction his canine counterpart gets from retrieving a duck.

From a career standpoint, one is highly unlikely to find a Retriever on Wall Street. They have absolutely none of the personality traits needed to succeed in business, and they are simply not all that interested in money, anyway.

Besides the aforementioned politics, they are often found in education (they make great teachers) and in medicine, where they are more likely to be drawn toward family practice and pediatrics than cardiac surgery or emergency medicine. Because they are altruists, they are often found teaching in inner-city schools, and practicing medicine in godforsaken places that need doctors.

Some of them are lawyers, but here again, they see law as an opportunity to do good rather than to make buckets of money. Lots of them seem attracted to wildlife and marine biology, as well as other fields that require being outdoors. Those who are scientists tend to be the guys in the field rather than the guys back in the lab.

Retrievers are all animal lovers, and they make wonderful veterinarians. In fact, this PSP probably makes up the largest percentage of men in that field, which would explain why so many female dog breeders adore their vets.

If a guy with lots of money is important to you, though, this is probably not the right PSP for you - money isn't all that important to a Retriever, and they never choose a career based on salary.

Mating Habits

Emotionally, Retrievers wear their hearts on their sleeve.
They fall in love pretty easily, which is no doubt a result of an abundance of oxytocin receptors. Sex, of course, releases oxytocin, and especially when they are young, these guys tend to fall in love with anyone they sleep with - at least temporarily.

This can be problematic for them, as they are also pretty easily *seduced*. (Remember, oxytocin makes men more trusting.) And because they are attractive, kind, and good listeners, they are more apt to be seduced than a lot of PSPs. Women just find themselves wanting to go to bed with Retrievers, and they're pushovers. (These guys have a hard time saying no in general, much less when they are being seduced.)

The famous lover Don Juan, by all accounts, owed his reputation as a great lover mostly to his ability to actually listen to women, which was apparently an even rarer trait in men during his time than it is today. Personally, I've always suspected he was a Retriever.

Now, if you put those two things together, you start to see the problem - Retrievers, especially young ones, can find themselves in love with more than one woman at a time. This causes them no end of distress, and it doesn't exactly make the women involved ecstatic, either. The Lovin' Spoonful's "Did You Ever Have to Make Up Your Mind?" was undoubtedly written by a Retriever.

Once they *do* finally make up their minds, they make wonderful husbands - loyal, loving, sensitive and supportive. In fact, they'd be perfect if it weren't for that "pushover" part, which they never outgrow, unfortunately. All their lives, needy women have a way of attaching themselves to Retrievers, and because they are inherently kind men and good listeners, they have a really hard time shaking them off.

Retrievers have no problem with *strong* women at all - they admire them, are not threatened by them in the least, and are in fact usually surrounded by them all their lives. (These guys often have strong mothers, whom they adore.) In fact, they usually do best when *married* to a strong woman - one who can put her foot down when necessary to keep him from being used by those with a tendency to exploit his altruistic nature.

Retrievers as a group are supportive of their wives, and generally not threatened by their careers. (Bear in mind, however, that they probably share few if any interests with urban career-minded businesswomen, and would likely have more in common with a kindergarten teacher who collects stray cats.)

Retrievers are good lovers.

Like Alphas, they are pretty conventional in their sexual tastes, but proficient. And, as with Alphas, there's that *altruism* thing.

Face it, a guy who derives pleasure and satisfaction from pleasing others is simply going to be better in bed than one whose main goal is to please himself. Which is why as a group, Democrats are better lovers than Republicans - an accepted fact among women that a whole lot of men (mostly Re-

publican men) are uncomfortable with and really don't want to see in print. Oh well.

Unlike Alphas, Retrievers are also good at expressing themselves emotionally, which many women see as a plus. In fact, next to the recliner thing and the difference in the size of their thighs, it's one of the main differences between the two groups. If you want an honest (bearing in mind that dishonest men have no problem saying *whatever* it takes to get laid), classically masculine guy who can say "I love you" without embarrassment or without you having to say it *first,* these are your boys, no doubt about it.

But it has to be weighed against the fact that their natural tendency toward monogamy (and most Retrievers only have one wife over the course of their lives) needs to be pretty strictly *enforced* by their mates. Unlike Leglifters, Retrievers will not actively *seek* extramarital affairs, but they won't be able to easily turn down the opportunity should it present itself, simply because they have a hard time saying no to anything.

Like their canine counterparts (and every woman who breeds Retrievers can attest to this) Retrievers tend to view every wag of the tail as an invitation they cannot turn down, no matter how inappropriate the bitch.

A woman married to a Retriever needs to be vigilant about any stray women who seem to need advice, or financial help, or special tutoring, or she will become a major problem, sure as God made little green apples.

As one would expect, Retrievers make great fathers. They are nurturing, and natural lovers of kids. (Many of them are pretty good with babies, even, which is pretty rare in men.) Like Alphas, though, they are extremely tolerant and not great disciplinarians, preferring to leave that aspect of childrearing to their wives.

Being trustworthy to a fault, Retrievers can be safely left in charge of even very small children with no fears for their safety or well-being. All in all, a strong-minded practical woman who wants a life filled with friends, family, food, kids, and animals could do worse.

7

Perpetual Puppies

Everybody loves a puppy.

Mother Nature, in her infinite wisdom, intentionally makes puppies cute so that we can't get as angry with them for their misdeeds as we might if they looked more like maybe *opossums* - a singularly unattractive critter by anyone's standards - or *cockroaches*, neither of whose young have any more charm, at least to our eyes, than their adult counterparts. *("Oh, Harvey, don't squash it - it's just a baby cockroach!"....yeah, right. Has anyone but me ever noticed how even people who won't eat meat because they think killing animals is cruel draw the line at cockroaches? Like, what - it's somehow bad to kill CUTE creatures, but really UGLY ones are fair game...? There's a piece of fluid morality for you.*)

In the world of dogs, Perpetual Puppies are the ones who have lots of promise as puppies, but for some reason take forever to actually *realize* that promise. Every show breeder has had one or two over the years, and they are frustrating as hell. You "run them on", waiting and waiting for them to mature into the spectacular specimen you are just *sure* they're gonna turn into, and somehow they never quite get there; instead, they just seem to stay stuck in that stupid "adolescent puppy" stage forever. Sooner or later most breeders give up, and pass them on to someone with more patience or lower expectations.

The same thing often happens with men - in fact, they account for a lot of first husbands. (You remember him - that cute guy you married in college, who was so funny and smart...before you realized he wanted to spend the rest of his *life* there so as to avoid having to get a real adult job in the real adult world.)

Men who are still "cute" past the age of 16 are usually Perpetual Puppies. Perpetual Puppies are a charming group for the most part, and although I suspect no guy wants to wear a sign around his neck identifying himself as one, many Perpetual Puppies have actually gone on to great success and fame in our modern society. They are always attractive and possessed of lifelong 'boyish charm', often bright enough to get by, and a pack animal through-and-through.

What sets the Perpetual Puppy apart from all other PSPs is simply his inability to ever really reach full maturity, either emotionally or intellectually. He might have the individual genes and brain chemistry that would ultimately have made him a Beta, or a Leglifter, or even a Junkyard Dog...but *he never quite gets there* because he's permanently immature. This is important to remember, because there's a fair amount of difference between a Beta Puppy, who is pretty easy to housebreak and live with, and a Leglifter Puppy, who is not.

The success or failure of a Perpetual Puppy is entirely dependent upon the competence and skill of his handlers. These handlers are most often wives and mothers, although in the political arena, they are often specifically hired for the purpose.

In fact, one of the most successful Perpetual Puppies in modern history was none other than:

Ronald Reagan.

Although an amazing number of people guess The Great Communicator for an Alpha, they are quite simply *missing the obvious* - "Ronnie" Reagan (there's your first clue to his PSP, by the way) was an *actor*, and the part he played for a full and successful 8 year run was the part of *John Wayne* who, as it happens, probably *was* an Alpha. Even though John Wayne was an Alpha and Ronnie Reagan was not, *Reagan was by far the better actor.* Why?

Well, although Reagan played the Duke really well, John Wayne could not have played Reagan if you put a *gun* to his head.

This is mostly because John Wayne, like Clint Eastwood, Sean Connery, and Arnold Schwarzenegger, bless their hearts, *can't act.* (Many actors, like our 40th President, are in fact Perpetual Puppies, although these three guys most definitely are not.) They've made some great flicks over the years, and made a whole lot of money doing it, but let's face it - did any of them *ever* fool you into thinking they were *someone else*, even for a minute?

Nahh...We dropped the price of admission to see *them*. Could any of them ever have played...say...*Tootsie*, like Dustin Hoffman did? Or Mrs. Doubtfire? Not in *this* lifetime. Hell, John Wayne even turned down the role of the Waco Kid in Blazing Saddles, although he thought the script was hilarious. He explained to Mel Brooks that he simply couldn't do it. Why not? *Because he was John Wayne.*

Perpetual Puppies are the product of a phenomenon known as neoteny. The word *neoteny (nee-OT-eny)*, like so many English words, is borrowed from the Greeks - in this case, the prefix *neo*, meaning "young", and *teinein,* meaning "to extend". It simply refers to the retention of juvenile characteristics into adulthood.
(And by the way, you might want to put some Windex on that...)

Neoteny, which most women have never even heard of, is critical to understanding Perpetual Puppies, and several other very important things about men (and women) that have probably never occurred to most of us, but will make perfect sense in a minute.

I am dead serious, here - if this stuff was required reading for all girls in 8th grade or thereabouts, we'd all be a lot better off. Better late than never, though...so here goes:

Back in 1983, a Dr Dan Kiley published a book called **The Peter Pan Syndrome**, about men who refused to grow up. Although the book enjoyed a lot of popularity and women recognized the phenomenon immediately, for some unknown reason it never gained the support of the mainstream psychology community (probably because Freud never wrote a paper on it), and consequently Peter Pan Syndrome is not listed in the Diagnostic and Statistical Manual of Mental Disorders. This is probably a good thing in the long run, because Peter Pan Syndrome, although real enough, is *not* a mental disorder - it's entirely biochemical, and purely genetic. *The Peter Pan Syndrome is simply neoteny.*

Neoteny is dependent on mutations in a small handful of genes that determine the onset of maturation in any species, and has long been believed to be responsible for the domestication of the dog. For years evolutionary biologists held to the theory that our early ancestors chose for domestication those wolves which were both most trusting of man and least threatening *toward* him - both characteristics of the juvenile wolf that, for purely practical reasons of survival, are missing in the adult. Years of more or less selective breeding for these traits, they believed, ultimately produced what we now know as the domestic dog.

In addition to being a whole lot more affectionate and trusting than your average wolf, the domestic dog retains many *physical* characteristics of the juvenile wolf as well - shorter, broader muzzles, floppy ears, and the retention of barking into adulthood. But since early man didn't exactly keep good written records, it was a theory that was, by necessity, pretty hard to actually prove. Then a fascinating experiment, conducted in Russia on foxes, proved it right beyond a shadow of a doubt.

One of the problems with raising foxes commercially for their fur is that they never really 'tame up', which means that the people who have to feed and otherwise take care of them get bitten a lot, which is both annoying and painful, and makes it hard to keep reliable help. So in an effort to produce fur-bearing foxes that were easier to handle, these Russian guys started selecting breeding stock based on *temperament* rather than quality of pelt - they chose adult foxes that were most friendly and trusting of humans (traits usually found only in juvenile animals) and bred them together for generations.

Within *twenty years,* they had achieved, through deliberate selection, in the fox what had taken about 20,000 years of considerably more haphazard selection in his cousin the wolf - the creation of what amount to a *new domesticated species*, in effect the 'foxy' version of a domestic dog.

These new 'fox-dogs' were friendlier, easier to handle, and most surprisingly, *looked entirely different.* As well as retaining the juvenile characteristics of the fox kit in terms of temperament, after several generations they started to retain the *physical* characteristics of the immature fox as well - most notably the floppy ears, shorter muzzles, and curlier tails. They were, in a word, CUTER.

They also started producing *parti-colored* foxes, which has no bearing that I can think of on men, but which will no doubt be of interest to Cocker breeders, many of whom have noticed subtle temperament between the various coat colors and patterns in the breed. (Cockers as a whole are the quintessential Perpetual Puppies of the purebred dog world, with their floppy ears, short, plush muzzles, and lifelong immaturity. They are also famously hard to housebreak. Duhh.)

That they managed to pull all this off in so few generations would indicate that the genes for neoteny are not single point mutations, but are more likely controlled by non-Mendelian genetic variations known as trinucleotide repeats, a fact which will, lamentably, be of interest to really only one person I can think of and who, now that I actually AM thinking about it, probably already knows about it anyway.

Not surprisingly, the 'friendly foxes' selected for breeding were also found to carry higher serotonin levels than the rest of the population.

Perpetual Puppies in the world of men display many of the characteristics of high-serotonin levels as well. Unlike Alphas, though, their serotonin levels stay high and their cortisol levels stay low no matter what, which is not necessarily a Good Thing. It's the "Look, Ma, no hands!" sort of idiotic self-confidence displayed by boys that drives mothers crazy and inevitably leads to trips to the emergency room.

That neoteny exists in humans has been a generally accepted fact for decades among anthropologists, evolutionary biologists, and maybe parking-lot attendants for all I know. Yet it's *complete news* to most women, who could really *use* this information. Figures.

Homo Sapiens, it turns out, is the most neotenous of all primates. We take longer to reach maturity than any other mammal on the planet, and when compared to other primates, we retain many juvenile characteristics (including sparse body hair and enlarged heads) well into adulthood.

Now, WHY, you might wonder, would neoteny exist at all in humans? And how would the genes that incline one to a lifetime of immaturity manage to survive among pack-hunting predators?

The 'why' part is simple, actually. There is an evolutionary advantage to neoteny - at least up to a certain point, after which it becomes a decided liability as well as an annoyance. Immature animals are more adaptable than adults, more playful, and have a greater inclination to explore. In humans, the brain actually continues to grow long after it stops in most other species, which is a definite plus. This combination probably accounts for a lot of man's creativity and, indeed, Perpetual Puppies are usually pretty creative guys when compared to the rest of the PSPs...especially when they're lying.

Adaptability is considered to be primarily responsible for the evolution of man - without it, we'd probably still be digging termites out of hollow logs with sticks, and sleeping in trees. But in the world of pack-hunting predators, which is where man set down his roots once he'd gotten over that termite thing, a playful nature and creativity just ain't all that important, especially when compared to the genes necessary for, say, actual *hunting.* I mean, think about it - how many shamans, drummers, and cave-painters does a hunter-gatherer tribe need? (In succeeding millennia, you can substitute artists, minstrels, and court-jesters, here... followed by artists, actors, musicians, and lamentably, all-too-many politicians. Same guys, different centuries.)

So HOW did these genes manage to survive? In humans, just as in the Russian foxes, the genes for neoteny have been deliberately selected for, *that's* how.

But not by women. Most women are tolerant of Perpetual Puppies, but relatively few actually deliberately choose them for mates, at least intentionally, and rarely more than once. In earlier times, when a mate was necessary for protection as much as anything, they were even more useless.

It's *men* who have selected for neoteny over the years. Think trophy wives. Think supermodels. Think of all the billions of dollars women spend trying to look younger than they are.

The physical and emotional results of neoteny are not found exclusively in males. (I bet that hadn't occurred to you until right this minute, did it?) Neoteny is an Equal Opportunity Genetic Phenomenon. Neotenous women, like neotenous men, retain the physical characteristics of children well into adulthood - they look cute and "girlish" well past the time when most girls are starting to turn into women, with adult noses and jaws, breasts, and ever-widening hips.

If they also happen to be really tall, these neotenous women can make an obscene amount of money as fashion models... you know, those long-legged girls with the big-eyed, heart-shaped faces of 6-year- olds modeling sexy lingerie in the Victoria's Secret catalogue. Lots of them in the entertainment fields as well - being narcissistic to a fault (part of being permanently stuck in adolescence) neotenous women are, like their Perpetual Puppy male counterparts, often attracted to the performing arts.

And a large proportion of the male population (oddly, the PSPs that would be excluded here are Alphas, Junkyard Dogs, and Perpetual Puppies themselves) is *seriously attracted* to neotenous females. Which is what led to the discovery of facelifts and tummy-tucks.

Evolutionary biologists have come up with two possible explanations for this: The first, and most widely-accepted explanation, is that youth translates to fertility, and so men are attracted to younger women in order to insure the future of the species. This idea, I am absolutely certain, is simply the product of a testosterone-soaked brain. **In other words...it's pure bullshit.**

The reason I know this is because Alphas, the one PSP who by this logic *should* be attracted to younger (and presumably more fertile) women, seeing as to how they are the ones genetically designed to pass on their superior DNA, are actually the PSP *least* attracted to sweet young things. (In fact, I've yet to meet an Alpha whose mate could by any stretch of the imagination be described as 'a sweet young thing', even when they actually *are* young things.) Duhh.

So the other possible explanation makes *much* more sense.

Very simply, neotenous females are less *threatening* to many males, and because they are for the most part more docile, they more easily dominated.

Less fear of rejection allows males to "display" their male attributes around females with more confidence.
(The reason Alphas are to a large degree immune to neoteny is probably because their serotonin levels are generally high and their testosterone levels only average - this means they are less easily threatened and have less drive to dominate. And being monogamous, they don't need to spend their lives trying to attract unknown females, anyhow. The PSP most attracted to neotenous females is, not surprisingly, the Leglifter. Which probably explains why so many rock stars marry supermodels.)

These displays, part of the competition to attract the attention of females and driven entirely by testosterone, are common to nearly all social species, no matter what their collective intellect. That this instinct to 'display' still exists in human males is evident at every urban construction site, where whistling, preening, and posturing every time a pretty girl walks by are simply the human equivalent of peacocks screeching and spreading their tails.

(Mooning, for the record, is also a form of masculine display common to many primate species besides ours, although I personally know very few human females who are particularly impressed by it...)

Once a male has attracted the attention of a neotenous female through displays of male superiority (which among more successful human males is likely to be via displays of the material trappings of status and wealth), she is far more likely to tolerate his testosterone-laden behavior without slapping him with a sexual-harassment suit than is a female who has reached intellectual and emotional maturity. This ultimately ups the odds he's actually going to get laid.

So what happens is this:

Men with high dominance-seeking personalities (successful Leglifters, usually) choose a docile and youthful 'trophy wife' as soon as they can afford one, both to increase their status with other men, and because having a wife who won't challenge them and will put up with their philandering is critical to their domestic happiness. As a result these are the men most likely to produce offspring who inherit the genes for neoteny.

Which is why the sons of successful Leglifters are so often *complete dodos*, and why their rich fathers have to shell out ten million bucks for a library or a sports stadium to get them into a decent college.

Neoteny is mostly tolerated (and actually encouraged) in advanced, post-industrialized economies like ours, as is the entire concept of *adolescence* if you think about it, whereas in societies where resources are scarce, children sort of jump right into productive adulthood as soon as they are physically capable. (*Rarely will you see a 19 year-old college student in a developing country walking around with a baby pacifier hung around his neck as some sort of neotenous fashion statement...*)

While this process of encouraging neoteny certainly has practical financial advantages for our more prestigious institutions of higher learning, the overall effect is probably less than advantageous in the long run to society at large. While the adaptability and curiosity that comes with neoteny has allowed our species to evolve and that is a Good Thing, one could probably argue that *if some is good, more is not necessarily better.*

Neoteny is not an either/or proposition controlled by a single autosomal recessive gene. If the genes responsible for it are indeed controlled by trinucleotide repeats, as appears to be the case, expansion of those repeats will be amplified every time the genes are passed on, resulting in an exaggeration of neotenous traits with each succeeding generation.

(You want proof of that? Look at Pugs, a cheerful and neotenous short-nosed breed whose muzzles have gotten SO short over the years that they have now pretty much disappeared...or look at the poor Pekinese, which have evolved into flat-faced fuzzy caterpillars. Or simply take a look at the Bush dynasty, where each generation appears to be turning out dopier and more chronically immature than the one preceding it...)

OK, now you know where Perpetual Puppies come from, and why they are still around. Whether or not you actually *want* one is entirely up to you, but either way, it pays to be able to identify them right out of the gate.

A middle-aged man who still wants a birthday party is probably a Perpetual Puppy. Normal males outgrow that desire about the time they can successfully ride a bike without training wheels.

Plumage

Perpetual Puppies are probably the easiest of all the PSPs to spot in a crowd - they're really pretty hard to miss once you know what you're looking for. These are the guys who are *cute* from the day they're born until they day they die. In fact, I've never yet run into a guy who was cute much past puberty who *wasn't* a Perpetual Puppy, because it is the single defining characteristic of the PSP.

"Cute" much beyond puberty is the unmistakable mark of neoteny. However, this developmental lag actually gives the Perpetual Puppy an edge in high school and college, when most of the other guys their age (many of whom will ultimately "finish out better", to borrow a phrase from dog breeders) are in an awkward stage of maturation where none of their parts seem to really fit together, and this is usually the period in his life when the Perpetual Puppy is most popular, especially with girls. (This is helped in no small measure by the fact that these guys seem to be immune to teenage zits.)

Neoteny gives the Perpetual Puppy a fairly distinctive face, no matter what his ethnic background. In general, handsome or not, it's proportionally the face of a male *child* rather than a male adult. Like puppies, they're fairly wide between the eyes, usually with ears they haven't quite finished growing into, a proportionally small nose (often still dusted with freckles), a broad unclouded brow, and a wide, easy grin that displays both trust and eagerness.

A Perpetual Puppy is easy to pick out 20 years later in his grade school class pictures. Unlike a normal adult male, the face of a Perpetual Puppy is extremely mobile and the expressions always a little exaggerated - kind of like those disgustingly cute kids on TV commercials.

For instance, if he is being thoughtful (or wants to appear thoughtful) his face will immediately shape itself into what is almost a 'caricature of thoughtfulness' - head cocked, with a furrowed brow and pursed lips, maybe squinting a little with one eye. *(If it seems vaguely familiar, that's because it's the exact same expression you'll find on a puppy examining a toad who's suddenly plopped into his water bowl...in neither case does it actually represent highly complex thought.)*

Worried? They do that face, too - you can always tell when they are worried about something. Outrage? They're *great* at that one. Hurt? No other mere mortal can look as flat-out hurt as a Perpetual Puppy - it's positively *heart-rending*. Contrite? No guessing needed. (This is the expression they use all their lives when they are in trouble, incidentally.) In fact, you can always tell *exactly* what these guys are thinking (or what they want you to *think* they are thinking) just by watching their faces - they have the most expressive faces of any PSP.

Once you get past the boyish face, you'll find the rest of him is equally boyish as well. The Perpetual Puppy has a fair amount of energy, and a springy, eager stride that's hard to miss. Because he's usually stuck somewhere between puberty and adulthood, when testosterone levels are starting to rise, the Perpetual Puppy is a fairly high-T guy, with the energy and competitiveness it brings to the party, although rarely with the focus, courage, and overall toughness that accompany testosterone in adulthood. So these guys are by definition pretty energetic and athletic, with teenage bodies. Rarely does he sport a beard or mustache, unless he is deliberately trying to look mature and can actually grow one. (A lot of them can't.)

Left to his own devices, the Perpetual Puppy wears his hair the same way he's worn it since high school, when his taste in *all things* was pretty well set. (He can't really help it - that's where he got "stuck" in the maturation process.) And, for reasons that probably have something to do with the biochemistry of neoteny, these guys rarely have to worry about losing their hair as they age - they seem to be physically, as well as mentally and emotionally, stuck in adolescence, so they always look (and usually dress) young for their age.

An adult male who wears a baseball cap backwards is very likely a Perpetual Puppy. This is a *not* a look favored by normal mature men.

Ditto for super-baggy hiphop pants.

Males, once they are old enough to vote, generally do not reveal an appalling amount of their butts when they bend over unless they're actually mooning someone or maybe fixing your plumbing, in which case it is not a fashion statement; it's more like a tool-belt-to-pants-weight-ratio problem that the whole industry apparently has yet to resolve.

By and large, though, Perpetual Puppies don't have strong feelings about personal style, and are generally pretty good-natured about letting women choose their clothes. (These women can be mothers, sisters, girlfriends, or wives.) Given their own personal taste, or lack thereof, this is a Good Thing for the most part. If the women in their lives have reasonably good taste, they'll usually be pretty well-dressed.

On their own (which they almost never are for any length of time) Perpetual Puppies will simply wear What The Other Guys Are Wearing. This is because Perpetual Puppies are pack animals through and through, and like all puppies, they mimic the behaviors of other pack members. (This is a double-edged sword that can get them into a lot of trouble on occasion throughout their entire lives, in areas that extend far beyond their wardrobes. It results in the sort of behavior that has led generations of mothers to ask in exasperation, "If Johnny jumped off a cliff, would you jump off a cliff, too?" The big difference is that most boys eventually outgrow what animal behaviorists call *allelomimetic behavior* and these guys never do...)

The one fashion area in which Perpetual Puppies do have an opinion is *costumes*. They love 'em. Show me a guy who'll wear a silly costume when someone is not actually pointing a loaded gun at his head and I'll show you a Perpetual Puppy. (OK, Betas will if their wives make them, but they'll be uncomfortable.) Ronald Reagan, the quintessential Perpetual Puppy, actually had his *picture taken* in full cowboy regalia that would have made John Wayne blush - here the guy was, the Leader of the Free World with access to nuclear weapons, *dressed up in an outfit that made him look like Roy Rogers in drag,* and he wasn't even *embarrassed...*(And, yeah, Ronnie actually did ride horses. So what? John F. Kennedy was in the Navy, and spent a lot of his free time on boats, but you never saw him dressed up in a sailor suit like some demented Donald Duck...why? *Because he was an adult male with a sense of personal dignity, that's why.*)

Habitat

The den of a Perpetual Puppy is also pretty hard to miss. Unless there is a woman running the show, their taste in the home décor department often runs to Early Frat House, if not actually Peewee's Playhouse. Usually short on accoutrements associated with mundane things like cooking, their digs will inevitably be full of toys and games. These guys actually consider a foosball table a perfectly normal piece of living room furniture and feel no need to apologize for its presence therein. Dartboards are considered wall art. Beer signs provide needed lighting.

They own the usual electronic toys, of course, but like many adolescents, they really like *physical* stuff - toys you can *do* things with. They usually have a lot of sporting equipment. A punching bag is always fun. Guns are fun. So are swords.

Perpetual Puppies virtually never live alone. If they're single, they far prefer a couple of their frat brothers to solitude once they've moved out of their actual frat house due to eventual graduation. (Did I mention this is the PSP most likely to belong to a fraternity during their college years?)

Perpetual Puppies, in fact, are not good at being alone under *any* circumstances. Like all puppies, they have strong social needs and absolutely no affinity for solitude. If they are alone in a room or a car, odds are good they're on the phone, or emailing someone.

Even sports like hunting and fishing, which many men with an affinity for the outdoors consider an opportunity for quiet solitude, are more like team sports for Perpetual Puppies, and they usually turn them into a party, complete with beer. (This often scares the fish, but they've never figured that out.)

Perpetual Puppies *love* parties. They're party animals. They like to throw parties, and they like to attend other people's parties. They even like kids' birthday parties. (As previously mentioned, Perpetual Puppies take their *own* birthdays as seriously as any 6-year-old well into middle age and beyond, which is an important thing to know if you are thinking of marrying one.)

But the truth is, Perpetual Puppies are rarely single. Attractive, charming, and affectionate, they tend to marry early - unlike many men, they have no fear of marriage. This is mostly because they see women as having been put on this earth *to take care of them*. A fair number of them marry during college, which account for a lot of women's disastrous first marriages. (The ones who honestly thought he just needed to grow up a little...)

Finding themselves single again, Perpetual Puppies either move back home or in with a couple of buddies (and these guys always have plenty of buddies) until they find another woman. It's not so much that they're not domestic (once married, they can really get into the domestic thing) so much as they simply can't manage it on their own. The truth is, even if they are relatively bright, Perpetual Puppies can't manage very much on their own, including responsibility, which makes holding down a job without help a real challenge.

Unless you're pretty dense, you've probably guessed by now that two places one is likely to find a Perpetual Puppy are the theatre and politics. You'd be right, of course. Perpetual Puppies are about as common in those two professions as ants at a picnic... they're tailor-made for them.

Because they are attractive, charming, and radiate a sort of sunny optimism for the future, these guys are often

highly successful politicians. Even if they are totally *clueless* about the finer points of both domestic and foreign policy (which most of them are because they rarely pick up an actual book), they *can* read a script and insert all the right expressions into their speeches in the appropriate places if coached beforehand. And they usually look good in a suit and tie, assuming someone picks it out for them.

And unlike Alphas and Junkyard Dogs (who generally have a far greater understanding of world affairs than they do) Perpetual Puppies have absolutely no problem being 'handled' by a bunch of Leglifters and Fearbiters who are simply too smarmy and unattractive to get elected to any public office themselves. *(In fact, 'easily-handled' is the hallmark of this PSP.)* Their basically trusting puppy-like nature makes Perpetual Puppies extremely useful (in truth, absolutely critical) to these guys for the advancement of their personal agendas.

But because he never really matures, the Perpetual Puppy needs to be handled, coached and guided pretty much all the way through his life, and his ultimate success or failure in the political arena is completely and utterly dependent upon the skills of his handlers. And whether or not he ultimately serves the public good (which he really *does* want to do) is again totally dependent upon the collective agenda of his handlers.

Because he maintains pretty high serotonin levels under all circumstances (a function of neoteny) being in a position of leadership is not particularly stressful for a Perpetual Puppy - he simply enjoys the attention that comes along with it, and trusts his handlers to advise him.

Acting is another field where the Perpetual Puppy can find success, because they've never outgrown the ability to play make-believe, which is all acting really is. They are also drawn to art and music - lots of artists and musicians in this PSP. Here, of course, they are again dependent upon someone else to handle their careers or they'll end up as waiters, but a lot of them really *are* talented, because creativity is part of neoteny.

But many Perpetual Puppies aren't actors, artists, musicians or politicians - instead they end up with a real job sooner or later, even if they hold off as long as possible. They tend to be especially good in sales, where their enthusiasm and sincerity serve them well. They are often drawn toward the toy industry, and they can make great designers - after all, they *like* toys. A fair number find careers in the computer industry for the same reason - computers, to these guys, *are* toys.

What they *can't* do successfully is run their own business. Since many of them have rich parents to bankroll them, a lot of them try it, and it's almost always a complete and total disaster. Every single one of these guys will ultimately run a business into the ground, and the reason is simple:

Perpetual Puppies all suffer from fiscal irresponsibility - it's another hallmark of the PSP. If you are (or were) married to one, you probably already know this. If you are *planning* to marry one, you might as well be prepared to be in charge of the family finances, or brace yourself for bad credit and financial ruin. If a Perpetual Puppy has two hundred dollars worth of overdue credit card bills on his desk and two hundred dollars in his pocket, he'll take the two hundred bucks in his pocket and blow it on something stupid every single time.

Any man over the age of thirty with bad credit is most likely a Perpetual Puppy. This is reflected in the cars they drive - although like any teenager they really *like* cool cars, they rarely own one. The problem here is that unless they are married or they got it as a graduation present, Perpetual Puppies have a hard time *keeping* a car because they never get around to actually making the payments.

Mating Habits

Perpetual Puppies are always fun dates, assuming their credit cards can hold the dinner tab. Lots of dates with them actually don't *involve* dinner, though - they are usually more inclined toward "fun" dates, which might include a water park, or bumper cars.

Adult men who will visit Disney World without children in tow are usually Perpetual Puppies.

However, you might want to be wary of the ones who want to take you bungee-jumping or sky-diving - Perpetual Puppies with a copy of the novelty-seeking gene (these would be Junkyard Puppies) are a pretty dangerous bunch...lacking maturity, they often have chronic run-ins with the law even as adults, and they usually end up plagued by substance-abuse problems.

Perpetual Puppies fall in love pretty easily, and are creative, affectionate, and playful lovers - these guys are rarely boring in bed. And don't forget cute.

They're also not afraid to propose marriage. In fact, most of them do it more than once in their lives. Many Perpetual Puppies, believe it or not, actually don't make bad husbands married to the right woman. They are affectionate and loving, fun to be around, and generally good-natured. If you want a guy who will make you laugh, massage your feet after a long hard day at the office, and tell you how wonderful you are and how much they love you, these are your boys. They *are* irresponsible to an alarming degree, especially with money, but the upside of that is most of them don't mind if their wife controls the money. In fact, most of them don't mind if their wife controls pretty much *everything.*

Perpetual Puppies are tailor-made for women who need to be in total control. They're *never* chauvinists - these guys truly respect women, and are not threatened by strong-minded, controlling ones - in fact, that's their favorite kind, and certainly the *only* ones they can successfully live with for any length of time. *In fact, President Reagan used to call his wife Nancy (a woman renowned in the White House for her personal strength and strong will) "Mommy" with no apparent embarrassment at all, which ought to tell you something....*

Women who joke that they have three children, one of whom they are married to, are invariably married to Perpetual Puppies.

They are generally supportive of their wives' careers, and are usually more than willing to be the stay-at-home parent if her career is higher-paying than his.

Perpetual Puppies all make good fathers, and great stepfathers. They are patient, affectionate, and they genuinely enjoy the company of children and dogs, with whom they share a natural affinity. Their kids usually adore them because they are more *fun* than most adults - and so do all the neighborhood kids. Most of them are not particularly good disciplinarians (but then neither are Alphas) but they are generally pretty protective of them and sensitive to their needs.

Although they're not naturally housebroken, they *can* learn the basics of housekeeping and cooking, and some actually enjoy sharing household responsibilities, especially the cooking part. (Unburdened by the sense of fiscal responsibility that usually plagues this particular PSP, Beta Puppies in particular are absolutely wonderful at being Mr. Mom - they are both domestically talented and nurturing.)

The bottom line is this - although these guys will drive a lot of women to distraction, for others they are absolutely perfect. Women who have high-paying careers they enjoy and a strong need to be in control but who don't particularly enjoy being single probably can't do much better.

And don't forget, they're cute!

8

Sentinels

As any owner of multiple dogs knows, in every "pack" of domestic dogs, whether they are in a house or a kennel, one animal assumes the role of Sentinel for the entire pack.

This guy functions as the group's "automatic alarm system" - at least several times a day this dog (who is, by definition, one of the least dominant but most vocal pack members) will sound the alarm, waking everybody up and often causing short-term chaos while the extent of the threat to the pack is evaluated. (This "threat" can be the mail carrier, a squirrel outside the window, or any odd noise whatsoever.)

Most of the time there is no real or immediate threat to the safety and well-being of the pack, and everyone settles back down. This deters the Sentinel not in the least - the next time he sees or hears anything worth reporting, he'll go off again like the Fourth of July, and the pack will once again rouse itself sufficiently to check it out. It's his job.

This phenomenon is not limited to domesticated packs, by the way - many wild species, it turns out, actually *assign* particular pack members to stand guard, warning the rest of the group against the approach of predators.

Sentinels are a critical PSP to the safety and well-being of any pack.

The characteristic that defines a good Sentinel in any species is a hair-trigger startle (or "flight-or-fight") response. The Sentinel probably carries only average testosterone levels at best, which is a good thing. Being a highly social animal, with at least one copy of the altruism gene variant and lots of pack loyalty, the Sentinel responds by *warning* the rest of the pack of danger, rather than attempting to deal with it himself.

In many species, including ours, this is a position that carries significant risk, although ironically these are *not* guys who display the classic characteristics of risk-takers, and they rarely take risks just for the hell of it. It's mostly the combination of altruism, which engenders pro-social behavior, along with heightened sensitivity to their environment (at least compared to most guys, who rarely notice if the living room is a different color unless it's actually pointed out to them) and a well-developed startle response that creates this personality.

This would probably be as good a point as any to explain that a whole lot of my female dog breeder friends thought that "Anklebiter" was the most descriptive name for this group, and some of them were actually disappointed that I ultimately discarded it in favor of "Sentinel". Although "ankle-biting" describes their follow-up technique (after shrill barking) for both getting their own pack on its feet and moving it in the direction of safety, I discarded it because it sounded vaguely derogatory somehow (making one think immediately of annoying little yappy dogs), and because it misses the primary and very important function of this PSP within the pack.

In a society as complex as ours, the Sentinel's duties are a lot more complex and varied than they would be in a hunter-gatherer society. Rather than sitting in a tree somewhere and yodeling when they perceive a threat, Sentinels are more likely to put their warnings into publication for dissemination to the rest of the pack, or to employ other media outlets like radio, internet, and TV.

So what defines a Sentinel in the biochemistry department? Usually chronically low serotonin levels. Most Sentinels suffer from many, or all, of the symptoms of Serotonin Deficiency Syndrome. As a result of their hair-trigger flight or fight response, these are high-cortisol guys, and because cortisol blocks the production of serotonin in the brain, this is a fairly angst-ridden group of worriers. Depression is often a very real problem for them, as are panic attacks, chronic anxiety, weight problems, and insomnia. Lots of carb junkies in this PSP.

Any guy who actually mentions his shrink by name on the first date is very likely a Sentinel.

These are the males most likely to voluntarily avail themselves of the services of a mental health care professional.

They're also the ones most likely to be in a 12-step program or two, with AA being a fairly common one. (Although a pretty wide cross-section of PSPs are actually represented at the average AA meeting, Sentinels are the ones most likely to mention it in casual conversation.) The fact that a guy is "in a program" of one sort or another really indicates a willingness to at least recognize and deal with his problems, and shouldn't necessarily be a red flag on a date, assuming it's not the main topic of conversation.

The exception here would be even the most offhand reference to "one of the guys in my Anger-Management program", which nine times out of ten is court-ordered and a pretty good indicator you are not in the company of a Sentinel at all, but rather a Fearbiter, who is an entirely different biochemical kettle of fish. In this case, bail out immediately and gracefully or you could be sorry in the long run. Nobody signs up for an anger management course unless they've had some fairly serious problems managing their anger, and you sure don't want to be around if (or when) this guy falls off the anger-management wagon.

The reason a fair number of Sentinels end up in AA (or should) is the same reason they often suffer from depression and anxiety - too little serotonin, too much cortisol. These guys drink to self-medicate; alcohol will temporarily blunt the unpleasant effects of cortisol and also temporarily raise serotonin levels. Unfortunately, the result is short-lived, after which serotonin levels plunge and cortisol levels rise even farther than they were in the first place, and it's no more effective than years of psychoanalysis, for which many of these guys have shelled out big bucks. What they *really* need to do is balance their brain chemistry.

If you are attracted to, or already involved with, a Sentinel whose depression, and/or general craziness, is in danger of driving you crazy (which it ultimately will) it's worth knowing a little about their basic brain chemistry, so you can understand that it's really got nothing to do with you, his mother, or his job. It's his overdeveloped personal security system.

Referred to by guys with PhDs in things most people can't even pronounce as the *hypothalamic-pituitary-adrenal (HPA) axis*, this security system relies on several key players, which are in reality various specific areas of the brain. Basic operations are the same for everyone, often resulting in the following scenario inside the brain, and which everyone has probably experienced at one time or another, although odds are they didn't know what was really going on:

SCENARIO INSIDE THE BRAIN
Cast of characters:
THALAMUS
AMYGDALA &
HIPPOCAMPUS, all areas of the *limbic*, or "emotional", brain, and
CORTEX, an area of the "rational" brain responsible for executive function

When the body receives sensory input of a potentially dangerous nature (let's say the ears pick up an ominous rattle in the grass during a walk) *it sends the message first to* THALAMUS, *who functions sort of like a dispatcher.*
And THALAMUS *always sends this information out over two routes simultaneously.*
The first route is the shortest one, sort of like sending the message to the closest squad car to check out the situation and secure it if need be.
Riding in the squad car are AMYGDALA *and* HIPPOCAMPUS, *a pretty conscientious pair, but neither of whom are particularly bright.*
These two guys have very different styles. AMYGDALA *relies entirely upon 'emotional' (and often faulty) memory to make rough assessments of each situation - consequently, he has a tendency to over-react.*
His partner HIPPOCAMPUS, *on the other hand, relies mainly upon 'contextual' memory, and assesses danger based entirely on previous experiences encountered in similar physical situations.*

So AMYGDALA, *who's always in charge of the radio, takes the message from* THALAMUS *concerning a report of an ominous rattle, digs quickly through his memory for the last time he heard a similar noise (in this case an old Western he watched on Cable), comes up with "holy shit, a rattlesnake!" and immediately pulls out his gun and snaps the safety off in case he needs to shoot a rattlesnake.*

(As a result of this response, stress hormones are released- the heart rate doubles in the space of two beats, respiration quickens, muscles tense, the immune system is temporarily shut down, and blood sugar rises, all in preparation for emergency action.)

HIPPOCAMPUS, *meanwhile, is sitting next to* AMYGDALA *calmly eating a jelly donut.*

Now, while all this is happening, the report about the ominous rattle has also, thankfully, been sent to CORTEX, who's sitting at a desk back in the "executive" part of the brain drinking his usual Double Serotonin Latte, which is what keeps him functioning on the job.

As soon as CORTEX gets the message, he contacts the squad car, listens to AMYGDALA babble about rattlesnakes for a minute, and then tells him to put HIPPOCAMPUS on so he can get a halfway reasonable assessment of the situation.

"We're in Central Park, for Crissake," mumbles HIPPOCAMPUS, swallowing the last of his jelly donut, "not West Texas. It's probably a just a paper bag rattling in the wind. I noticed last time I was over here that the litter's just terrible in this part of the park, they really oughta do something about it. We'll check it out, though. AMYGDALA'S got his damn gun out already - the guy's a basket-case, he really needs to cut down on his caffeine."

"You got that right," sighs CORTEX. "Put him back on the line." When AMYGDALA comes on, CORTEX says, "It's OK, John Wayne, it's probably just a paper bag. Now put your gun away before you hurt somebody." He hangs up and takes another sip of his Double Serotonin Latte, shaking his head.

So AMYGDALA (who's never yet fired the thing in the line of duty) breathes a sigh of relief, holsters his gun, and the stress hormones dissipate almost immediately.

And for the next six months, every time they pass that spot HIPPOCAMPUS says, "Hey, is that a rattlesnake over there in the grass?" causing AMYGDALA to panic and immediately reach for his gun before he realizes that HIPPOCAMPUS is just yanking his chain.

Now, that's how the system is supposed to work. (And it also explains why, when you find yourself in the same situation where you previously had a frightening or unpleasant experience, you will experience an actual physical stress response - blame your hippocampus, and don't worry about it.) But with the Sentinel, who is way more *alert* than average, there is a constant barrage of sensory input to the brain, and the system gets overloaded, resulting in the following scenario:

CORTEX, who's been working overtime trying to make rational decisions on the nonstop calls coming in, drains the last of his Double Serotonin Latte and abandons his desk to go see if he can find some in the coffee shop around the corner.
This leaves AMYGDALA and HIPPOCAMPUS out in the field taking the calls, trying to assess each potentially dangerous situation without any rational input from CORTEX on how to proceed.
With no one to keep AMYGDALA calmed down, the level of stress hormones, especially cortisol, just gets higher and higher.
If CORTEX doesn't get back to his desk in time, these high cortisol levels will cause AMYGDALA to, sooner or later, come unglued and, goaded by HIPPOCAMPUS, he'll start acting on his emotional impulses, inevitably with unfortunate results.

The *reason* cortisol rises in the previous scenario is because it is essentially the "do nothing" stress hormone. Although it hardly ever occurs to anyone, when faced with a potentially dangerous situation there are really *three* possible responses, not two. (This is probably because it's usually called the "fight-or-flight" response, which sort of makes it sound like there are only two options, fight or flight, when in reality there are three.) And in modern society, the third response is apt to be the one most often utilized.

Adrenaline provides the body with what it needs to flee, *noradrenaline* with what it needs to fight (this one maintains a close relationship with testosterone, not surprisingly), while *cortisol* provides the body with what it needs for the third option, which is "inhibition of behavior".

This is what happens when a field mouse, sensing a hawk overhead, decides it's safer to sit tight and wait for him to pass than to either fight or flee.

It's also what happens when a dozen cops hunker down with guns drawn behind their squad cars waiting for the hostage negotiator to show up. In most cases it's the result of *somebody's* executive brain function and, in principle anyway, usually represents an intelligent option, especially in an "under siege" situation.

Behavioral inhibition is usually the result of two things - either it is an "executive decision" reached by the cortex after examining the situation, or it can be a temporary solution while the cortex is trying to gather and process enough information to make a rational decision on how to proceed.

Problem is, in both cases, behavioral inhibition was designed as a *short-term solution*, and cortisol, the primary hormone released by choosing this option, is pretty toxic to the body and brain over time. Cortisol increases blood sugar and blood pressure, stimulates the colon, suppresses the reproductive and immune systems, and deactivates the body's disease-fighting white blood cells. While all this makes biochemical sense in the short term, it should come as no surprise that chronically high levels can result in serious health problems. (Diabetes, heart disease, stroke, irritable bowel syndrome, autoimmune disease, and even cancer have all been linked to chronic stress.)

The overproduction of cortisol also blocks the body's ability to make serotonin, which is needed to both maintain a sense of calm well-being and to deal with dangers rationally. Because of this, high cortisol levels have been shown to impair cognitive function in numerous studies. As if that weren't bad enough, chronically high cortisol levels are toxic to the brain over time, causing the destruction of brain cells, especially in the hippocampus, resulting in memory loss, cognitive problems and disorientation. (Alzheimer's Disease, which is characterized by high cortisol levels, ultimately results in pretty total destruction of the hippocampus.)

Sentinels are extremely susceptible to chronic stress, partially because they are usually found in careers that involve tons of sensory input, most of which really cannot be acted upon. Most of this sensory input comes from the media, which I'm sure Mother Nature simply could not envision when she designed the whole system.

Turn on CNN *for 5 minutes* - in that space of time on a typical day you can learn about:

1. A terrorist plot to blow up transatlantic passenger flights, resulting in no one in America being allowed to carry toothpaste in their carry-on luggage;
2. 12,000 lightning strikes *in one hour* reported in the Chicago area;
3. Wildfires burning out of control in California;
4. 34 Iraqis killed by a bomb in Baghdad;
5. Continued bombing in southern Lebanon.

You also get to see *graphic images* of all of the above, complete with blood and gore whenever possible, thereby insuring that these potential threats are being transferred to the thalamus through at least *two senses simultaneously*, rather than just one. (Ain't TV great?) And the standard brain response to all this danger, about which we can actually do little or nothing, is *behavioral inhibition,* which raises cortisol levels.

(But never fear - all this good news is helpfully followed by ads for expensive pharmaceuticals that will normalize your blood pressure, your cholesterol, your reproductive, digestive, and immune systems, and take care of that pesky depression, although they may cause dizziness and blurred vision in some patients, and you probably want to be sure and inform your doctor if you have liver disease.)

Sentinels, because of their genetic makeup (very likely including a copy or two of the APOE e4 allele, a cholesterol-transporter gene which has been linked to increased risk of both heart attacks and Alzheimer's Disease) are hard-wired to be more sensitive to this input than most other PSPs. And rather than fighting, fleeing, or doing nothing, they respond with a *fourth* option - they warn the rest of the pack. *Unfortunately, the HPA axis, being about 10,000 years out of date, is simply not set up to provide for dissipation of stress hormones by either typing or talking, unless you happen to be actually running really fast at the same time.*

Not only are most Sentinels news junkies themselves, most of them are the guys actually *collecting and disseminating it* so the rest of us can keep *our* cortisol levels up in the stratosphere as well. Which pretty much guarantees that *everyone's* cortex will be draining the last of that Double Serotonin Latte well before lunchtime.

Plumage

The Sentinel is not one of the high-T PSPs, so don't expect a lot of brawn, here. Although they may be attractive enough, they are generally not jocks. These were the guys in high school who sat in the back of the room making wisecracks, and they usually worked on the school newspaper.

They are nearly always bright, and often *very* funny - their humor is usually pretty self-deprecating, which is not possible with really high-T types. (Testosterone by definition gives a man a fairly high opinion of himself.) All in all, it adds no small amount of charm to their personalities, and which is why so many women put up with their craziness.

Sentinels notice things before the rest of us, because they are hard-wired to do so.
Take a walk with a Sentinel some time: "Wow, did you see that guy - he looked exactly like a goldfish!" ... "Watch out, don't

step on that!" … "What kind of a dog do you think that is?"… they will do this nonstop, I swear to God, which can drive you nuts. On the other hand, they'll also probably notice if you got a new haircut, or if you lost ten pounds, which puts them one up on a lot of other PSPs.

Adolescence is particularly difficult for Sentinels, because adolescence is the *one time* when testosterone is critical to male pack status, and these guys just don't carry a lot of it. (Adolescence is a pretty primitive period; this is because there is actually no appreciable brain growth during those years, which every parent has probably already noticed…)

In high school, Testosterone Rules, and Leglifters will rarely have more status in life than they do at that point in their lives. Most women will admit to having crushes in high school on guys they would walk across the street to avoid today. (This is often LITERALLY true, since a lot of these former high school jocks are probably the same guys eating lunch at a construction site and wolf-whistling at passing women…)

On the other hand, the qualities that make Sentinels attractive to women, like intelligence and a sense of humor, tend to be things most women find sexy only after they've reached adulthood and are pretty well past swooning over lifeguards and hometown football heroes. So popularity with girls comes a little late for these guys, many of whom were downright awkward teenagers and significantly improved with age. However, years of adolescent insecurity has a tendency to make them pretty vulnerable through their twenties, and sometimes well beyond that - as a group, Sentinels are probably more attractive to women than they think they are. (Omegas have the same problem, and for the exact same reason.)

Because they are discriminating by nature, Sentinels generally have better taste than most PSPs, and they often develop a fair amount of personal style as they mature.

Samuel Clemens, aka Mark Twain, was a Sentinel who developed an incredible personal style as well as a much cooler name, and lots of Sentinels seem inclined to emulate him.

In terms of attire, the average Sentinel is almost always "in uniform". Once they reach adulthood, these guys all seem to choose a personal style and stick with it. They probably spend more money on their wardrobes than many other PSPs.

The uniform they choose often depends upon their particular occupation - there's the Banana Republic look favored by journalists, the Natty Bow-tie look favored by theatre and food critics, and the Woody Guthrie look favored by left-leaning social critics and most writers. But they are *all* uniforms, make no mistake about it….

'Personal style" with these guys is a very deliberate and carefully cultivated undertaking. Physically, Sentinels can be tall or short, fat or thin, but odds are they won't have six-pack abs or bulging biceps, because these guys don't much like to break a sweat if they can avoid it. (This is really too bad, because exercising to the point of breaking a sweat has actually been proven to lower cortisol levels.)

A fair number of them grow mustaches, although I am not sure why. This is about the *only* trait they share with their old high-school nemesis, the Leglifter.

You see a cop with a mustache, odds are pretty good he's a Leglifter.

Of course, if you see a cop without a mustache, odds are pretty good he's a Leglifter, too.

For some reason the Sentinel is the PSP most likely to wear a hat, which they can actually pull off with style. The sort of hat depends on the persona previously established.

Sentinels rarely sleep in the buff, which is interesting. Unlike the Beta, this is not because of personal modesty. They'll *walk around* in the buff, they just won't *sleep* that way. They usually just strip down to their shorts before climbing in bed. (Some of them will actually put their shorts back *on* after sex so they can sleep comfortably, honest to God...)

This is most likely for the same reason most of them sleep lightly (or rarely) and can be totally awake in a flash: Given their hard-wiring, they need to be able to fly out of bed at a moment's notice, and this way *they're already partly dressed*. For this reason, Sentinels don't generally wear pajamas. Pajamas would be worse than sleeping in nothing, because they'd have to take them *off* before they could throw on the rest of their clothes, which they invariably leave in a pile right on the floor next to the bed. (Don't try to talk them out of that habit, either - it won't work.)

I personally know one Sentinel who used to keep a rope ladder right next to his second-story bedroom window, just in case of a fire in the middle of the night, honest to God.

Habitat

Because they have better taste than most guys, Sentinels often have pretty comfortable digs, especially as they mature, usually characterized by antiques, squashy leather furniture, Persian rugs, a wine rack, and lots of books, magazines, and newspapers. Sentinels always have subscriptions to numerous magazines and at least one daily newspaper. (These guys are by definition readers, a trait they share with both Alphas and Junkyard Dogs.) They tend to have decent art around them and they are both culturally and politically literate. (Sentinels *always* know what's going on in the world; it's part of being generally sensitive to their environment.)

Do not confuse good taste with good housekeeping skills, though - Sentinels are by nature pretty disorganized, and they can work and live in chaos better than many other people...it's that ability to absorb sensory input from many sources at once. They create chaos from order as they go along, which is important to remember if you're thinking of sharing space with one.

They're usually fairly solvent, as material success is necessary to the level of creature comforts they desire, and they generally have both the intelligence and energy to be successful in their chosen field.

They usually drive nice cars, mostly late-model imports as soon as they can afford them, with silver being the preferred color. Now, although they appreciate the fine engineering and design that goes into them, these guys have little or no real affinity for the internal combustion engine, and generally can't so much as change the oil in their own Beemer, relying on primarily upon the Leglifters who work in the bay at the dealership to do so.

This might be a good time to point out that Sentinels are not usually what is referred to by women as "handy". Changing a light bulb often represents the sum total of their mechanical skills. Although some of them may actually own tools, it's really safer to hire a Leglifter if you have anything that needs fixing around the house. Alphas generally can perform home-improvement tasks if pushed, prodded, nagged and cajoled - they just don't like to. Sentinels, on the other hand, often overrate their own abilities regarding home-improvement, usually with disastrous results.

Unlike Betas, they're not really interested enough in cars as a concept to own more than one at a time, especially if they're single. (Married Sentinels with kids will actually own a minivan without embarrassment, although in all fairness it's usually their *wife's* primary vehicle, and they'll personally drive something with more style. But at least they don't consider them emasculating.)

Lots of cat-owners in this PSP, although most usually like dogs well enough. But I've never yet met one who could stay on a horse.

The range of careers suited to the temperament of the Sentinel is pretty varied, but they absolutely always include communications of some sort, because these guys are natural-born communicators. One of the most obvious is journalism (the modern equivalent of sitting in a tree yelling out warnings), a talent they honed early on, raking muck for their local high school newspaper.

In fact, there are probably very few successful journalists who *aren't* Sentinels. In addition to their superior powers of observation, these guys are articulate, and are better spellers than the male population at large, which is largely a function of their low/average baseline testosterone levels. (Someday they are going to find an inversely proportional link between testosterone levels and spelling ability, mark my words...)

IMPORTANT: When we talk about "low testosterone" in males, that level is still roughly ten times higher than the testosterone level of your average female, so don't get your hopes up - unless testosterone levels are pathologically low for some medical reason, virtually every human being with a penis still has more than enough to ensure that he will do stupid competitive guy stuff that even the highest-T woman wouldn't think of doing.

Remember, nearly all male dogs lift their legs to mark territory unless they've actually been neutered. The high-testosterone ones are just a lot more obsessive and obnoxious about it. Sentinels may not play hockey, but they are every bit as likely to get in a pissing contest over a parking space as your average jock.

Being both pro-social and pack-dependent, Sentries are naturally attracted to the political arena, where they serve as political speechwriters, lobbyists, campaign strategists, and political "handlers" whose clients are likely to be Perpetual Puppies far less intelligent and well-informed than themselves. In fact, inside the Beltway, where this PSP is as common as ants at a picnic, Sentinels actually *travel in packs*. The DC bars are full of them, if one is interested in tracking down a bunch of them at once - they're pretty much a dime-a-dozen there. The easiest way to separate them from the lawyers, who generally make up the *other* half of the patrons in every bar in Our Nation's Capitol on any given day, is by looking for that element of "style" which sets Sentinels apart...by and large, *government lawyers don't have any*. Government lawyers are generally Betas.

Politics have *always* appealed to Sentinels (the largely misunderstood Machiavelli was one), and they are scattered throughout our own nation's history from its very beginnings:

One if by land, and two if by sea,
While I on the opposite shore shall be
Ready to ride and spread the alarm
Through every Middlesex village and farm.

(What, you thought Paul Revere was a *Leglifter,* maybe? And he was possibly the last Sentinel who could stay on a horse.)

Outside the Beltway, where politics is not an all-consuming passion, Sentinels tend to be attracted to the Arts, especially in cities like New York, where one can actually make a *living* in them. Lots of them are writers, of course, and even more are editors.

They're rarely *performers,* though - actors have some of the highest baseline testosterone levels of any occupational group short of NFL players, which pretty much excludes your average Sentinel. And they aren't particularly good at playing someone else - the role they've mastered is their *own* persona, usually well-honed.

No, these guys are generally paid to do what comes most naturally to them - they're *critics*. Theatre critics, Art critics, literary critics, social critics, food critics - you name it, these guys can *criticize* it. They've been doing it all their lives.

The reason these guys are such good critics is two-fold: One, they're hard-wired to notice things the rest of us don't. And two, they're compulsive communicators and generally good writers, which inclines them to share what they've noticed.

Whether or not they have a well-developed sense of humor also determines to a large degree where they end up, career-wise. A Sentinel with no discernable sense of humor is likely to end up as a theatre or food critic, warning the rest of the pack about the dangers of imminent food poisoning or, at the very least, the prospect of a dull evening, or maybe as an editor, where one's powers of criticism can be turned loose with abandon on hapless writers, no sense of humor required.

Those who are a little less tightly laced, but who still take life, and themselves, fairly seriously, are often inclined to investigative journalism, and there are certainly some superstars here.

Those blessed with a well-developed sense of humor (no doubt this is a gene yet to be discovered, but clearly linked to this PSP, as I can think of very damn few truly funny guys who are *not* Sentinels) are often the best-known. They are inevitably social critics, specializing in satire.

No one, of course, did it better than Mark Twain.

Jerry Seinfeld, a relative lightweight as a social critic, but probably the *quintessential* modern urban Sentinel, actually made this PSP *cool*. And even when he had his own TV series, Jerry Seinfeld only played Jerry Seinfeld.

Garrison Keillor is another Sentinel who has made a career of noticing what no one else does, and his personal style is just about inimitable.

And South Florida's Dave Barry, of course, has over the years raised the concept of the Sentinel as Social Satirist to a level of sheer genius surpassed only by Mark Twain himself. Of course, being in South Florida, he's got a lot of good local material to work with.

Anyhow, this heightened ability to notice what the rest of us don't is really what sets this PSP apart. It also often makes them a little...well...*intense* compared to the rest of the world. Which is something to consider if you plan to start dating one.

MATING HABITS

Being involved with a Sentinel is generally a bit of an emotional roller-coaster ride, which is probably why most of them blow through more than one wife over the course of their lifetime. I personally know a couple who've had *four*. In fact, a guy with more than two marriages under his belt (assuming he isn't a Leglifter running through a series of ever-younger trophy wives) is probably a Sentinel by definition, since there is no other PSP defined quite as neatly by what could best be called *serial monogamy.*

The same hair-trigger cortisol response that makes Sentinels particularly alert to their environment also makes them hard to live with. The same guys who seem bright, funny, charming, and interesting while dating often turn out to be moody, anxiety-ridden, depressive, and insecure once you really get to know them. Unfortunately, by this time, you're generally already married to them.

These guys generally don't ditch their wives for a younger model, or even cheat on them - what they usually do is make their wives totally crazy until they finally say something like:

"Eric, I love you but I can't live with you any more, you're making me totally crazy." And they pack their stuff and leave, which completely *devastates* the Sentinel, who really doesn't like living alone.

He can't sleep or eat for weeks, and becomes depressed. He has a hard time concentrating on his job. His life is empty. He drives his friends, family, and shrink totally crazy trying to analyze what went wrong. And then he meets another woman who invariably finds him bright, funny, charming, and interesting, falls in love and marries her...*and promptly proceeds to drive her crazy.*

For some reason, though, most Sentinels have pretty good relationships with their ex-wives and ex-girlfriends...probably better than any other PSP. This may have something to do with the fact that the failure of the marriage didn't involve adultery, which it almost never does.

In fact, any guy who still has a warm relationship with his ex-wife (or wives) is probably a Sentinel. A lot of their ex-wives and girlfriends are still honestly *fond* of them, and probably feel vaguely guilty about walking out on what they know is really a decent human being they simply *can't live with.*

Because they are sensitive and basically altruists, Sentinels are not selfish sexual partners, and really do try hard to please the women they care about, insofar as they can. They can be very romantic and, unlike a lot of PSPs, they don't have a real problem expressing their emotions - mostly because they don't have a real problem expressing *anything*. For a lot of women, that's a *very* big plus.

Unfortunately, as with Betas, the Sentinel's sex life is often affected by the other things going on in his life, and when they're really stressed, they simply can't get into it. (High cortisol levels automatically suppress the entire reproductive system.) Which is probably a good thing to know if you're involved with one, so you don't start wondering if it's somehow *your* fault, when it's really because the campaign he's managing is going badly. Unlike Leglifters, for Sentinels sex really *does* involve the thought process, rather than being a sort of mindless physical reflex, like belching.

It's probably also useful to remember that like vigorous exercise, sexual intercourse has also been shown to keep cortisol levels and resulting blood pressure low in the face of stress for up to a week afterwards. Getting him to actually do either one when he's stressed is usually the challenge.

Sentinels make pretty good fathers, and can generally be trusted with the care of small children, since they are alert to danger at all times. They worry a lot about their kids' safety from the moment they're born, and they worry about their future in a dangerous and uncertain world. The fact that they are more aware of the danger and uncertainty of that world than most men only makes it worse. For this reason, some of them are literally afraid to have kids at all, which is important to know. (This is probably the *only* PSP that is afraid to bring children into the world...)

All in all, the Sentinel is probably a good choice for women who want a partner they can actually *communicate* with on both an intellectual and emotional level. (You can spend forty years with a Sentinel and never run out of conversation, which is not something you can say about a lot of PSPs.)

And God knows no woman ever leaves a Sentinel because she's bored.

They may be a lot of things, but they're *never* boring.

Women who are successfully married to Sentinels are usually exceptionally calm, even-tempered, and pragmatic. Although bright and every bit as politically astute as their mates, they're rarely chatterbugs (as one explained with a smile, "one talker in the family is enough") especially in large social gatherings, where they're inclined to listen rather than talk.

What they provide for the Sentinel is an emotional "anchor". An amazing number of them seem to be from Minnesota and Wisconsin, although that's probably not a prerequisite.

9

Omegas

> AND THE MEEK SHALL INHERIT THE EARTH.
> — MATTHEW 5:5

For probably the first time in the history of our species, Omegas are now viewed by many perfectly intelligent and attractive women as desirable mates.

Not surprisingly, Omegas seem to be especially favored as *second* husbands, usually by women weary of a lifestyle dominated by seemingly endless rounds of playoffs, beer parties, and philandering. These women are really suffering from a very old but surprisingly under-diagnosed female malady called TES, or Testosterone Exhaustion Syndrome, and those afflicted ultimately decide it's easier to simply *pay a guy by the hour* to fix the water heater or the transmission on their car than it is to actually live with one who can.

Now initially (like when the ink is still wet on the divorce papers) these women are pretty convinced they don't want a guy around *at all*, and during this phase are likely to wear T-shirts emblazoned with witty sayings like:

> A WOMAN WITHOUT A MAN
> IS LIKE A FISH WITHOUT A BICYCLE

and to listen to Uppity Blues Women CDs around the clock, but this is really just part of the normal progression of the disease, and it ultimately passes.

And sooner or later it occurs to them that it's probably not fair to lump all men into the Neanderthal category just because their ex-husband practically dragged his knuckles on the floor when he walked, and that what they are really tired of is not *men in general* so much as *high-testosterone men in particular*. And this is where the Omega has an actual physical advantage over most other men, a situation he's, frankly, not had much prior experience with.

The Omega is a low-testosterone guy. He's not a risk-taker by any stretch of the imagination, because it's testosterone that facilitates risk. (Women with a bad case of TES generally see this as a definite plus.)

He's an altruist but, because he probably carries fairly low oxytocin levels and has high harm-avoidance tendencies, he's pretty much of an introvert. The Omega is pro-social enough; he's just not socially *confident,* and usually hasn't had the opportunity to learn many social skills. (In fact, although he doesn't have the hair-trigger fight-or-flight response of a Sentinel, certain social situations - like dates - will send his usually adequate serotonin levels plummeting and his cortisol skyrocketing, effectively rendering him pretty much incapable of coherent speech.)

This unfortunate tendency is more than balanced out by higher-than-average prolactin levels, which make him unassuming, essentially *nice,* and a guy who'd much rather stay at home than go out cruising the bars. (In the wild, it is the Omegas who baby-sit the cubs while the higher-testosterone animals are out hunting.) He's nearly always extremely intelligent, generally excelling in math and science from an early age.

If one were to use a more traditional psychological approach like Meyers-Briggs to identify and categorize this PSP rather than the genetic/biochemical approach, the Omega would be an INT type - an Introverted Intuitive Thinker, which is not coincidentally also the standard Alpha personality. INTs are stimulated by ideas and concepts rather than people, inclined toward abstract concepts, and more adept at logic and reason than emotion. (Both subgroups INTP and INTJ would include Omegas, with INTJs more likely to be aware of and to follow social rules than INTPs, who consider them mostly irrational and irrelevant - like the guy who shows up to fix your government-issue computer at the Commerce Department sporting a ponytail, an earring, and a T-shirt with a picture of an alien on it.)

In other words, he's a geek.

It's also entirely possible that he's a billionaire. This last piece of information reflects a fascinating scenario that Mother Nature quite frankly never envisioned. The truth is, the main difference between an Alpha and an Omega, who share a whole lot of traits, is that along with higher levels of serotonin and the confidence it brings to the party, Alphas carry higher levels of testosterone, which adds the physical superiority traditionally required for leadership. Of course, Mother Nature never exactly envisioned industrialization or technology either, when she was equipping men with testosterone.

If the human serotonin system is 10,000 years out of date, and its fight-or-flight response is 10,000 years out of date, the whole testosterone/dominance system is a virtual *dinosaur* in modern society.

In the "formative years" of our species, when muscle mattered, machines were unimaginable, and *homo sapiens* lived primarily in caves, dominance was determined by BRUTE FORCE, **a result of testosterone in the primitive limbic brain.** In the post-industrialized society in which we now live, this is pretty much only still true on playgrounds, in maximum-security prisons, and in the foreign policy of the Bush administration.

Dominance in the *rest* of the modern civilized world is determined primarily by IQ and serotonin, both of which involve engagement of the prefrontal cortex, and like Alphas, Omegas have a definite advantage here. Which probably explains why most of the richest men in America appear to be either Alphas or Omegas (with a couple Sentinels like Ted Turner thrown in courtesy of the Communications Industry), but rarely if ever Leglifters any more.

It also probably explains the attraction, by a percentage of Leglifters of limited intellectual capacity, to the weird hobby known as "survivalism" - filling their basements with dehydrated food, flashlights, guns, and ammunition with which to feed and protect their families "after the trucks stop rolling". (Not surprisingly, Fearbiters are also found in great numbers in this venue.) The theory of course, is that in a post-apocalyptic world where technology no longer exists - anybody remember Y2K? - testosterone and the particular skills it engenders will again determine survival, and they want to Be Prepared. (For some reason I've never been able to figure out, in this future low-tech world everyone will be required to wear Vietnam-era army surplus clothing.)

Unfortunately, until that happy day when a total breakdown of society as we know it occurs, most survivalists are stuck enduring what they ironically refer to as the Revenge of the Nerds - in other words, their paychecks are signed by the very guys they once chased from the playground. Assuming they're even *getting* a paycheck - remember, the highest T-levels of all were found among *unemployed* men.

So let's take a minute and look at the places where high T-levels still do provide an edge:

On playgrounds, bullying and victimization based entirely on relative size and strength occur with appalling regularity (mostly among boys) because childhood is pretty socially primitive, and testosterone still rules. This is because children do not yet have well-developed prefrontal cortexes, where rational thought takes place, so have to rely mainly on their limbic (or "primitive") brains, which is why children have so little impulse control.

Not surprisingly, research has shown that our maximum-security prisons tend to be overwhelmingly populated by males with high testosterone levels, low IQs, and little discernable impulse control. You can draw your own conclusions about the foreign policy of the Bush Administration.

Testosterone-driven dominance-seeking in males is a hangover from much more primitive times and, unfortunately, we're pretty much stuck with it and stuck with the guys who display it, although we really no longer need to marry them unless we're so inclined.

On the other hand, pack order *can* be managed, which lessens the physical bullying on the part of the high-testosterone animals. In the human world, we refer to this management as "civilization", and the poor beleaguered U.N. tries to manage it on a global scale.

It's always seemed to me that the whole effort would be more successful if the U.N. representatives from each and every country were required to be GRANDMOTHERS, the world's undisputed experts in coaxing civilized behavior from rambunctious little boys.

In facilities where wolf packs are actually managed for research purposes, rather than allowed to develop on their own, there is inevitably an Omega Pack, separated from the higher-ranking wolves by high fences. Wolf-park managers do this purely for the safety and well-being of the Omega animals. In the wild, these wolves are inevitably targets for the aggression of the higher-testosterone pack members; in other words, they tend to get beaten up and have their wolf-lunches stolen on a pretty regular basis.

Although an argument can be made that the job of the Omega is to absorb the free-floating aggression in the pack and thereby help to maintain harmony within the pack, allowing nature to take its course is not a Good Thing when a facility is dependent upon financial support from good-hearted folks who care about wild animals but are not entirely comfortable with the basic brutality of the natural world. Basically, in both a wild wolf pack and on a playground, it pretty much sucks to be the Omega.

On the other hand, when grouped together in a managed facility, without having to deal with the more aggressive animals on a day-to-day basis, these guys usually do pretty well, and sometimes actually manage to reproduce.

Experienced breeders of show dogs generally manage their domestic "packs" in a similar manner, although very few breeders actually maintain an Omega pack. Instead, an animal who seems to have been born with a *kick me* sign on his back is often sent to a pet home for his own well-being, where he invariably blossoms into the World's Smartest Dog.

In the world of purebred dogs, where so much of the emphasis is placed on purely physical attributes, this ultimately results in little damage to the gene pool, as the animals of higher pack status are usually the better physical specimens anyway.

The fact that many of the Omegas in the purebred dog world are highly intelligent and make wonderful companions, while a lot of Leglifters are dumber than the proverbial box of hammers and cannot even be housebroken, matters little at a dog show, where the finalists rarely have to submit to an interview on current affairs as part of the adjudication process. (In fact, all they really need to do is trot around a ring on a leash with their tail up and then stand still for a minute while staring intently at a piece of liver, neither of which, quite frankly, requires much brainpower.) Because of this, show dogs are getting better-looking but dumber with every succeeding generation, although nobody involved really seems to notice or care. (There's probably a cautionary message in here somewhere.)

In the civilized world of *homo sapiens*, your average American public school pretty much resembles your average wolf park, only not usually as well-managed. Here Omega packs often start forming around middle school, and generally last through high school, college, and most post-doc programs. Before computers, when these were the "AV Guys", the Chess Club probably represented the quintessential Omega Pack. Now, of course, there are a lot more options, most of which involve computers and virtually *none* of which involve competitive physical sports.

One of the biggest myths about Omegas is that they are social misfits with no friends. They're not - the Omega is a pack animal through and through. Although they are innately uncomfortable around high-testosterone males (the latter often a result of having been hung upside-down in their locker one time too many), Omegas more often than not have a circle of male (and sometimes female) friends who share similar interests. Typically, most of these friends are also Omegas (the classic Omega Pack), but some may be Retrievers (the big softies who stuck up for them back in grades school), Betas, or Sentinels and, within this group, they are pretty relaxed. It's important to remember that while all Omegas are by definition geeks, *not all geeks are Omegas.*

All in all, Omegas have lots going for them, especially once they have outgrown the general physical awkwardness that seems to plague them through adolescence. They may not be able to fix your transmission or re-roof your house, but according to the statistics, Omegas are more likely to stay married, and more likely to describe their marriages as "happy", than their high-testosterone brethren. So they are worth a look, especially if classic machismo and hard muscle are not particularly important to you, and you have no personal interest in watching NASCAR and/or endless series of year-round playoffs in sports you can't even identify. And most of them make a pretty good living.

Plumage

Omegas are usually pretty easy to identify - they display all the physical characteristics of a low-testosterone male. There's been lots of research showing that, in males, it's pretty easy to tell the difference between an high-testosterone guy and a low-testosterone guy just by looking at his face. The face of the low-T male is less intense in its expression, and considerably friendlier. They smile more easily, with characteristically "upturned" smiles. And unlike high-T men, their smiles extend all the way to their eyes, crinkling them at the corners with those lines radiating down in what women refer to mournfully in themselves as "laugh lines". (Women, of course, are low-testosterone by definition when compared to men, and as a result have thinner skin, which is more prone to collapse. Women also smile more than men, as a rule.)

In terms of body type, Omegas may be whippet-slim or pretty pudgy, but they are rarely broad-shouldered, or hard-muscled, because those physical traits are the result of higher testosterone levels than Omegas generally carry. Also, hard muscle usually requires hard physical exercise, and about the only exercise Omegas get is maybe riding their bikes to work.

Fashion-wise, although there is a stereotype of the nerd as a skinny little guy with his pants hiked up under his armpits and the ubiquitous pocket-protector in his shirt pocket, this image is really a couple of decades out of date. The modern Omega is defined as much by his T-shirt collection as by anything else. Your younger Omegas *adore* T-shirts with obscure (to the rest of the world anyway) references emblazoned on them - in no other area are they as likely to reveal their usually politely well-hidden (and honestly well-deserved) intellectual arrogance. Unless they are required to, Omegas rarely will wear a suit. They're casual, "jeans and a t-shirt" kind of guys who really don't care much about impressing anyone with their looks or wardrobe. (In this regard they are a lot like Alphas.) In fact, if you asked around, you'd probably find most Omegas probably think Armani is a computer game - their cultural awareness rarely extends to fashion.

This general lack of interest in appearance is also reflected in their hair. Some Omegas wear their hair pretty short, and some sport a ponytail halfway down their back. In both cases the motivation is pretty much the same - they really don't care about it. One group doesn't want to bother with haircuts, the other doesn't want to bother combing their hair. Neither group owns mousse or hair gel.

Lots of Omegas wear glasses, but I've yet to meet one who bothered with contacts. Again, this is reflective of a total lack of narcissism. On the other hand, for most women (especially those on the second go-round) looks are rarely as important as a sense of humor, loyalty, intelligence, and dependability, and in all these areas Omegas have a definite edge.

Habitat

Where you most likely *won't* find an Omega:

1. Running with the bulls in Spain
2. At the Daytona 500
3. In the House or Senate
4. At an NFL game
5. Drinking beer in the local pub
6. At a heavyweight title fight
7. At a strip club
8. In the Marine Corps
9. At a construction site
10. At an all-night poker game
11. Watching a Three Stooges movie
12. At a WWF wrestling match (often hard to tell from #11.)
13. In a duck-hunting blind

The reason, of course, is that these are all places inhabited mostly by pretty high-testosterone men. Now, this really shouldn't pose much of a problem for most women since, for the most part, *women generally don't frequent any of these places either*, nor are they likely to at any point in the foreseeable future. *The larger question might be why women are even attracted to guys who think any of these things actually constitutes a fun time...*

So where are you likely to find an Omega?

Most likely at home or at work. Occasionally at the wedding of a friend or relative. (He'll find the whole thing extremely painful, but he'll show up because he's a nice guy, and a loyal friend.)

Although these guys spend a lot of time in front of a computer, you're highly unlikely to find a picture of one on a garden-variety internet dating site - actually putting their name, photo, and a line of bullshit designed to make them sound sexy out there for the whole non-Omega world to see is *totally* not their style.

That said, I did manage to locate a very cool internet dating site specifically designed for geeks wishing to meet other geeks for the purpose of dating, however...well worth a look if you think you'd qualify. Photos are not included - apparently, looks actually ARE less important to these guys than brains and character.

However, most women who end up with an Omega mate seem to have met him through work, a mutual friend, or his sister. I've yet to encounter a woman who's met an Omega in a bar, although maybe internet cafes might have some potential...

A lot of Omegas live at home well into adulthood. In the wild, it is the highest-status young males who are the first to disperse, while the Omegas are most likely to stay with their birth pack, and the same phenomenon can be observed in people. Since Omegas rarely have an active sex life when they're single, this doesn't pose much of a problem for them.

Omegas who don't live at home usually have a job that would make commuting difficult. They rarely have a roommate. Single Omegas are usually financially able to pay the rent without splitting it and, although they're pack animals, they are perfectly comfortable with their own company, a quality they share with Alphas. They'll usually live in a modest modern apartment (even when they make a salary well into six-figures) and are often what you might call "domestic" in a charmingly inept way.

They do their own laundry, usually in the laundry room in the basement of their apartment. (Some women have actually met them there.)

They generally don't eat out a lot, nor do they live on takeout. *What they do is go to the supermarket and buy only those things that they can microwave.* These guys are the *backbone* of the microwaveable dinner industry.

Unlike single Leglifters, who tend to live on pizza and beer, Omegas actually shop for groceries and keep basic food staples in the pantry. They eat cereal for breakfast (when we say "cereal" we're talking Cheerios or Cap'n Crunch here, not granola, by the way) and usually have milk and cookies in the house. They buy orange juice because they're bright guys and they know vitamin C is good for them. They usually own a few dishes, which they actually wash, and sometimes put away.

But odds are good that an Omega living by himself has never *once* used the conventional oven that came with the apartment, even if he has a PhD in something most people cannot even pronounce. I have no idea why, or what they did before the invention of the microwave.

The Omega's idea of furniture is pretty basic, because these are neither comfort-seekers like Retrievers nor are they status-seekers like Leglifters. (The ones with lots and lots of money have taste that runs to sleek and high-tech, with gray being the universally preferred color.)

They're usually relatively tidy except for their workspaces, which are invariably a chaotic jumble of electronic equipment and wires and cables all stacked halfway to the ceiling.

Computers are a fact of life for Omegas, and rarely are they found in a field that does not rely on them to a great extent.

In fact, the guys who currently *design* computers, as well as computer programs, systems, and software, are most likely Omegas.

It is important to understand that this was not always true - most of the early pioneers of the PC industry back in the 70s, many of whom took huge personal, professional, and intellectual risks and made huge fortunes as a result, were clearly not Omegas (it's testosterone that facilitates risk), although they are certainly a bright bunch of geeks and the heroes of Omegas everywhere. This goes back to the fact that although all Omegas are geeks, not all geeks are Omegas, which is important to remember. The high tech "geek-world" is also populated by Alphas, Betas, Sentinels, and even a few Junkyard dogs, although in lesser numbers.

As far as hobbies go, most Omegas are attracted to hobbies that involve computer technology, as opposed to hobbies that involve fishing tackle, golf clubs, or bowling shoes. Omegas, of course, more or less *invented* the whole role-playing game thing, which I would explain here if I actually understood anything about it, which I do not.

But a little research on my part produced some interesting stuff - these guys actually have pretty varied interests, some of which were entirely unexpected. Some of them are *gamblers*, which frankly surprised the hell out of me. Not only do they gamble online, but some of them actually like Las Vegas, and will drop some serious money there in what amounts to a mathematical battle of wits with the casinos. Gambling is an intellectual game for Omegas, I found out, and the game involves higher math. (Apparently, casino owners are less than thrilled to see a bunch of MIT geniuses show up in their establishments, because they win more than sheer statistical probability would predict.)

Horticulture and plant genetics is another fairly popular hobby with this bunch - some are into hydroponics, while others grow rare orchids or other less exotic plants indoors under entirely artificial light in their basements. Geology is also a popular interest - lots of rock hounds here.

There are a fair number of movie-buffs in the Omega world - in fact, cultural trivia is more or less their personal domain, especially if it involves science fiction and quirky cult-classics. Their affinity for comic-book superheroes is of course legendary. (Clark Kent was probably the quintessential Omega.) Omegas are particularly fond of quirky humor.

Fantasy appeals to Omegas, of course. As far as I can tell, they've all read the entire Lord of the Rings Trilogy and all the Harry Potter books - the difference between Omegas and the rest of the world is that they remember the most astonishing details about each and every book. Not surprisingly, Douglas Adams is another popular author among Omegas. (Junkyard dogs are also fond of his stuff for no reason I can think of.)

Because they are so very bright as a group, Omegas are actually a lot more interesting, and have a wider range of interests, than most people would expect.

Mating Habits

Omegas probably have a harder time dating than most other guys. They're not innately comfortable with women they don't know well, and in a standard dating situation have a tendency to be awkward to an astonishing degree.

Generally, it's better to get to know an Omega pretty well before you go out on an actual date with him, or his social discomfort level will cause the evening to be a disaster for both of you. Nothing is worse than having a guy with an IQ of 150 and a PhD start hyperventilating on you in an expensive restaurant. Some have actually been known to pass out cold from the stress. You need to proceed very slowly with these guys, meeting them informally during the day in non-threatening situations where they're comfortable before moving on to dating, which is very scary for them. Think of it like trying to get a chipmunk to eat out of your hand - move too fast and they'll bolt in terror. So why bother at all? Read on.

Omegas are not guys who are particularly comfortable talking about sex, I found. Especially with a woman they hardly know. So in order to get an accurate picture of the mating habits of Omegas, I went online. Logic told me that since traditionally Omegas find out whatever they need to know via their computers, there might actually be some useful information there.

That was an understatement. What I found was a treasure-trove. In their own world (cyberspace) these guys are articulate, insightful, funny, and quick on the uptake. They also spell better than most men. Among the best finds was a website that actually listed the top ten reasons geeks make better lovers, which included some pretty good stuff.

- According to this guy (who sounds like he ought to know), *geeks don't cheat*.
- They are just grateful that some woman actually wants them in the first place, and most don't have the social skills

necessary to pull off an affair even if they wanted to.
- They like to learn new things, which is certainly an advantage in bed.
- They don't give up easily if something doesn't work the first time - they try to fix it, using logic and their problem-solving skills.
- They don't judge women by their looks because they don't judge *anyone* by their looks.
- They generally like their jobs, and are usually well-paid.
- They like to stay home in the evening.
- They like to give gifts. (Who knew?)
- And of course, they can fix your hard drive if it crashes.

Another site I found included a Geek's Guide to Sex. In my opinion, they ought to put this one somewhere where *all* men could read it, because it was a masterpiece.

Written without hyperbola in the clear and concise language one might use to discuss a computer systems problem, it covered the basic differences between men and women sexually - for example, women, it was explained, do not have a single major erogenous zone as men do, and therefore respond to generalized stroking and massage more. It went on to explain (in the same clear and slightly technical language) the gender differences in arousal and length of time necessary to reach orgasm and then, in an absolutely breathtaking piece of Omega logic, proposed a solution to the problem that was equitable to both partners.

The obvious solution was *cunnilingus* (to use the author's term) and a set of fairly technical and anatomically sophisticated instructions on how to successfully perform this procedure on one's partner followed. Once the female partner had already reached orgasm via this technique *prior* to intercourse, it was explained, she was unlikely to be critical of the shorter amount of time the male partner needed to spend in actual intercourse before achieving the same result, thereby saving him from the undue embarrassment of too-swift ejaculation.

Good Lord. Talk about creative problem-solving. Somebody really ought to send that to the *Marines*. (Their websites, I noticed, were fairly devoid of such useful information.)

Anyway, should you happen to become involved with an Omega and decide you want to marry him, you'll be pleased to know that unlike a lot of higher-testosterone guys, they have no real fear of commitment. Omegas *like* to be married, and they are more likely than any other PSP (with the exception of Alphas) to *stay* married.

Omegas also make great fathers - remember, in canines, they are the PSP that usually assumes the baby-sitting duties, even when they haven't sired the cubs themselves. They are patient, responsible, and very conscientious in the care of small children. Because a lot of Omegas now enjoy the sort of job flexibility that allows them to work from home, many of them are the primary child-care parent in families today, and it seems to work out well for all parties involved.

Omegas are a good choice for women with demanding careers because, as husbands go, they're pretty low maintenance guys; comfortable with their own interests and not panicked by solitude, they rarely need constant contact with their partners and are not particularly emotionally needy. Nor are Omegas threatened by a woman's success - like Alphas, they *admire* intelligence in a woman.

If, on the other hand, you want a snappy dresser who's comfortable in large social gatherings who will be willing to attend social, business, or political functions several nights a week, you're going to be disappointed. These guys would rather be home surfing the web.

10

Leglifters

In the world of dogs, leg-lifting is a behavior that has absolutely nothing to do with the actual need to pee (most bitches manage to pee just fine without hitting every tree, lamppost, and fire hydrant for miles around) and everything to do with territorial marking, and the desire to dominate.

Leg-lifting is, very simply, caused by an abundance of the androgen hormone *testosterone*, most of which is produced in the testes, which is why a male dog who is surgically castrated prior to adolescence (when testosterone levels climb rapidly) will rarely become a chronic Leglifter. This option, unfortunately, is not widely available for men, which is why we will never, as a species, manage to achieve World Peace.

As long as we have Leglifters, we will have wars - the old ones *start* them, and the young ones *fight* them.

Back in the sixties, there was a popular T-shirt whose logo read:

JOIN THE ARMY.
TRAVEL TO NEW AND EXCITING PLACES.
MEET NEW PEOPLE.
AND KILL THEM.

Some guys honestly *didn't get it*. Invariably, *they* wore T-shirts that read:

> KILL 'EM ALL.
> LET GOD SORT 'EM OUT.

Those guys were Leglifters. Not necessarily the *smartest* ones maybe, but Leglifters nonetheless. In fact, this single slogan pretty much sums up the basic effect of testosterone on the male brain.

Testosterone facilitates action which is, in the words of Car Talk's Magliozzi brothers (who have lots of first-hand experience with the stuff), *"entirely unencumbered by the thought process"*.

Men who join the military to defend their country, and who may consequently actually *die* defending that country, are not necessarily altruists. Because they make "the ultimate sacrifice" we have a tendency to view this behavior as altruistic, but it is not. Dying for a particular political cause, even a good one, does NOT automatically make one an altruist. *(On the other hand, dying because you threw yourself on a grenade to save someone else's life DOES, even if you happened to be wearing the uniform of the Third Reich at the time.)*

Pretty much like chimps (a primate species where the males carry high T-levels across the board), guys who are "defending their country" are really just aggressively competing for *real estate*, and access to the available resources it contains. In almost any species, the scarcer the resources and the higher the collective testosterone level in the males, the more likely this is to happen.

The fact that the willingness of these guys to defend their territory is on occasion *advantageous to the rest of pack* still does not automatically make it pro-social, or altruistic, behavior, because the motivation is different. It's motivated, not by a dopamine release from helping others, but by testosterone, a hormone that pretty much has its own agenda.

If there is no outside threat to their territory, or no pressing need for the expansion of it, these same males will aggressively compete to maintain or gain status within their *own* pack, which can hardly be viewed as altruistic behavior by any stretch of the imagination. Or, barring any opportunity to defend or expand their territory, or raise their status within their pack, they will aggressively compete over sexual access to females (which happens both in the wild and in every redneck bar in the country with appalling regularity.)

Lacking "acceptable" territory to defend and means to gain pack status (both of which are provided by military service, especially in times of war), young high-testosterone males are likely to seek other outlets, which probably explains both inner-city and prison gang violence.

Leglifters are hard-wired to *enjoy* competition, and they are aggressive competitors. *James Dabbs did an analysis of the T-levels of over 4,000 Vietnam Veterans. Across the board, those who saw the most combat were the ones with the highest testosterone levels - and these levels were measured more than twenty years later, after they had fallen significantly. (That this occurred in spite of the draft, when the Army had to take pretty much whatever it got, is a testament to the military's well-honed ability to recognize testosterone and put it to good use.)*

Words like "honor" and "defense" represent some testosterone-laden concepts - very often they are not about *helping others* (i.e. pro-social behavior), as much as *maintaining one's own pack status* and *protection (or expansion) of one's own territory.*

Now, to be fair, the word *honor* actually has developed two very different meanings over the years:
One implies a sense of *integrity*; of understanding right from wrong *as determined by the society in which one lives* and doing the right, or "honorable", thing. Because it varies from culture to culture, this sort of personal honor is not pre-installed hardware in most males, but has to be *learned.* In many social species besides ours (including canines, other primates, and elephants) appropriate pro-social behavior is taught to the young males by the older dominant animals of both sexes.

Any experienced dog breeder knows that the most efficient way to cool the jets of an obnoxious young male is to simply move him temporarily into a pen full of old bitches, who can be depended upon to smack that boy upside the head as soon as he steps out of line.

Most Leglifters who've had good role models take personal honor pretty seriously, and try to behave honorably, which is a good thing for society.

The *other* definition of honor, though, is really the *original* one, from the Latin word honor, which literally means "repute or esteem", and accounts for Webster's primary definition:

1. high regard or great respect given, received, or enjoyed; especially a) glory; fame; renown. b) good reputation; as opposed to dishonor, disgrace.

In other words, *this* sort of honor is entirely about maintaining one's male pack status position, and does not have to be learned - it comes as pre-installed hardware in males with high testosterone levels, sort of like getting Windows XP for free when you buy a new computer. Which is probably why most women, who carry about *a tenth* of the testosterone that men do, can go for *years* without ever using the word "honor" in an actual sentence, or feeling the need to risk their lives defending theirs.

The reason women have traditionally tolerated this whole "honor thing" is probably because, in most species, the testosterone-driven status-seeking of males can actually provide an evolutionary advantage for females, who reap the benefits through greater access to resources for their offspring - in other words, it furthers both the male and female biological agendas. As women have gained access to the job market, this is probably less true today than it once was. Some women view this change as a sign of continuing evolution of the species.

"Defending one's honor" is really about defending one's status within the pack. And the absolutely *stupidest* form of defending one's honor, and thereby maintaining one's pack status, ever to be developed and codified in the history of testosterone surely must be:

The Duel.

A duel is defined as "a formalized type of combat between two individuals, usually developing out of a desire for the challenger to redress an insult to his honor" and dates back at least as far as the written word. *Because it is about establishing dominance, and dominance is driven by testosterone, which men carry roughly ten times as much of as women do, these 'individuals' are invariable male.* But dueling is not limited to the *human* male by a long shot.

For example, both wolves and man's best buddy, the domestic dog, practice dueling. In the canine world, duels between males are extremely formalized rituals, starting with posturing and eye contact. If that fails to establish dominance, they move on to growling and circling, and then progress to actual combat (using their teeth as weapons) ending only when one guy rolls over on his back and bares his throat, at which point the winner, rather than ripping it out, usually just pees on him and saunters off.

Now rams, bless their hearts, are much dumber than canines and are *ferocious* duelers - lacking the sort of teeth needed for ripping flesh but blessed with extremely thick skulls, they will engage in a duel consisting of repeated short charges and skull-bashing (which can be heard for miles) UNTIL ONE OF THEM FALLS DOWN. *This is, no doubt, where the idea for professional boxing came from.*

And the absolute *epitome of absurdity* in dueling is practiced by the bull elk, a very large and not-too-terribly-bright animal possessing an extraordinarily large rack of elaborately designed horns, which serves no earthly purpose other than as a very expensive display of testosterone.

Most of the time, the bull elk does not really have to fight - all he has do is walk around displaying this ridiculous headgear, and the guy with the biggest "rack" sort of wins by default. (It's the elkish equivalent of a guy wearing his Corvette, or in some cases his actual *penis*, strapped on his head.) But sometimes in the fall, when elk testosterone (and corresponding stupidity) levels are at their highest, two bulls will actually "lock horns" in a magnificent battle for territory and breeding rights to the available cows, who are themselves hornless and who appear fairly bored by the whole affair.

Unfortunately, one major pitfall of these magnificent and terrible forest duels is that the splendid racks will sometimes become *entangled* during the battle. Then the bull elk, lacking as they do opposable thumbs, are sometimes unable to untangle themselves and can end up *permanently stuck* in this position, standing nose to nose with their adversary in a mutual testosterone-soaked rage, completely unable to eat or drink, until they both die of dehydration and/or starvation, whichever comes first.

So as not to be outdone in the Animal Kingdom in the stupidity department, men have been dueling pretty much since the day they first picked up a club.

Over the course of history men have dueled with heavy claymores while dressed in short plaid skirts and no underwear; with elegantly-wrought swords while dressed in jerkins and tights; and with pistols inclined to misfire while dressed in velvet jackets and outsized hats with feathered plumes.

Over the years, as men became more civilized, they developed actual written *rules* for dueling. According to these rules, the offended party was known as "the challenger", and the challenge was declared with a glove.

Back in Medieval days the challenger would literally "throw down the gauntlet", although in later years when gloves were no longer made of heavy metal and you could actually whack the other guy with one without knocking him silly, a "slap in the face" became the challenge of choice. That both terms are still widely used today is very telling...

And by the rules, it was the challenger who decided the level of violence required to assuage his honor. A duel could be ended at *first blood*, in which case the first man to bleed would be the loser (this worked better before the invention of the pistol) or alternatively *to the death*, in which case the winner was the survivor. Duhh.

In the case of pistol duels, each party would generally agree to fire one shot, after which the duel was declared, thankfully, over. However (your average female reader immediately sees the obvious answer for avoiding bloodshed here) Rule 13 of the Code Duello of 1777 clearly states "no dumb firing or shooting in the air is admissible in any case." Oh well.

So standard dueling protocol was for the two parties to be placed back to back (by their respective "seconds") with loaded pistols at their sides, walk a specified number of paces (the greater the insult, the fewer the paces), turn, and simultaneously *shoot* at each other. In this manner, one man's honor is defended, and the slower man is dead - the fact that these might well be *the same man* apparently managed to escape notice.

And we let these guys run the planet?????????

It has always seemed to me that it would be far simpler to just have the two parties involved turn, simultaneously whip their respective dicks out of their pants, slap them on a table, and let the guy with the biggest one be declared the winner. No bloodshed required.

Hey, I'm dead serious here - since wars are really no more than duels with a whole bunch of guys getting in there on both sides to support the two who started it (sort of like a bar fight on a global scale), think of all the innocent lives that could have been saved over the years...many of them belonging to women and small children.

Even in the United States, dueling was an acceptable form of determining male dominance until the late-nineteenth century. Alexander Hamilton (yup, the same one whose face adorns the ten-dollar bill to this day) was fatally wounded in a duel while defending his honor. First Secretary of the Treasury or not, the guy was a *complete idiot,* and they put his face on the ten dollar bill?! Amazing.

During the Revolutionary War, George Washington opposed dueling and in fact encouraged his officers to refuse challenges, as he felt that the inevitable loss of life would be detrimental to the revolutionary war effort. (George was an Alpha.)

To give you an idea how prevalent this insanity was, Abraham Lincoln was once challenged to a duel by a political opponent while he was a member of the Illinois Legislature. He was saved only by the fact that his serotonin levels and IQ thankfully exceeded his testosterone level. To have refused the challenge was unthinkable - it would have ended his political career. In fact, challenging politicians to a duel over imagined slights was a popular way of getting rid of one's political enemies back then. (And for God's sake don't tell Karl Rove - lots of states still allow dueling in their statutes to this day.) So how did Mr. Lincoln think his way out of it, thereby managing to stay alive at least long enough to preserve the Union?

Under the established Code Duello (or: Rules for Duels) the guy being challenged, rather than the challenger, gets to choose the venue and weapon – THE FACT THAT *THIS* PARTICULAR RULE IS REALLY STUPID SHOULD COME AS NO SURPRISE TO WOMEN - and rather than the popular "pistols in a field at dawn", Abe chose, I kid you not:

BROADSWORDS
IN THE MIDDLE OF THE
MISSISSIPPI RIVER.

The logistical difficulties involved with arranging this particular METHODUS PUGNANDI *(to say nothing of the physical advantage held by the 6'4" Lincoln over his significantly shorter-limbed opponent in a swordfight even on dry land) resulted in the duel never actually taking place, thank God, or a whole bunch of us would be sending our Federal tax returns to Richmond and buying our groceries with currency featuring pictures of Bobby Lee and Jeff Davis.*

Duels are the sole province of Leglifters. Duels are, by definition, stupid and entirely self-serving and Leglifters are a high-testosterone PSP usually lacking a copy of the gene variant associated with altruistic behavior. This "altruism" gene occurs in roughly 65% of the population worldwide (although, not surprisingly, distribution varies from country to country) and what this really means is that 35% of the population is *not* carrying it. And roughly half of *those* people are men, some of whom are carrying T-levels that would probably get them thrown out of the Tour de France.

These guys, like the rest of their gender, are also somewhat hampered by a smaller cerebral cortex (which controls rational thought) and a larger amygdala (which controls aggression and sexual desire) than females, both effects of testosterone on the developing embryo.

Although some Mental Health Care Professionals who are making a lot of serious money off Freudian bullshit will dispute this, the truth is the male and the female brain are physiologically and biochemically different, and most intelligent people know it.

What is less well-known is that the "default" brain in nearly all mammals is actually the female model. All brains start out female, and are altered in the second trimester in those embryos carrying a Y chromosome by the appearance of large quantities of testosterone. (So much for the "Adam's rib" theory...)

Toss in low male baseline levels of both prolactin and oxytocin, a copy or two of the novelty-seeking variant, and you've got a typical Leglifter. This particular genetic "stew" pretty much guarantees you're going to get a guy with strong dominance-seeking tendencies and a penchant for risk-taking, with little ability to communicate on an emotional level or to form strong social bonds, and completely lacking in domesticity and child-rearing capabilities. Without the high baseline serotonin levels and resulting impulse control of an Alpha, they are inclined to immediate action with little or no reflection whatsoever. They are extremely focused, because testosterone increases focus. (Unfortunately, it also hampers the ability to focus on more than one thing at a time.) And they have a strong sex drive. Given this combination, many modern women don't find Leglifters a really great bargain as husbands, even the straight ones.

What, it hadn't actually occurred to you that there were *gay* Leglifters? Actually, there are *bucket-loads* of them. The gay community probably contains about the same percentage of high-T men as the straight community because, although it increases sex drive, testosterone does *not* appear to have a damn thing to do with sexual *preference.* And unlike all the other PSPs, Leglifters can be divided into two sub-groups, or "varieties" as we say in the dog world:

PITBULLS and SPECIALS.

Now, anyone who doesn't spend every single weekend and all of their expendable income showing dogs (*in other words, a Normal Person*) is probably familiar enough with Pitbulls, but is also right now wondering what the hell a "Special" is...fair question.
In the weird world of show dogs, where an adjective can be used as a noun without anyone wondering why, a Special is a sort of "super-show dog". These are the dogs who continue to compete for top awards long after they've completed the requirements for their championships. Specials are the dogs you'll see in TV coverage of the big dog shows like the AKC Invitational and Westminster competing for Best In Show. They're good dogs with Something Extra.

In the dog world, the difference between a Special and an ordinary champion is sort of like the difference between Mick Jagger and the lead singer of a competent bar band - both are probably pretty good, but one of them is a superstar.

In addition to their physical attributes, Specials have something dog people call "presence" - they catch your eye, and they can take your breath away. Without presence, a show dog simply cannot be a Special, no matter how good he is. And experienced breeders can recognize that "look at me" quality very early on, no matter what the breed. (A Special is *not* a particular breed, although in fact some breeds seem to produce more superstars than others.) It's mostly a matter of attitude.

Just for the record, the canine Pitbull is not an AKC breed, either. In fact, it's hardly an actual breed at all...it's more like a *type* of dog, bred for a specific purpose. A hard-muscled, high-testosterone fellow with a singular love of combat, the modern Pitbull was never designed for fighting bulls at all, but rather was developed solely for the purpose of fighting others of his own kind in spectator-ringed arenas, or "pits" (an occupation which in all honesty he thoroughly enjoys), by guys who really oughta be slapping their *own* dicks on a table after letting spectators bet beforehand on whose is biggest - but, hey, that's just my opinion...some people like to watch professional boxing, too.

At any rate, under no circumstances should the Pitbull be confused with the Amstaff, the Staffordshire Bull Terrier, the Bull Terrier, or the Bulldog, all of whom are (in spite of their somewhat checkered pasts) perfectly nice breeds of AKC dogs with unfortunately similar names.

Both Pitbulls and Specials have the strong dominance-seeking tendencies that make a Leglifter a Leglifter. The *difference* between the two is that, like peacocks, Specials attempt to dominate primarily through "display" whenever possible, while Pitbulls don't seem to *mind* the possibility that they might get their nose broken on occasion. (Like a dueling scar, within certain socioeconomic groups a nose broken by repeated fighting is actually viewed as a badge of honor.) Specials, on the other hand, don't *like* to injure themselves - in fact, they don't even like to mess up their *clothes* if they can avoid it.

As a result, Pitbulls are more likely to attempt to dominate through physical violence, or the implied threat thereof, while Specials generally rely on their sheer *presence.* There's probably a gene or two that controls this difference, but damned if I know what it is. At any rate, the net result is the same: the overriding urge to dominate everyone else around them from cradle to grave by whatever means works best for them.

Both Specials and Pitbulls share a basic tendency toward narcissism, and tend to think very highly of themselves, whether fully warranted or not. And, like all narcissists, they have little or no ability to accept criticism, real or imagined, which they will immediately perceive as a threat to their status (or "honor") and which is, of course, what the whole dueling thing is about.

Whether they're Specials or Pitbulls, all Leglifters are entirely self-centered. A lot like your average two-year-old, their favorite words are invariably "I", "me", "my", and "mine", and all of them figure heavily into their conversation. *(This should be your first red flag on a date, by the way, along with some really serious over-tipping.)*

This self-centered view of the world is largely a biochemical function of testosterone, the most "selfish" of brain chemicals, whose evolutionary function after all is to ensure continuation of the species, primarily (in the case of males anyway) through dissemination of the sperm entrusted to its care.

Of course, not all high-T men are complete and utter narcissists, since testosterone's effects can be moderated by other neurotransmitters and hormones such as serotonin, prolactin, and oxytocin, but since these guys don't carry an abundance of any of them, Leglifters are pretty much completely, and utterly, narcissistic.

Which takes us neatly to:

Plumage

You're so vain you probably think this song is about you.
— Carly Simon (backup vocals by Mick Jagger)

Vanity, it turns out, is very much a function of testosterone. *(Astonishingly, this was found to be true in women as well as men. High-T women tend to be more concerned about their looks than their lower-testosterone sisters and, like high-T men, are more likely to "decorate" themselves with jewelry and flashy clothes. Some very classically sexy women carry surprisingly high testosterone levels - turns out it's virtually impossible to guess a woman's t-levels just by looking at her.)*

The same cannot be said for men, where testosterone is pretty easy to spot and, physically, Leglifters are very much defined by it. In men, high-T levels are responsible for lean muscle mass, which is usually carried in the upper body, causing Leglifters, no matter what their height (and there are a LOT of short Leglifters), to be broader through the shoulders. Testosterone also causes fat to be carried in the abdomen, where it is easily accessible for quick energy if needed, so when these guys do gain weight, it's always carried up front, right above the belt. (This is also why a man can lose a beer gut just by giving up his morning donut, while a woman can do crunches until she's blue in the face and never end up with six-pack abs...) But Leglifters, like all high-T men, are rarely obese.

There are lots of serious competitive body-builders in this group, by the way, especially among the shorter ones. And since research has shown over and over that bulging freakazoid muscle (often in weird places where normal well-built men don't even have muscles) is not particularly attractive to women, we can safely assume it's probably more about competition and display among males than any desire to attract or please females... sort of like the rack on a bull elk.

Testosterone is also largely responsible for male-pattern baldness, so unless he got lucky in the genetics department (easily determined just by looking at his maternal grandfather), sooner or later, the average Leglifter is going to start losing his hair, beginning in the front. Being vain to a fault, this is a pretty devastating occurrence for them. Leglifters as a group take great *pride* in their hair, and spend a lot of time and money on it - styling it, streaking it, smoothing it constantly, coloring it when it starts to go gray, and tossing it around when it's plentiful. So the balding Leglifter will generally try *anything* - Rogaine, hair transplants, strange hairdos (think Donald Trump here), a really bad toupee - to keep from appearing bald. Some of them, once they realize the battle is pretty much lost, will simply shave their heads completely.

With or without hair on top of it, the high-T face of a Leglifter is pretty hard to miss. It's not so much a matter of bone structure (although testosterone does generally produce a square jaw), as it is a matter of *expression* - whether classically handsome or not, there's virtually no softness of expression in their faces, or around their eyes. In fact, it's not a particularly *friendly* face, nor is it particularly expressive.

It has been shown in numerous scientific experiments that extremely high-T men do not smile as often, or as readily, as lower-testosterone men and, when they *do* smile, *their mouths don't turn up at the corners.* Instead, they usually grin, showing a lot of teeth. Pitbulls, like most high-T men, will invariably display a decidedly 'wolfish' grin when asked to "Smile!" for a photograph, and which isn't exactly the same thing, although I guess they don't know that.

Specials, on the other hand, are the masters of what is called *the gingival smile*, a peculiarly rectangular grin both deep and wide that's really a display of teeth and gums, and which has long been associated by psychologists with the personality trait of narcissism. (The "gingival smile" is seen in male animals of many species, including most other primates, and rarely is it associated with simple friendliness - the male orangutan at the zoo may be feeling pretty good about himself, but he *does not* want to be your friend.)

In neither case do these grins generally have the effect of being *disarming,* which is the underlying psychological purpose of a smile. As any internet-savvy person knows, a smile (a *real* smile, that is, where the corners of the mouth turn up like the little yellow smiley-face guy) is the universal human method of indicating a lack of aggressive intentions, and which probably explains why really high-testosterone men smile less frequently than the rest of the world. (I'd wager they never include smiley-faces in their emails, either...)

Leglifters also make more eye contact than most other PSPs, with the possible exception of the Retriever, although the intent is very different. Retrievers tend to make eye contact for the same reason women do - it's part of social bonding. With Leglifters, it's more like an impromptu non-violent duel, sort of like arm wrestling, and the person who breaks first loses a couple points. (Canine Leglifters do the same eye-contact thing.)

Like Junkyard Dogs, Leglifters will often spend a lot of money on their clothes, and Specials are always among the best-dressed men at any function, but the underlying *reason* for it is different. Where Junkyard Dogs don't feel the need to impress so much as the need to please themselves, Leglifters are positively *driven* by the need to "dress to impress", because it is a very basic way of raising their status among their peers. Whether they're decked out in Armani (designer of choice for all Leglifters,) or Harley-Davidson's finest (pretty limited to the Pitbull variety,) is probably determined by some "taste" gene yet to be identified, but the one thing they *will* be for sure is "decked out".

Leglifters are THE single most status-conscious PSP. They are the most label-conscious of men, and always seem to know who's in and who's out. These guys would drape Ralph *himself* over their shoulders and wear him to a party if they could get away with it...unless of course Ralph's out - it's hard to keep up. That's why they read GQ. (Specials, that is. Pitbulls read Sports Illustrated, and get a lot of tattoos.)

Once popular only among the lowest echelons of society (and sailors on shore leave), tattoos have always been associated with high testosterone levels. Although they've become a lot more trendy in recent years among people of both sexes from social classes unlikely to include felons and sailors, nothing much appears to have changed in regards to testosterone levels. Painting and decorating one's body for the purposes of intimidating other males has long been practiced among Leglifters from Borneo to Newark. Which is probably why you'll never ever find an Alpha with a tattoo, or wearing gold chains around his neck or wrists.

Pitbulls generally favor tattoos, while Specials generally prefer less permanent decor, like jewelry. *In spite of their strong self-preservation instincts, Specials will often grit their teeth and subject themselves to painful procedures that will improve their appearance (they often wear an earring, and lots of them have had nose jobs, Botox injections, and hair transplants), but they rarely get tattoos. The possibility that they may end up permanently stuck with a tattoo that may become dated or - yikes! - inexplicably déclassé in the future probably disinclines them to make that sort of commitment.*

Men who wear gold jewelry other than a watch and a wedding (or class) ring are almost invariably Leglifters of one sort or the other.

A Leglifter is a "brand-name" kind of guy. The brand itself doesn't matter so much as the fact that it *is* a brand, and besides, having a favorite brand of something often opens the door to a little friendly competition. Leglifters wear their brand-loyalties prominently displayed in all their casual clothing - with these guys, you never have to guess their favorite brand of anything, because it's usually on the front of their shirt or, in the case of Pitbulls, on their hat. (This is very handy for bartenders...)

However, these loyalties to labels and brands are always subject to change should the Leglifter rise in social and/or economic status.

So much for loyalty.

While some PSPs remain stubbornly loyal to their cultural roots long after they've made their fortunes and could easily afford to upgrade their look and maybe their taste in beer a little, Leglifters are upgrading *constantly*. A financially successful Leglifter who grew up in Wisconsin will often have precisely the same taste as a successful Leglifter who grew up in Connecticut - they'll drink the same Scotch, drive the same car, wear the same clothes, and buy the same tie at Barney's when they're in New York on business, because all of these things are immediately recognizable symbols of their status in the world. *(Immediately recognizable to other Leglifters, anyhow. Lots of other PSPs are totally oblivious to them, which seriously annoys Leglifters.)* In fact, Leglifters are the guys Vance Packard was writing about back in the fifties when he coined the term "Status-Seekers".

The major exception here is the Southern Leglifter. The South has its own unique rules for displaying wealth and/or social status, for both Pitbulls and Specials. If you really need to peek in that particular window, I'd suggest reading **Midnight in the Garden of Good and Evil**. *Or just rent the movie.*

Habitat

Contrary to popular belief, high testosterone does not guarantee financial success. In fact, it can be a decided *hindrance* in the twenty-first century.

Whether a Leglifter ends up on Wall Street, working construction, or doing hard time in a federal facility somewhere is mostly dependent upon his IQ and his male role models. Testosterone gives the Leglifter a lot of physical energy and a strong drive to dominate - he will jockey for the highest position in any pack he finds himself because that's how he's hard-wired.

Unfortunately, our modern warm and fuzzy educational methods are not really geared toward little Leglifters, who prefer physical activity to sitting still, generally have no great interest in reading, and are born with a natural tendency to challenge authority. They're competitive rather than cooperative, and their two favorite classes have traditionally been gym and recess. They need a pretty firm hand - little gold stars and time-outs are about as effective on these boys as they would be on a Rottweiler puppy. (If it weren't for the few military academies and Catholic schools still around, there'd be no place left for Leglifters to get a decent education.)

Which is probably why the higher his baseline T-level, the less formal education an American male is now likely to have. The brightest of them, especially those with strong role models who can set firm boundaries for civilized male behavior and guide them toward acceptable outlets for their energy (like competitive sports), will generally make it through high school and college and, once they have an education, their energy and competitive drive can serve them well.

The guys who have good male role models but aren't exactly rocket-scientist material (and let's face it - if the average IQ in this country is 100, half the people you run into on a daily basis have IQs under that), will generally do OK, too - they'll make it through high school as popular jocks, get laid a lot more than the rest of the guys, and spend the rest of their lives reliving those "glory days" over a couple beers with their buddies after work.

The ones least fortunate in both regards are usually in serious trouble as soon as they hit adolescence. Without job skills and strong male role models, the Leglifter is very likely to find his dominance-seeking tendencies frustrated at every turn.

This is because testosterone is responsible for dominance-seeking as a personality trait, not dominance itself, which is an actual position of leadership within a group which must be earned. Frustrated dominance-seeking leads to inappropriate aggression, which is why young high-testosterone males with insufficient education and guidance are over-represented among the incarcerated.

In a survey of testosterone levels and occupations, the highest average T-levels were found in NFL players and stage actors. *The quintessential Pitbulls and Specials, of course.*

And the highest T- levels of all were found in unemployed men.

So much for the myth that testosterone runs the world.

Assuming a Leglifter makes it through the educational system, he is pretty well-suited for a few careers that can make him serious money. Obviously, both stage acting and professional sports fall into this category, where extremely high T-levels are actually an advantage.

So does a peculiar form of "performance art" that seems pretty unique to our modern culture - or maybe it's just world-wide media exposure makes it seem that way, and what we're really looking at here is no more than Shamanism. (Invariably decked out in outfits that would make Elton John jealous, Shamans were probably the original Specials...) This career really involves no more than the development of a larger-than-life outrageous public persona. Whatever social/political agenda they may appear to represent is simply a part of the character they have developed - what you're really looking at is a Special playing to an audience.

Howard Stern, the Reverend Jerry Falwell, Ted Nugent, and Ann Coulter (all of whom display the characteristics of extremely high-testosterone Leglifters of the Specials variety and at least three of whom I'm pretty sure are actually biologically male) are all roaringly successful practitioners of this particular form of acting, and all of whom provide proof-positive that, like a good run on Broadway, it can be extremely lucrative.

So can clawing your way up the corporate ladder. Working on the floor of the Stock Exchange probably requires the sort of aggression and focus that testosterone brings to the party without much physical risk, and a lack of altruism probably won't be noticed much here.

Actually *managing* a business successfully on a day-to-day basis, however, requires a degree of diplomatic finesse and attention to detail that Leglifters may be short on and which is far more likely to be found in Betas, whose T-levels are generally on the low end of the normal range. (*These* T-levels, contrary to popular belief, are the ones currently associated with the greatest number of high-paying white-collar jobs, based on analysis of almost 4,500 hundred men in over 500 different careers in the US.)

Professional athletes, rock stars, and popular cultural myths notwithstanding, actual statistical data reveals that very high-T men are far more likely to be found in traditional "blue-collar" jobs than anywhere else, and there's nothing wrong with that except a lot of those jobs are being outsourced now, which is probably why so many very high-T men are currently found among the unemployed.

(These are more likely to be Leglifters of the Pitbull variety, of course; out-of-work actors usually end up as waiters in trendy restaurants where they can still practice their craft, rather than standing on street corners donating testosterone samples to grad students.)

Leglifters of the Pitbull variety have always dominated the construction trades. These are the guys, after all, who literally *built* this country with sweat and muscle. And they have traditionally defended and protected what they've built, which is why a lot of them are also veterans.

Pitbulls are the absolute backbone of both the Marine Corps and the Army. The physical and mental effects of testosterone are honed into a "lean, mean fighting machine" in the armed forces, at least for those Leglifters who don't suffer from strong harm avoidance tendencies. And a Marine in full-dress uniform rivals only the peacock in the "male display" department.

Protect and serve?

Both cops and firefighters are more apt to be Leglifters than any other PSP. Both are physical, high-risk jobs where the ability to act quickly without undue reflection can mean the difference between life and death. (For obvious reasons, Pitbulls tend to outnumber the Specials here, too...)

So what do Leglifters drive other than heavy equipment, Bradley tanks, fire trucks and squad cars? *(Long before they're old enough to drive, you may notice little baby Leglifters pushing small replicas of these particular vehicles around sand piles, going "Brrm, Brrrm!" and merrily crashing them into each other.)*
On their own time, Leglifters of both varieties favor anything with a ridiculously high horsepower-to-weight ratio that will make other men jealous. (*Brrrm, brrrrm!*)

In fact, with an HP/weight ratio of .11 , GM might as well just slap a factory-installed bumper sticker that reads "I'm a Leglifter" on every Corvette as it rolls off the line. The absurdly overpowered Dodge Viper, the Trans Am, and every muscle car Detroit ever produced were all designed for (and mostly sold to) Leglifters. Leglifters who can afford them invariably display a penchant for fast Italian cars like the Maserati and the Testerosa, which are the internal combustion engine's version of Armani. (Specials pretty much limit themselves to expensive imports, whether they can actually afford them or not. These guys carry a fairly heavy debt load as a rule - as they have no fear of risk, this bothers them not at all, but is something to consider before marrying one, especially if you tend to be of a financially conservative bent.) Hummers are popular with Leglifters, as are 4WD pickups with big Hemis and oversized tires - especially with Pitbulls. Volkswagens,

Volvos, and minivans are not popular with Leglifters. They'd rather walk. The auto industry has tried to rise to the challenge here by coming up with a minivan that boasts a Hemi and all-wheel drive. Personally, I don't think it's gonna fly.

Mostly what the Leglifter cares about is horsepower. *This also applies to lawnmowers. Computer RAM is viewed by Leglifters as horsepower. So are BTUs on a gas grill. And CCs in a motorcycle engine. And more is always better, which is why their wives get stuck with overpowered household appliances.*

Hobbies? Anything competitive, whether they're actually playing it themselves, or just watching it. If it doesn't involve competition, they're simply not interested - what's the point? Leglifters are especially fond of competitive sports that involve any sort of target, because the ability to hit a target, whether using a pistol, a dart, or a golf club, is a high-testosterone skill. (These guys ALL own guns, by the way.) Sports that involve physical contact are also favored, mostly by Pitbulls. Hockey is a very high-testosterone sport...it's fast, brutal, and very competitive.

These guys are so competitive they'd cheat a five-year-old girl at jacks if that's what it took to win.

A Leglifter friend of mine who owned some top-winning wire-haired dachshunds actually gave me that line, along with a lot of the other information in this chapter - he is an ex-Marine and former NFL tight end, with an MBA from Harvard and three ex-wives. By the time he hit 60 he'd developed a pretty good sense of humor about himself and his fiercely competitive nature. Unless his dog was in the ring.

Cooking, housekeeping? *That's what God made women for.* If they don't happen to have one of their own, they'll simply *hire* a couple...after all, a man's home is his castle, right? And the bigger and more impressive the castle, the better.

Because Leglifters are extremely status-conscious, they care a whole lot about *where* they live - not only must their house be impressive, but they want to live in the right *neighborhood* as well. A Leglifter will cheerfully take on extra debt (which he may or may not be able to afford) simply to live at the "right" address.

Not they'll spend much time there - Leglifters are not domestically inclined at all; the young, single, and less-affluent ones (none of whom have a woman around full-time to do the basic housekeeping) are among the *least* housebroken of men, and live entirely on take-out and pizza delivery. Older, richer ones either hire a housekeeper or eat out a lot. Once they are married, their culinary skills develop to the point where they can grill meat, provided their barbeque grill is bigger than their brother-in-law's.

Which takes us neatly to:

Mating Habits

Testosterone is pretty much entirely responsible for sex drive in both genders, and so it's not really a surprise that Leglifters have more of it than most guys, and that it shows up pretty early on.

Being very competitive guys, sex (like almost everything else) is mostly perceived as an actual *competitive sport* by Leglifters. This can work either *for* women or against them, depending on whether the Leglifter in question wants to be the *best* lover in the world, or simply the most *prolific. Don't laugh* - there are rock stars (most rock stars are Specials, in case you haven't already figured that out) who've famously had sex with *6 or 7 different women in a single day*, with a few world-class Pitbull NFL players not far behind. (The biochemical reason for this, of course, is both their high testosterone and low prolactin levels - no prolactin surge, no refractory period.) The guys who view bringing their partner to orgasm as scoring a sort of Sexual Touchdown are generally a better bet from a female point of view. But either way, sex is competitive for these guys, and they *all* keep score.

Research shows high-testosterone men are twice as likely to end up divorced as low-testosterone men. They're also twice as likely to cheat. Clearly, there's some cause-and-effect here. This is not because they're bad guys, or because they necessarily *want* to end their marriages.

Like a lot of other things they do, sex for Leglifters is pretty much action unencumbered by the thought process. Especially extramarital sex. Women *really* need to understand this right out of the gate if they are attracted to Leglifters as a group, because they are not going to change no matter what - they *can't*.

They're responding to the biological imperative of testosterone, whose purpose is to ensure the survival of the entire species, and they are hard-wired to Do Their Part. For a fair number of them, this means they're gonna cheat. The ones who *don't* cheat probably have more vasopressin receptors, and they tend to run to jealousy, which can be annoying.

And I should probably point out here that cheating *on* a Leglifter is just plain *stupid*, even if you're not married to him. It's very important to understand that given their hard-wiring, these guys view a woman's infidelity primarily as *a loss of status* on their part. This perception can lead to real nastiness, legally or physically. A Leglifter who believes he's been cuckolded is a pretty dangerous animal.

There seems to be two kinds of women attracted to Leglifters, and one kind generally fares better than the other.

The first group are pretty, docile, not-very-bold women attracted to Leglifters because of the power and strength they convey - as one woman put it, "they make you feel like Lois

Lane". For a lot of women this is frankly a turn-on, especially in the early days of the relationship. And these guys certainly *are* protective of their wife and kids - they're protective of *everything* that's theirs. (That's why they own guns.)

What they're not is *attentive*. A Leglifter, whether of the Pitbull or Specials variety, is a basically self-centered man and pretty incapable of guessing what a woman's emotional needs are, so if you're not good at expressing yourself clearly and succinctly without whining (Leglifters *really* hate whining), and incapable of having a life that doesn't always depend on his (although he of course expects you to always "be there" for him), you're gonna end up feeling pretty ripped off.

This is what usually happens with "trophy wives", by the way - Leglifters are attracted to gorgeous young women the same way they're attracted to gorgeous new cars, but as soon as they detect a whine in the transmission they're gonna trade 'em in for a new one - they're not going to spend a lot of time or energy trying to figure out what's causing the whine.

The other group of women who are attracted to Leglifters generally fare better. (They're usually the second or sometimes the third wife, and the one who stays.)

High-testosterone men are most likely to *stay* married to high-T woman who are pretty tough themselves. *This applies to both Specials and Pitbulls.*

High-testosterone women don't mind the fact that they may occasionally have to yell to get what they want or need out the relationship, because they actually *don't mind a good fight once in a while*. (According to these women, it clears the air and the sex is really good afterwards.) Like the women who marry Junkyard Dogs, they're essentially tough, confident women who happen to like tough men.

Their strength also makes it easier for them to cope with the fact that their husbands aren't always around when they'd like them to be, like on Christmas, or for the kid's birthdays, because of The Job. (The Job can be in an urban or foreign combat zone or shooting on location somewhere, doesn't matter - they're still not home.)

Women who are successfully married to cops and firefighters are especially tough women - they send their husbands off to work every morning knowing full well they may not make it home that night.

Hell, you want to meet a *really* tough bunch of women, visit any military base in the country and start talking to soldier's wives. Not only do these chicks *not whine,* they're proud of the men they're married to, and the dangerous job they're doing. And not a single one would trade theirs in for an Omega no matter how many millions he'd made in the dotcom industry. They see raising the kids and taking care of the house for a whole year all by themselves as simply "doing their part".

Women successfully married to Leglifters usually *don't* feel like Lois Lane - most days, they feel more like Superwoman, and just hope the plumber shows up before they've got to pick the kids up from Little League, otherwise they're gonna have to take the damn sink apart themselves.

But although their guys are not exactly *romantic* (there is probably no PSP that has more difficulty actually saying "I love you" - and those who can have been trained like parrots, with patience and positive reward), the sex is frequent and usually good, and these seem to be women who know instinctively that everything in life is a tradeoff.

As fathers, Leglifters are fiercely protective but also dangerously inattentive, which is important to know. This is *not their fault.* Testosterone focuses attention, but does *not* allow for multi-tasking, which is a critical skill in the care of small children. All men have a problem with this, but it's much more severe in Leglifters. *These guys cannot watch the playoffs and a toddler at the same time, and if you try to make them, everyone will be sorry.*

A guy who buys a complete drum set and/or a dirt bike for his two-year old is probably a Leglifter. In fact, come to think about it, it's probably best not to entrust small children to their care *at all* until the kids are old enough to have developed some survival instincts of their own.

Once the kids are completely toilet-trained ("you didn't *say* anything about changing his damn *diaper,* how the hell was I supposed to know...?") and big enough to play a few competitive sports, they tend to do a lot better, though.

These guys can really get into coaching their kid's sports, although being fiercely competitive themselves they often tend to take the job a little too seriously, and may actually get in fistfights on occasion with the Leglifter coaches from the other team.

And God help the poor guy who wants to marry their daughter.

11

Fearbiters

My friend Googie, who's a realtor, once had a listing that was such a dog on the market she thought for sure she'd end up being BURIED with the damn thing. This otherwise nice house, unfortunately, overlooked the local NASCAR Speedway which, from a desirability point of view, is a lot like overlooking a major airport, only louder.

Prospective buyers would stroll out unsuspectingly onto the spacious deck, gaze down on the track for a minute with dawning horror, and then scramble back through the house and out the door like they were being chased by swarms of angry hornets, which is pretty close to what it sounded like out there every weekend when the NASCAR guys really got going. It got to the point where she really hated showing the place.

And then one fine day a prospective buyer (this would be Prospective Buyer # 9,647 by her recollection) walked out onto the deck, surveyed the unfortunate view, and grinned in absolute delight. "Well, look at that! I could sit out here on my own deck every weekend, drink my own beer, and watch the races in comfort - for free!" The guy promptly made an offer, proving yet again that, in this life, *THERE IS A BUTT FOR EVERY SEAT*, which is Googie's motto when it comes to real estate.

The basic tenet of this book (in case you've somehow missed it) is that every guy on the planet displays the characteristics of a particular PSP that are genetically hard-wired in and really *cannot be changed,* no matter how hard you try. Each PSP has its own merits and shortcomings, and no particular PSP is intrinsically more desirable than any other - it's mostly a matter of figuring out which one best fits your own personal needs. Not *wants,* mind you, but *needs.* There's a big difference.

As Mick pointed out decades ago, you can't always get what you want. A big part of maturity is understanding that that's often a *good* thing...as any woman who's fantasized about Mel Gibson or Tom Cruise has probably figured out. Happiness, which is really no more than a state of biochemical homeostasis (or balance) in the brain, is much more dependent on having your emotional needs met than having your desires fulfilled. And although they're all very different, each PSP really does have an individual set of qualities that meet some woman's emotional and intellectual needs.

Except for Fearbiters and Lone Wolves. Trust me on this:

THERE AIN'T NO BUTTS FOR THOSE TWO SEATS.

Although very different biochemically, Fearbiters and Lone Wolves have one major thing in common - no sane woman can ever hope to be happy in a relationship with one over the long haul. So what you really need to be able to do is identify them early on so you won't get sucked in.

The major problem with both PSPs is that these guys can appear so *normal* at first that women get deeply involved with them before they figure out what they are really dealing with.

Fearbiters

This PSP is fairly easy to identify, if you know what to look for.

Fearbiters are, by definition, very high-testosterone guys (it's testosterone that *facilitates* aggression, including the defensive aggression that characterizes the PSP) and they tend to display all the physical and behavioral characteristics of high-T men.

Lots of them sport a more or less permanent five o'clock shadow and, according to Harry Truman, who particularly loathed them as a group and could spot one at thirty paces, they are a "shifty-eyed" lot. (Old Harry was, as usual, dead-on about this…the Fearbiter's odd pattern of eye contact is often a dead-giveaway, characterized by a vacillation between a dominance-stare and a total lack of eye contact that's pretty unique to the PSP in both domestic dogs and men.)

Like all high-T men, they display strong dominance-seeking tendencies - they're extremely competitive, high-energy guys and, if they're also bright, they can get pretty far in life before they ultimately self-destruct in both their personal and professional lives. (The dumber ones end up running afoul of the law pretty early on and usually end up incarcerated.) But whether he's sharp as a tack or dumber than a begonia, the Fearbiter is a singularly self-centered and paranoid guy, pretty much lacking in altruism for the most part.

This probably goes a long way to explain why most of the really classic examples, like former President Richard M. Nixon and Senator "Pint-a-day Joe" McCarthy (to name a couple of comfortably dead ones - hey, do I look stupid ???), have all been high-ranking members of the GOP, where defense against enemies both real and imagined traditionally takes precedence over bleeding-heart liberal social programs like feeding and educating small children. These are defensive guys by definition and, as far as Fearbiters are concerned, a good offense is always the best defense.

Now, the self-centered part may not show up immediately, especially if he's trying to make a good first impression, but the lack of altruism should be pretty apparent right from the get-go, and so should the paranoia, once you know the signs.

Much like the Sentinel, the Fearbiter's personal security system is on permanent overdrive. Extremely alert to his environment, he sees potential threats everywhere, and lives pretty much in a state of constant emotional siege. As with the Sentinel, this constant assault on his HPA axis keeps his cortisol levels chronically high and his serotonin levels correspondingly low, the latter inclining him toward both a lack of impulse control and alcohol abuse. (In the case of the Sentinel, who is wired differently, low serotonin is more likely to result in overeating and depression.) As alcohol further lowers inhibition levels, you *really* don't want to be around these guys when they start knocking back the bourbon or scotch...it makes them much worse. *And, trust me, you never want to go hunting with them...guns, a hair-trigger startle response, and alcohol don't mix well under any circumstances but with these guys, it's a deadly combination.*

What also makes him different from the Sentinel is both his general lack of altruism (Edward Hart famously said of Joe McCarthy "he asked himself only two questions - what do I want and how can I get it") and his overdeveloped *noradrenaline response.*

Not only does the Fearbiter too often sense a threat where no sane person would (witness Nixon's weirdly paranoid perception of 21-year-old college student and Vietnam vet John Kerry as a significant "danger" to his administration) they usually respond to these nonexistent threats with immediate overt aggression rather than behavioral inhibition.

Noradrenaline (also known as *norepinephrine*) is one of the so-called "stress hormones" and, indeed, it is released by the adrenal glands as part of the stress response - fed by testosterone, it facilitates the "fight" option of the "fight or flight response". Like most hormones, it also acts as a neurotransmitter in the brain. And like most neurotransmitters, problems arise when levels are poorly regulated.

Noradrenaline heightens attention and increases focus, both of which are advantageous to survival and which probably served our early ancestors well in a hostile environment. In fact, they're *still* pretty handy in a lot of situations (like when walking down a dark street alone) which is probably why the gene which produces noradrenaline is still part of the human genome.

Not surprisingly, an insufficiency of noradrenaline is associated with ADHD - in fact, many drugs currently being used to treat ADHD are *noradrenaline reuptake inhibitors.* By keeping noradrenaline in the brain longer, the ability to focus and actually pay attention is increased, allowing ADHD kids to function better in school.

But, as with pretty much everything else in life, if some is good, *more* is not necessarily better, especially when it comes to noradrenaline Biochemically, noradrenaline release is facilitated by testosterone. On its own, we know that testosterone is responsible for dominance-seeking tendencies. In Fearbiters, who carry high baseline levels of testosterone, excessive noradrenaline production in response to perceived threats to their status results in inappropriate aggression, and this is the MO of the Fearbiter in both the canine and human world.

In fact, clonidine, a drug which lowers noradrenaline levels, is actually prescribed as a *treatment* for this sort of aggression in boys with Fragile X Syndrome, a complex genetic disorder where both noradrenaline and testosterone levels are often abnormally high.

Low serotonin, as we have learned, can manifest itself differently depending on the number and distribution of serotonin receptors one has. The behavior of a Fearbiter would be consistent with a glitch in the production and distribution of the 5-HT1B receptor, where a knockout has been shown to produce both aggression and a high attraction to alcohol.

In the world of traditional psychology, about which I honestly know just slightly less than nothing, Fearbiters would probably be diagnosed with *Intermittent Explosive Disorder*, which falls under the category of "Impulse-control Disorders" in the **Diagnostic and Statistical Manual of Mental Disorders**, should you actually want to bother to look it up. (Not surprisingly, this disorder is most common in young men, which probably has something to do with the high testosterone levels of youth.) Studies suggest that patients diagnosed with this disorder respond best to a combination of behaviorial modification (the old "anger management course") and drug therapy, with a combination of drugs that raise serotonin and lower noradrenaline levels being most effective. Duhhh.

My personal opinion is that if every Fearbiter was required to swallow 300 mg of 5-HTP and slap on a clonidine patch before he got behind the wheel of a car, it would pretty well take care of the Road Rage problem in America, and driving home from work would be a much more pleasant experience for everyone else. But I'm just a dog breeder, what do I know.

There's a conventional wisdom regarding black bears among woodsmen that probably applies here. Here's what these guys all know:

A black bear won't attack you unless he feels threatened. Trouble is, *you just never know when a bear is feeling threatened.*

Most wild animals have a well-developed fear response, and those who sit pretty high on the food chain, as most predators do, are apt to respond with aggression when threatened. Without this response, which is largely absent only in the juveniles, their very survival would be in jeopardy. In wolves, fearbiting is the rule rather than the exception, and the response develops fairly early on, when testosterone levels start to rise during adolescence. Without it, the species would probably be extinct.

Domestication, of course, has been largely a matter of deliberately selecting for neoteny (the retention of juvenile characteristics into adulthood) and so the fear/aggression response has been diminished in most domestic species, including man. When faced with novel stimuli, both man and his buddy the domestic dog will usually tend to respond with curiosity and/or caution (behavioral inhibition) as puppies do, rather than with the aggression of an adult wolf.

It has been shown in numerous experiments that breeds which most *physically* resemble the wolf are more likely to respond with a fear/aggression response when faced with novel and potentially threatening stimuli than those which display the short muzzles and floppy ears associated with extreme neoteny. The reason is simple - the more wolf-like breeds, which are genetically closer to "wild type" and less neotenous are simply more likely to produce individuals which revert to wild type in this regard as well.

Man, of course, is considered to be the most neotenous of primates, with W being the uncontested hands-down winner here. *I mean, come on, I know he's the Leader of the Free World and all, but there are entire websites devoted wholly to the guy's uncanny resemblance to an immature chimpanzee, for God's sake…*

It is interesting (although probably unnoticed by anyone but me) that Fearbiters of the human persuasion rarely display much neoteny - neither of my favorite two examples, Joe McCarthy and Tricky Dick, were characterized by any discernable boyish charm, by any stretch of the imagination. In fact, in the looks department, these often beetle-browed guys run decidedly to the Neanderthal, perhaps representing a reversion to wild type physically as well?

Pop Quiz: Which member of the current administration's shifty-eyed sneer, scowling brow, and increasingly aggressive paranoid rhetoric most resembles that of old Pint-a-Day Joe and Tricky Dick?

In domestic dogs, the response of a Fearbiter is always disproportionate to the actual threat. Because of their overdeveloped fight-or-flight response, they often feel threatened by things that simply don't bother most dogs - like the mailman, the UPS guy, or the poor vet...and they react with inappropriate aggression. *In other words, they attack and bite out of fear - hence the term Fearbiter, which I certainly didn't invent.* Because of their high testosterone levels, what they fear most is loss of pack status at any and every level.

The same can be said for the PSP known as Fearbiters - whenever they feel the least bit threatened, they react with inappropriate aggression *and, sooner or later, they are going to find something that you do threatening.* (Most women unfortunately figure this out the hard way, and usually way too late.) "Inappropriate aggression" is a nice way of saying that these guys are abusive - psychologically, emotionally, and frequently physically.

Relationships with Fearbiters all too often end with a restraining order. If you're lucky.

In the world of dogs, fear biting can sometimes be corrected if caught early by a knowledgeable trainer who is willing to put a lot of time and energy into the project. And many breeders believe it can be *prevented* with early intervention in those puppies that appear at risk, which may very well be true. (Neurological hardwiring can be altered in immature animals, since new pathways may actually develop in the brain in response to positive conditioning.) But every responsible breeder *also* knows that puppies displaying an overactive fight-or-flight response should never be kept as breeding stock, as they will pass on these tendencies to the next generation, whose owners may not be quite so astute about identifying high-risk pups in a litter.

An adult dog who's a Fearbiter invariably comes to a bad end. The overwhelming majority of them end up either euthanized by the family vet after they've bitten the neighbor's kid, or they end up in a shelter somewhere, where they are usually euthanized because they are unadoptable. Even the most soft-hearted rescue organizations are loathe to take on Fearbiters - they're afraid to place them for adoption even after rehabilitation, because Fearbiters can never be entirely trusted, and there's a real liability issue should they come unglued again.

Which they probably will.

One of the oldest rules of dog ownership is this:

Once a dog has bitten someone, no matter what the circumstances, he can never be trusted not to do it again.

The same is true of human Fearbiters. A guy who comes unglued once will do it again no matter how bad he feels about it afterwards (not lacking in empathy, he's always genuinely sorry), and odds are good that *sooner or later you are going to get hurt or killed,* in which case how sorry he is really won't matter to you one way or the other. Intelligent women stay as far away from Fearbiters as they possibly can. Which probably explains the following (absolutely genuine) quote:

YOU WANT A WIFE WHO IS INTELLIGENT,
 BUT NOT *TOO* INTELLIGENT.
 -PRESIDENT RICHARD M. NIXON

Warning Signs

Here are some "red flags" which may tip you off that you just might be having dinner with a Fearbiter:

1. Normal men do not use the term "anger management" in a sentence. (With the exception maybe of the psychologist teaching the course, any guy who *does* has most likely been through the program, which is usually court-ordered.)

2. Most waiters rarely ignore a customer *intentionally* - odds are, they're simply busy. Guys who view poor service as a deliberate act of subtle aggression, aimed at them personally, are almost always Fearbiters.

3. Fearbiters are emotionally comfortable only when they feel like they are in control – it's a form of dominance-seeking. Any man who tells you what to order (or what *not* to order) is probably a Fearbiter.

4. Outside of the movies, parking valets are rarely actually part of car-theft rings - any guy who tells you they all are is probably a Fearbiter.

5. Mentally healthy men do not examine the restaurant's silver and glassware for dirt or germs - in fact, unless there's actually a cockroach skewered on his fork when he puts it in his mouth, the average guy won't even *notice* the silverware. A Fearbiter will.

6. Normal men *never* criticize a woman early in a relationship. (In fact, most men will wait until they've actually *married* a woman and sired her children before they finally tell her that it makes them crazy when she picks the croutons out of a salad.) Fearbiters will do this from the very first date, under the guises of good-

natured "teasing" or being "helpful". It only gets worse, and it quickly stops being good-natured.

7. Unless they are off-duty cops, most normal men (even redneck Leglifters with a gun rack in their pickup) do *not* have a carry-permit for a handgun. Those who do are usually Fearbiters. Guys who carry a handgun *without* a permit are even scarier - virtually anyone who is not actually a felon or a certifiable nutcase can obtain a carry permit in most states.

8. Normal men do not suggest a few exercises their date may want to consider for toning her thighs. (In fact, happily married men *who don't want to end up like John Bobbit* generally don't even suggest it to their own wives.) Attempts to "improve" you early on should be viewed as a major red flag.

9. Normal men do not become possessive early on in a relationship. Nor do they call ten times the day after the first date just to "see what you're doing" at that particular moment. No matter how flattering that may seem at first, it's the mark of a Fearbiter.

10. Fearbiters rarely have cordial relationships with their ex-wives and girlfriends. Beware the man who does not know *exactly* where his ex-wife and children are currently living. Odds are, she didn't just leave him... she *escaped.*

Assuming you missed these red flags on the first few dates, and actually find yourself in a Fearbiter's *apartment*, there are usually a couple red flags there as well that you might want to be alert to:

Normal guys do not have six locks on their door, a sophisticated security system, and bars on their windows unless they live in a neighborhood that's a war zone (in which case you'd probably have to wonder why they lived there.) Fearbiters do.

Fearbiters are often *way* neater and cleaner than normal males - verging on the obsessive - and so an overall aura of *sterility* in a guy's digs should be viewed with suspicion if not outright alarm.

Even Specials, who often live in gorgeous surroundings befitting their gorgeous selves, rarely have a kitchen floor so sparkling clean you could actually *eat* off it, or acres of gleaming countertops spookily devoid of anything at all, including a coffeepot. And they do not shriek "Don't put that there!" in alarm if you foolishly attempt to place a wineglass on an end table without a coaster, or pick up and put back in its "proper" place anything you accidentally "rearranged". *Fearbiters do.*

Spending the night in a man's apartment that you're afraid to make yourself comfortable in is *extremely* foolish.

My advice is *not to* - even if it means you have to suddenly remember you have a cat at home that you forgot to feed...

Now, unless you're pretty dense, you've probably got an idea of what we're looking for here - little glimmers of paranoia, dominance-seeking, control, and aggression in his actions or conversation. These little glimmers are not in actual fact *little* at all. Trust me, nobody's "a little bit" paranoid - it's like being "a little bit" pregnant.

What you're *actually* seeing is the tip of a very large iceberg, most of which is still below the surface.

And dating a Fearbiter is "a little bit" like rearranging the deck chairs on the Titanic.

12

Lone Wolves

The romantic myth of "the Lone Wolf" is pretty much bullshit. If all women understood this, less of us would end up as their unwitting victims. Because they are so hard to identify early on, remembering *this one fact* is absolutely critical.

To understand the Lone Wolf, we need to look at *wolves* rather than dogs, because this is one place where domestication gets in the way. (A domestic dog with this PSP is pretty hard to identify when he's the only dog in the house.)

And in the wild, where survival depends almost entirely on being a member of a pack, there are really only two sorts of wolves generally observed traveling alone.

The first are young high-status animals who willingly disperse from their respective packs once they reach adulthood in hopes of finding an unrelated mate from another pack. *(Young wolves, like young humans, have a hard time getting laid when they're living at home. And, as is the case with humans, it's the lower-status animals who are likely to live at home longer.)*

This voluntary "dispersal period" is an extremely high-risk time for these young wolves, as they are vulnerable to both attacks from other packs and possible starvation, lacking as they do ready availability of Chinese take-out and pizza delivery. Besides, as with humans, enforced solitude for long periods is a form of psychological torture for wolves, and they will attempt to find a mate or new pack ASAP. If wolves could avail themselves of internet dating services, they most assuredly would - they don't seem to like the "singles scene" any more than we do.

Although these young animals often travel singly or (*in the case of young Betas*) in pairs for short periods during normal dispersal, *they are not really Lone Wolves*, and it's very important to understand that distinction, especially if you're looking at guys in the 18-30 year old category, many of whom are in the corresponding human "dispersal" period, when the higher-status ones may be living alone.

The second category of wolves observed traveling alone, the REAL Lone Wolves, are the animals whose inability to follow the rules of wolf society result in their being *driven from the pack*. Unless they can find another pack to take them in, these "social pariahs" are forced to live on the periphery of the pack and survive primarily by stealing and scavenging. Their overall mortality rate is pretty high - even assuming they can avoid starvation by stealing, Lone Wolves are often killed as soon as they invade the territory of an existing pack.

So much for romantic myths. Wolves are amazingly like humans socially; although they may not all have individual mates, each wolf spends most of his life as part of a pack - either the one he was born into, one he joined as an adult after leaving home, or one he formed on his own. Barring misfortune, wolves form long-term social attachments, not only with their mates and offspring but, with their unrelated fellow pack-members as well.

In the wild, where avoiding starvation is, by necessity, the result of cooperative effort, a lone wolf is a dead wolf, and most wolves would rather be the Omega than not part of a pack at all. (This is probably true of humans as well.)

In social species where survival depends on the ability to be part of a pack, Lone Wolves represent a "genetic anomaly". They display an unfortunate collection of personality traits which, when inherited all together, are *maladaptive to living cooperatively in a group for any extended period,* which is why they are driven from the pack.

In the human world, these Lone Wolves are called *psychopaths*. In fact, you probably know a couple of them personally.

I know, "psychopath" is a pretty loaded word, and odds are good it just made the hair on the back of your neck stand up. Don't worry about it - that happens to almost everybody. It probably creeps us out because it sounds a lot like "psycho" (which is actually short for *psychotic*, a pretty severe form of mental illness that probably can afflict any PSP) and so we tend to use the more neutral-sounding *sociopath* instead, which is not the same thing at all, but probably sounds better if you're talking about your brother-in-law.

Sociopaths are basically people (usually young males) whose *behavior* reflects a total disregard for the accepted rules of society. There are invariably social factors involved - lots of them (upwards of 70% by some estimates) are raised in fatherless homes, and they are traditionally likely to have grown up "below the poverty line". If they were dogs, breeders would say they lack proper early socialization.

Sociopaths are usually high in the testosterone department and often low in the IQ department (in other words, the not-very-bright Leglifters with no male role models discussed back in that chapter) and they are very apt to end up either in gangs or incarcerated. Falling into the loose, catch-all category of "antisocial personality disorder" (and Lord knows their behavior is often extremely anti-social), most sociopaths "age out" of crime as their testosterone levels drop, which is a good thing for society. They probably make up a large percentage of the prison population on any given day. In the world of dogs, they fill shelters from coast to coast. And many of them are salvageable, given enough time and effort.

Psychopaths, on the other hand, are identified not so much by their behavior, as by their *personalities*. In fact, the term "psychopath" is not found in the DSM-IV for the simple reason that it is not a mental illness. Nor is it really a personality *disorder,* although these guys can be pretty destructive to the rest of society, but more likely represents a particular extreme on the personality spectrum.

Most serial killers are psychopaths. On the other hand, so are many corporate raiders and high-level law-enforcement types. Researchers usually use the term "unsuccessful psychopath" when referring to the first group, so as to differentiate between a psychopath like Ted Bundy, who ended up in the electric chair, and a psychopath like J. Edgar Hoover, who ran the FBI until he died of old age, at which point he was laid out in the Capitol Rotunda and eulogized by many Important People, all of whom were unutterably relieved that the old bastard was finally dead and could no longer blackmail them.

It's really a personality *type.* Like every other PSP, Lone Wolves (a.k.a. psychopaths) are more a result of genetics than environment. Most psychopaths have had relatively normal, if not perfect, childhoods, and they can -*and do*- turn up in perfectly normal families from time to time.

This confusion of terminology (even by mental-health types and criminologists) is really unfortunate, because although some sociopaths are psychopaths, *not all psychopaths are sociopaths*, and there are probably more of them in corporate America than in prison on any given day.

There are a lot of checklists used by professionals to identify psychopathy, but most of them (like the "gold standard" CLP-R developed by Dr Robert Hare, the world-renowned guru on the subject) are geared toward *criminal psychopaths,* and the truth is that the overwhelming majority of psychopaths *are not criminals. In fact, it's been estimated that this particular personality type makes up anywhere from 1% to 5 % of the population, which amounts to several million people in the US alone.*

So who *are* these Lone Wolves?

Most experts agree that psychopaths all tend to display the following personality traits:

- **superficial charm**
- **a self-centered view of the world**
- **deceptive behavior & lying**
- **skill at manipulating others**
- **little remorse or guilt for their actions**
- **a shallow emotional response**
- **a lack of real empathy for others**
- **a predatory or parasitic lifestyle**
- **a lack of normal fear and nervousness**
- **poor self-control**
- **promiscuous or socially inappropriate sexual behavior**
- **a lack of long term goals and direction**
- **impulsive behavior**
- **a tendency to blame others for their actions**
- **an inability to maintain long-term relationships**
- **poor judgment**
- **an inability to foresee the consequences of their actions**
- **failure to learn from experience**

OK, if you're like most people, it's probably occurred to you at this point that you've actually *known* a psychopath or two over the years - in fact, you probably know one right now. It could be your boss, your neighbor, your brother-in-law, or a guy you were involved with recently. Psychopaths are everywhere, and they're not limited to our species.

Trust me, it's a lot less creepy if we call them Lone Wolves.

Although Lone Wolves are usually incapable of being part of any particular pack for any length of time (which should have logically made them extinct ions ago) they are still found in small numbers in all social species, including man, most primates, and both wolves and domestic dogs. This is because what Lone Wolves really represent is a *collection* of personality traits that may not be all that maladaptive to pack life when inherited individually, and many of which show up in other PSPs to some degree.

Because of this, psychopathy is currently considered to be both incurable and untreatable by mental health professionals. Unlike sociopaths, who actually can be rehabilitated, attempts to "treat" criminal psychopaths simply result in significantly higher recidivism rates, because it provides them with tools to become even better manipulators.

Biochemically, Lone Wolves are high-testosterone animals (human research has shown them to carry higher T-levels on average than either non-psychopathic criminals or normal controls), with correspondingly high narcissistic and dominance-seeking tendencies, although they usually hide both under a mask of charm. They really *want* to be leaders, and being narcissistic to a flaw, they believe they *deserve to* be. Their need to control and dominate is pathological in its intensity.

But as everyone reading this knows by now, since leaders tend to lead by consent, the desire to dominate generally results only in frustration if the *rest* of the qualities needed for leadership are lacking. And by a cruel quirk of Nature, most Lone Wolves are lacking *each and every one of them.*

The first and most *important* trait needed for successful leadership of any social group is altruism. And Lone Wolves are totally devoid of altruism. The simplest explanation of altruism is that it represents *pro-social (unselfish) behavior,* which is the opposite of anti-social (otherwise known as "selfish") behavior. However (and this is very important to remember) if someone performs good deeds primarily to gain recognition and thereby elevate his own status in the community, *it ain't really altruism.* It's a manipulative form of dominance-seeking, and Lone Wolves use this technique all the time, mostly when they are on their way up. (Once they have actually achieved the level of dominance they seek, they don't bother any more.)

By all accounts, the handsome, bright, and charming Ted Bundy, undisputed poster boy for psychopathy, volunteered at a rape crisis center, served as assistant to the chairman of the Washington State Republican Party, and was commended by the Seattle Police for saving a three-year old from drowning. Between college (where he graduated with an honors degree in psychology) and law school (he was actually in law school at the time of his arrest), Ted was appointed to the Seattle Crime Prevention Advisory Committee, where he helped develop a pamphlet on rape prevention, and once even chased down and captured a purse-snatcher.

Unbeknownst to those who assumed from his actions that he was both a caring person and a rising star in Republican politics (although probably nobody in the state of Washington wants to remember this, it's been reported that his name was actually being tossed around as a future gubernatorial candidate), old Ted was at the same time also busy viciously murdering and sexually mutilating every co-ed he could find who resembled the girl who had dumped him in college. (Talk about frustrated dominance and redirected aggression!) Before he was finally stopped, he had cold-bloodedly stalked and killed dozens of young women.

Hardly anyone would call Ted Bundy pro-social. He was, in his own words, "the most cold-blooded son-of-a-bitch you'll ever meet." Yet he was so incredibly charming that he received a average of 200 fan letters a day from women while he was on trial for mass murder, and even found a woman so convinced of his innocence she was willing to marry him and bear his child (which she actually did) during that time.

The take-home message here is probably that niceness and good works should never be automatically considered pro-social behavior - it may well be manipulation, which is no more or less than an indirect form of dominance-seeking. Lone Wolves are simply not pro-social, which represents a major lethal anomaly in a social species, although it may be perfectly OK in bears.

The other main characteristic of Lone Wolves is a complete and total lack of conscience.

In fact, Dr. Hare's classic and definitive book on psychopaths is actually titled **Without Conscience - the Disturbing World of the Psychopaths Among Us**. *It should be required reading for all women. Maybe men, too.* All social animals have a conscience, by definition. Conscience is really just the ability to feel remorse for an action, and anyone who doesn't think animals are capable of remorse has simply never owned a dog.

Feeling bad as a result of displeasing or hurting those with whom we feel some measure of affiliation or social bond is hardly limited to *Homo sapiens*. (Admittedly, for some that represents a wider group than it does for others - Retrievers both human and canine feel a social bond with just about *everyone they encounter,* as far as I can tell - but it's a normal response, to some degree at least, in almost everyone.)

Of course, in order to have a conscience, *one must be able to form genuine social bonds in the first place,* and one must also be able to feel *empathy.* Empathy is the ability to actually feel what someone else is feeling. It's dependent on reading pretty subtle cues, either verbal or non-verbal, so that one can actually *understand* what someone else is feeling in the first place. (Both dogs and wolves are especially good at the non-verbal part, probably because they have limited powers of speech. Within their own species, canines can accurately assess the meaning of a mere flick of another animal's ear and adjust their behavior accordingly.)

These sorts of responses usually take place in the limbic brain, where emotional and contextual memories are stored. The hormones strongly associated with social interaction, empathy, and pair-bonding are, of course, our old friends *oxytocin* and *vasopressin*. And Lone Wolves are pretty deficient here. Their inability to form long-term pair bonds is very likely related to a deficiency of vasopressin receptors, and their inability to "feel your pain" probably represents a deficiency in oxytocin receptors. (Women, who generally produce more oxytocin and probably have more receptors, are invariably both more empathetic *and* better at reading subtle social cues than are most men.

Testosterone, which blocks oxytocin to some degree, probably doesn't help either, which is why low-T men are generally more "sensitive" than their high-T brethren.) Now, being an insensitive lout is really not all that maladaptive to pack life if a guy's basically pro-social - *hell, a visit to your average sports bar ought to dispel that notion!* - but once again it's only the *combination* of deficits that's deadly.

Lots of emotionally insensitive people get by pretty well without being a blight on society, even if they maybe don't represent your average Dream Date. What they *do* have, though, is a normal fear/aversion response.

There are a whole lot of reasonably insensitive people who obey the rules of the society they live in not because it will make someone they don't even know feel bad if they don't, but because they understand that the consequences of not doing so will be personally unpleasant to them . Odds are, they'll never turn into Mother Teresa, but they'll probably get by just fine. This is a learned response in most social species, taught to the young by the adults (in fact, it represents the "old school" of both dog training and child-rearing), and almost everybody can learn it.

Except for Lone Wolves. Numerous experiments using MRIs and PET scans have shown that there is simply no biochemical response in the limbic areas of the brains of psychopaths to those stimuli which produce an aversion response in "normal" people. Nor do they show a normal physical (or parasympathetic) response like sweating in anticipation of an electric shock, even when they have *just received one under the same circumstances.*

In other words, when it comes to foreseeing the negative consequences of their actions, even on themselves (which *should* matter to a person who is totally self-centered and narcissistic), *they just don't get it.* Apparently, they just *can't* get it because of the way they're hard-wired. And this makes them fearless. Not *courageous,* which is the ability (usually facilitated by testosterone) to resolutely focus on a dangerous goal while ignoring frantic messages from the amygdala and hippocampus to cease and desist before you injure yourself, but actually *fearless,* which is in nearly all species, a Bad Thing from an evolutionary fitness point of view.

You don't have to be a theologian or a philosopher to figure out that major deficiencies in the areas of pro-social behavior, empathy, and aversion/fear response when inherited together pretty much negate the possibility of ever developing a conscience as we know it. And of course, a conscience not only causes us stress after we have done something that is antisocial, *it also ideally prevents us from doing it in the first place.*

In other words, it *inhibits* our tendency toward anti-social behaviors. (Cortisol is the hormone responsible for behavioral inhibition, and psychopaths show little cortisol response in controlled studies. Nothing seems to really stress them out except the frustration of not getting what they want...)

Because they lack a functioning conscience, Lone Wolves are incapable of feeling real remorse for their actions, no matter what they've done or who they've hurt. The only person they can ever actually feel sorry for is themselves, when things don't turn out the way they'd planned.

In addition, success in raising one's status within a pack (which is the driving force of the Lone Wolf) depends on the ability to control one's impulses (one of the prerequisites of the Alpha PSP is good impulse control) and Lone Wolves have little or none. In canines, this lack of impulse control usually manifests itself in stealing food (the snatch-and-grab) and attempting to copulate with the mates of higher-ranking animals, neither of which are tolerated by the rest of the pack, where impulse control on the part of lower-ranking animals is both required and enforced. (It doesn't tend to produce better results in the human world, either, come to think about it - screwing the boss's wife and stealing from the company are usually not great career advancement moves.) It's also not generally associated with coalition-building among one's peers, which is critical to advancing one's pack status position in most species.

Lack of impulse control has long been associated with low serotonin levels, and several studies have shown psychopaths to be low in the serotonin department when compared to controls. A mutation in the serotonin transporter gene has been recently implicated as a possible cause. Somewhat surprisingly, low impulse control is not necessarily maladaptive by itself, especially for the lower-status animals. Indeed, some evolutionary biologists have hypothesized that it might actually provide an evolutionary *advantage* in their case, as it often represents their best logical option for both eating and getting laid.

And when low impulse control is combined with "positive" traits like altruism and pro-social behavior, for example, you simply end up with a guy who'll quite literally give you the shirt off his back even when he can't afford to, which does not generally constitute a problem to society. However, it is *entirely* maladaptive to raising one's status within a pack, so when low impulse control is, unfortunately, inherited along with a strong need for dominance, it will invariably result in frustration for the individual. And that frustration in a Lone Wolf is what causes them to be so destructive toward the end, when their pathological need for dominance is ultimately unmet in spite of their best (or worst) efforts.

OK, so now we have the basic biochemical recipe for a Lone Wolf. And you've probably figured out why you really, *really* don't want to get involved with one. Even if he's not in the Ted Bundy league (which very honestly most of them are not) a guy with no working conscience, no empathy, no impulse control, and no ability to form long-term attachments is probably *not* great husband material, no matter how charming he may be. So how do you recognize one on a date?

Unfortunately, you probably can't. Outside of the superficial charm, virtually all of the personality traits of a Lone Wolf only become obvious after the fact. But let's see what we can do anyway.

Plumage

This PSP is high-testosterone, and that generally goes along with a fair degree of vanity. Lone Wolves will often spend a lot of money on their clothes and personal grooming, both because they're vain and because they need to make a good appearance in order to gain status.

And the Lone Wolf is totally status-driven. Like the Leglifter, they only want the best of everything. Unlike the Leglifter though (who may not be in the Mother Teresa-department as far as altruism goes but who generally possesses a working conscience), they will attempt to get what they want by fair means or foul. And because they have little impulse control, if they want something, they want it *right now.*

A Lone Wolf's money is rarely a result of honest effort, even if it reflects a salary - odds are, the money a Lone Wolf throws around (and they are notoriously extravagant and wasteful) recently belonged to someone else who'd probably just as soon still be in possession of it. But that does not stop the Lone Wolf from spending it on himself with no feelings of guilt whatsoever. (Think Ken Lay here.)

Like the Special, the narcissistic Lone Wolf also has no problems with cosmetic surgery of any kind to improve his appearance. After all, he's *worth* it. And even without cosmetic surgery, they change their appearance or "look" often, and fairly easily, to fit whatever "part" they happen to be playing at the time. (In fact, psychopaths are often described as "chameleon-like" for this reason.) One of the weirdest things about a Lone Wolf is that you can look at photographs of them taken at various times in their adult life, sometimes just a few years apart, and not even realize you are looking at the same person.

Which makes them pretty hard to spot by appearance alone.

Habitat

There are a few more clues in the habitat department, although they're not really easy to ascertain on a first date. Lone Wolves tend to move around a lot. Rarely, if ever, do they live in the same community they grew up in, because they've usually burned too many bridges there. Of course, in a mobile society like ours, *lots* of people don't live where they grew up, so that's really only useful for exclusionary purposes. Which also explains why nobody gets high-level security clearance without some guy in a suit showing up in their hometown to interview their grade-school teachers and neighbors.

The armed forces at least (bless their hearts) try very hard not to give high-level security clearances to psychopaths, and they are well-aware that the first symptoms show up in early childhood. Otherwise they wouldn't ask those subtle bed-wetting questions which, along with cruelty to animals and starting fires, is part of the "McDonald's Triad" of psychopathy...)

Not only do Lone Wolves tend to move around a lot in terms of their personal digs, they also tend to move around a lot in terms of their careers as well, although God knows this is not a hard-and-fast rule. *Successful* psychopaths can stay in the same job for decades if they manage to get all the way to the top before they're stopped - J. Edgar Hoover being a case in point. To say nothing of the boys from Enron and WorldCom, and Adelphia. (In fact, because the environment actually *rewards* many psychopathic personality traits, the corporate world today is so full of these guys Dr. Hare himself recently co-authored another book about them - it's called **Snakes in Suits**. Great title, and well worth reading.)

There's *a pattern of behavior* that is totally typical of the Lone Wolf, and recognizing that pattern is really the best way to identify one, more so than plumage or habitat. Whether we know it or not, we've all experienced the pattern firsthand, whether in a job situation, a social group, or even on the local School Board, and it's one of the best indicators that what you're dealing with is a Lone Wolf. Here's the way it works:

Someone with charm, excessive generosity, talent, and lots of good ideas comes on board and quickly starts working their way up the ladder, making lots of influential friends right out of the gate. This guy is a Lone Wolf, and dangerous, but no one knows that. The only real clue here (and it's an important one) is that they seem to come out of nowhere, and no one in the organization has ever actually spoken to anyone who's known them for any length of time.

Soon conflicts and little problems start to appear within the group that weren't there before. What happens next is interesting and predictable: a long-time, hard-working, and previously trusted member of the organization starts to lose the confidence of everyone else, and his performance and behavior come under scrutiny. Sensing himself under siege and without support, this person's cortisol levels start to rise, and the stress affects his performance and behavior. As he begins to self-destruct (and he often will), it looks like old Fred just doesn't have what it takes any more, and pretty soon Fred is more or less forced to retire. His place is taken by the Lone Wolf.

This scenario will often be repeated several more times as the Lone Wolf climbs toward dominance, and odds are good nobody realizes that the whole organization is being skillfully manipulated, and those members who may pose a threat to the Lone Wolf's ascent are being targeted and systematically eliminated. Eventually, though, it starts occurring to one or two people that maybe this new guy isn't as wonderful as everybody thought. There are clues here and there that maybe he's not completely honest, and that maybe his new "friends" are carrying the load for him. (It's worth noting these supporters are usually women. Unless of course the Lone Wolf is a female, which case they are usually men. Lone Wolves tend to gravitate toward the opposite sex, maybe because they find them generally easier to manipulate.)

When things don't get done, there's always a ready excuse and, for an amazingly long time, these excuses are accepted at face value. (Of course it's never the Lone Wolf's fault.) Conflicts escalate, and things get worse and worse within the organization. Higher-status members tend to leave, either to join another organization or to start their own.

How does it end? Unless the rest of the pack finally gets its collective act together and drives him off before he actually manages to claw his way to the top, a pack with a Lone Wolf in its midst too often ends up in total chaos. Lone Wolves, being devoid of any of the qualities needed for successful leadership, will ultimately destroy any organization they control.

Aggression, both internal and external, abounds as those with dominance-seeking tendencies of their own use the chaos to advance their own status. The whole process can take years, and the amount of damage they can do is mind-boggling.

In truth, wolves are usually a lot better at recognizing and dealing with a psychopath in their pack than people are. (Of course, for wolves, if their "corporation" ends up "bankrupt" due to bad management, the wolves are not unemployed - they're *dead,* which probably accounts for the difference.) But there are apparently exceptions, which should make us maybe feel a little less stupid about our own lack of instinct in this regard...

One of the earliest packs in Yellowstone, the Druid Peak pack, which was released into the park in 1996, was apparently led for several years by #40, a particularly successful and vicious female (sort of a Lupine Leona Helmsley). For several years, under her leadership, the pack was chaotic and terribly aggressive, staging raids on other Yellowstone packs and killing their members, which is fairly atypical behavior in wolves when resources are abundant.

One day, for reasons known only to himself, a young and confident collared Alpha (21M) from the Rose Creek pack, (which had suffered losses by the Druids over the years, including the murder of one of his pack-mates) approached the Druids and became the pack's new alpha in six hours flat. (Now there's a Board meeting a lot of people would probably love to have seen...) Under the leadership of 21M, the aggression ceased and the Druids became much better neighbors. (#40 herself, it should be noted, was permanently removed from the pack a few years later in a brutal political coup that the Plantagenets themselves could not have improved upon...)

The problem is that in a society as complex and mobile as ours, with its nearly infinite number of packs of all shapes and sizes, unless he's actually *executed* a Lone Wolf can usually find a new pack to accept him as soon as he gets thrown out of the last one.

And because they have a pathological need to dominate, Lone Wolves will keep moving from pack to pack, wreaking havoc as they go.

In order to identify a Lone Wolf, earlier rather than later (like after you've *married* him), you really need some solid background information to look for evidence of the characteristic psychopathic pattern of behavior. (You simply *cannot* take a Lone Wolf at his word, because he's probably a pathological liar.)

And the truth is, we've gotten sloppy about that part, mostly *because* our society is so very mobile. The days when you married a guy whose family and friends you've known all your life are pretty much gone, unless you live on a farm in North Dakota or somewhere and he grew up on the farm next door. But in spite of our mobility, most normal guys have old friends as well as new ones, representing various periods in their life - friends from school (in the case of Retrievers, these are often friends from *grade school*), old military buddies, co-workers from previous jobs, people they've shared a hobby or sport with over the years. For reasons of geography, they may not see all of them frequently, and most men are obviously not as good at "tending" friendships as women are but, like extended family, they *exist.* A man who doesn't seem to have *anyone* in his life who's known and trusted him for years should probably be viewed with suspicion.

Unless he's an orphan, the same is true for any guy who seems to have little or no real contact with his family (and I'd check out the orphan story myself). Most normal people spend holidays with their families when they can, even when they find it totally exasperating and swear *every single year* that they're going to spend *next* Christmas lying on the beach in Aruba with a couple of friends instead of subjecting themselves to the collective insanity of their blood relatives.

Close relatives are often viscerally able to recognize a Lone Wolf in the family early on (in fact, the Unabomber was ultimately captured because his own family contacted the FBI), and it's often the first pack they are driven from once they hit adulthood. So a good rule might be that any guy whose relationship with his entire family seems to consist of annual Christmas cards should be examined pretty closely before you get involved further. Hell, even *Fearbiters* are tolerated by their families. (In fact, the Annual Eggnog-Fueled Tantrum of the family Fearbiter is a cherished component of many family holiday traditions...)

Mating Habits

Lone Wolves are to a large degree *anhedonic,* which simply means they can't experience pleasure and satisfaction as normal people do. (This is believed to be a result of dopamine dysregulation.) About the *only* real pleasure they get is from being in a position of dominance and from inflicting emotional, financial, and sometimes physical pain on others, but in both cases the pleasure and the satisfaction are short-lived and the desire for it needs to be constantly fed.

Because they really can't experience either romantic love or sexual satisfaction to any great extent, sex is mostly a tool for them, and they use it to both manipulate and dominate. And they are often very good sexual partners, with a strong testosterone-fueled sex drive.

Lacking impulse control, they are usually pretty promiscuous, and have no scruples at all about seducing the girlfriends or wives of their boss, their enemies, or even their friends. (Bear in mind that since they are incapable of having real "friends" these are only people they use to gratify their own needs). In fact, these three groups comprise their *favorite* sexual targets. **Normal men do not attempt to seduce their bosses', their enemies',** *or* **their friends' wives or girlfriends - it is the mark of a psychopath.**

Should you find this happening to you, don't dismiss it as typically "stupid male behavior". This is not stupid - it's socially *aberrant* behavior indicating that this guy is NOT all right, and it's the one time you probably *should* report it to your spouse or boyfriend - he definitely needs a heads-up about this guy's true character.

Female Lone Wolves, it is probably worth noting, will exhibit precisely the same behaviors, and for precisely the same reasons. In a wolf-pack, it will invariably result in this female being literally torn to SHREDS by the targeted male's mate and her supporters. (The much-heralded natural tendency toward monogamy displayed by an Alpha wolf is ENFORCED by the pack's high-ranking females should he, by virtue of what Dave Barry has accurately dubbed "lust-induced brain freeze", temporarily misplace it when a low-ranking bitch with aspirations of grandeur approaches him with her tail flagging.) Oddly, the negative repercussions of this are experienced entirely by the errant bitch, not the male, probably because female wolves instinctively know that all guys, in the final analysis, are idiots.

Somebody probably should have explained this to that silly bitch in the infamous blue dress...she honestly thought we'd all actually buy her book and her stupid purses?? What a twit.

The most extremely psychopathic personalities, of course, are the serial killers who often rape and sexually mutilate their victims, usually after they kill them. If rape is not about sex, but rather an act of dominant aggression, *necrophilia,* which is non-consensual sex with a *dead person,* for Heaven's sake, surely takes that to the next level, and an amazing number of serial killers are necrophiliacs.

In a public interview that he'd specifically requested with a famous Christian psychologist (coincidentally the exact same guy who counseled Tom DeLay and Ted Haggard - talk about a "counselor to the stars"!) shortly before his execution, Ted Bundy publicly blamed his violent sexual tastes on pornography, but it's probably wise to remember that Ted was a stunningly talented pathological liar with an honors degree in psychology. (In fact, although the interviewers he talked with were probably unaware of it at the time, many of the more bizarre accounts he gave of his necrophiliac behaviors actually sounded suspiciously like those described in an obscure book on the subject published about 80 years earlier in Europe - apparently, Ted was pretty well-read in the history of abnormal sexual psychology. And bored. Which is why you shouldn't believe a Lone Wolf if he tells you it's *raining*.)

And although very few people on the planet besides me actually seem to *know* this, necrophilia is hardly unknown in the animal world. This pretty much excludes pornography as its cause, and strengthens the case that it's simply an extreme display of dominance and maybe an acquired taste, no matter how distasteful it seems to most of us. There are actually documented cases of necrophilia in species as varied as squirrels, mice, and mallard ducks.

The most famous of necrophiliac ducks was (I swear I am not making this up!) actually *photographed in the act*, since as luck would have it, it took place right outside a Natural History Museum in the Netherlands, after the first duck flew into a window and broke his neck. *And* both mallards were drakes, which was admittedly pretty weird. (Of course mallards are also well-known for the practice of gang-rape as well...and their high incidence of homosexual pairings is no doubt where the expression "queer as duck" comes from.) But at any rate, I'm pretty sure ducks haven't got much of a porn industry out there in duck-land, although Lord knows I could be wrong.

It's probably worth noting that there's no evidence that necrophilia is practiced by canines, but this is probably less an indication of their moral superiority than it is a matter of practicality - due to their physical limitations dogs really can only breed when both partners are standing up, and it's pretty hard to get a dead dog (or wolf, for that matter) to assume that position.

(Simple physical limitation may also explain why necrophilia, like rape, is practiced pretty exclusively by males in all species. Think about it for a minute.)

Most Lone Wolves you are apt to run into, though, are what would probably be termed "mildly" psychopathic (even most of the incarcerated ones only score in the "moderate" range) and so, statistically speaking, you are most probably unlikely to find yourself quartered-up like a chicken and stuffed into hefty bags should you accidentally end up in bed with one, which is good to know. But it's still wise to remember that *all* Lone Wolves are abnormal people who have mastered the art of appearing normal - it's a performance designed to draw others into their web. *What Lone Wolves are very good at is seduction, sexual or otherwise.*

If they tell you they love you, THEY ARE LYING. They don't love you. They *can't*, even if they *want to,* because they're biochemically challenged in the limbic department. They will lie to you and they will cheat on you, and they won't feel any remorse whatsoever, because they are simply incapable of remorse.

You can't change them, you can't help them, and you sure as hell can't *fix* them. No one can. If they *tell* you that you can, THEY ARE LYING.

Lone Wolves lie to everyone, especially themselves.

All in all, Lone Wolves are a bad bargain. Like the dementors they resemble, sooner or later they'll suck the happiness out of everyone around them.

Your best defense is probably chocolate.

13

The Final Chapter

ON OUR FIRST TRIP I TRIED SO HARD TO REARRANGE YOUR MINE.
BUT AFTER AWHILE I REALIZED YOU WERE DISARRANGING MINE.
 —JAGGER/RICHARDS, 1965

OK. Hopefully by now you know a little more about men, pack status, and the brain chemistry responsible for it than you did when you first picked up this book.

And the most *important* thing you need to remember from all of this (even if you can't remember *anything* else) is this single fact:

There is absolutely no hope whatsoever of changing anyone's PSP and it will just make you crazy if you try.

Why is it so important to remember this?

Because, according to raw data from the US Census Bureau, in 2005:

The marriage rate among Americans was 7.5 per 1,000.
The divorce rate for the same year was 3.6 per 1,000.
The median duration of a first marriage was about 8 years.

Now, you don't need a degree from MIT to figure out that those odds pretty much *stink* - at the very least, it oughta be enough to make any reasonably intelligent woman think twice about cashing in her 401K to spring for an expensive wedding gown.

Also according to the US Census Bureau, the *majority* of divorces were initiated by women. Among college-educated women the rate actually approached 90%.

That's a *lot* of women picking out the wrong dog.

Hell, if dog breeders had a lifetime failure rate of 50% in the placement of their puppies, they'd throw in the towel. *But they don't.* In fact, *most* purebred dogs purchased from responsible breeders stay where they're placed for their whole lives. Why?

Because *smart* breeders know that, no matter which particular breed of dog they personally love and pour a ridiculous amount of time and money into showing, breeding, and cleaning up after, it's *not* the right breed for everyone.

There are women who adore the perennially cute Cocker, while others find their chronic immaturity simply annoying. (For an awful lot of women, "cute" gets old pretty quickly when it's not accompanied by reliability.)

And while the tough and fearless Rottweiler might be the perfect breed for some women, certainly not every woman can handle one.

A friend of mine, who owns and competes in AKC performance events with two superbly trained Rotties, each roughly resembling a diesel locomotive in size and strength, has a husband of roughly the same muscle mass who hunts big game and drives a Corvette - and she handles them all with the same effortless sort of ease. In less competent hands, all three of them would probably be dangerous.

Responsible breeders try to collect as much information as they can about potential owners before agreeing to sell them a puppy, mostly to minimize the possibility that they'll get it back. (Unlike pet shops, responsible breeders will always take back a dog they've bred under any circumstances at any point in its life. There are some days when this seems like an incredibly stupid idea, but we do it anyway, because in the "dog world" it's what separates the good guys from the bad guys.)

And while choosing a particular breed will give you a pretty good idea of what to expect in terms of size, looks, and typical energy level - all of which are important - they are not enough, by themselves, to ensure a successful long-term relationship. Within any breed there are commonalities to be sure, because that's what defines breeds in the first place, *but no matter what his breed, each individual is still born with his own distinct pack status personality, or PSP, hard-wired in, and this can be every bit as important.* Sometimes more so. (Although they may *look* a lot alike, all Irish Setters unfortunately don't share a common PSP, any more than all *human* Irishmen do.)

In any breed, from Chihuahuas to Great Danes, each litter will include a mixed assortment of PSPs, from Alphas right through Omegas although, through years of deliberate selection, some breeds seem to produce a higher percentage of one than the other. Ultimately ending up with the right dog actually depends on selecting the right breed, selecting the right breeder, and then selecting *the right puppy from its litter.*

So what experienced breeders will do is *test* their puppies at 7 weeks to ascertain levels of personality traits like dominance-seeking, pack dependence, and stress-tolerance (sort of like a doggy Meyers-Briggs) so that they can make intelligent decisions for their placement. The best breeders out there are actually alot like professional matchmakers.

For example, puppies with strong dominance-seeking tendencies (i.e. Leglifters) are a poor choice for families with young children, because as they mature, these puppies will jockey for the highest position they can attain within the family pack, and the first pack-members they'll challenge are the lowest-ranking ones, who are the kids. This rarely ends well for the dog, even in the smaller breeds.

What good breeders do next is "interview" prospective owners, asking a lot of questions about their life, their family, and their lifestyle in general, so they have enough information to match owners with the puppy whose personality will best suit their needs.

They do all this because good breeders know that if the dog is a good fit to begin with, the odds of his staying in that home his whole life go way up.

Although it maybe sounds a little unromantic at first, if the divorce rate is ever going to improve, women really need to start doing the same sort of thing when choosing a man. (In fact, the odds of "romance" still existing in a relationship after a couple of decades are actually *improved* if there's a good fit between partners.)

The old bird-dog trainers have another expression that I'm fond of:

"It costs just as much to feed a sorry dog as a good one."
(In actual fact, it probably costs more.)

And the same is true with men - you'll expend a *lot* more emotional energy on a guy who's wrong for you than you will on one who's right for you, and you'll have a lot less to show for the effort you put in.

So what you have to do is ask yourself what's important to you, really and truly. (If you want it *all*, you'll probably need several guys at once, which pretty much excludes marriage as a possibility…) Again, it's not so much what you want as what you *need*.

Is financial security, social standing, and dependability more important to you than adventure or great (and frequent) sex? *You probably would be happiest with a Beta.*

Do you need a warm, friendly, social guy who can communicate with you on an emotional level? *Forget Alphas. You need a Retriever.*

Are you really only comfortable when you're in control? (Be honest, here…!) *You need a Perpetual Puppy, and God knows there are lots to choose from…*

Are you sexy, athletic, high-energy, and fiercely competitive? *Only a Leglifter will truly be able to keep up.*

Of course, if you're *already* married, the game changes a little because, unless you want to go through the unpleasant business of replacing him, you're pretty much stuck with what you've got, PSP-wise. In that case, understanding what you *do have* and the biochemical reasons for it can be a real advantage, and actually lessen the chances of ending up as a depressing US Census Bureau statistic.

This might be as good a time as any to tell the story of Zero:
Back when I was in college, I knew a guy - small, quiet, and slight of frame - who had always wanted a German Shorthaired

Pointer, which for the uninitiated is a sleek and elegant sporting dog with a short, glossy, liver-colored coat. It seemed like a good fit.

For some unfathomable reason, though, he thought that these dogs were also called Chesapeake Bay Retrievers. (This was before the internet, OK? And the guy was from New York.) So he went out and bought a Chesapeake puppy, who actually looked a little odd to him, but what the hell - he figured sooner or later this rough brown lump of a puppy would turn into the sleek dog he had envisioned. Of course, it didn't happen.

Zero grew up to be exactly what he was genetically intended to be - a hundred-plus-pound pile of tough muscle and testosterone with a head the size of a boulder and hawk-yellow eyes, covered in a thick, dull, totally waterproof coat the exact color of dead grass and blessed with a pain threshold that was off the chart - Zero was, for all intents and purposes, totally bulletproof.

Chessies, in case you've never met one, are a quintessentially American breed developed by early market hunters for the express purpose of retrieving large, uncooperative Canada geese out of the icy Chesapeake Bay, for hours on end, in the worst sort of weather, and Zero was well-suited to the task, both physically and mentally.

As a companion for an urban-minded apartment-dwelling college intellectual who drove a VW bug, he was significantly less well-suited, unfortunately. Things probably would have turned out badly here, except for two things.

The first was that, remarkably, Zero and his owner actually liked each other in spite of their essential differences. (In fact, by the time Zero was full-grown, their only similarity was that they weighed about the same, both tipping the scales at just over a hundred pounds.)

The second was that a knowledgeable dog person explained to Zero's owner that Zero actually was a Chessie, and a pretty good representative of his breed, rather than the truly terrible Shorthair his owner assumed he'd gotten stuck with.

Once that happened, and Zero's owner could accept Zero for what he WAS rather than hoping he'd somehow miraculously turn into something he simply could never be, things worked out a whole lot better.

Zero and his owner were often seen tooling around town in their little green VW bug, a mismatched couple if ever there was one, but apparently pretty respectful of each other's innate strengths and limitations.

Too often, men marry a woman hoping she won't change, while women marry a man hoping he *will*. And, in all fairness, it's usually the *man* who's victim of the old "bait-and-switch", rather than the woman.

As far as men go, unless he's totally dishonest about the fact that he prefers football to chick flicks, or maybe pretends he's tidy when he's really a pig, what the woman sees when she's dating a guy is pretty much what she gets after she marries him.

And most men (any worth having, anyway) are *not* dishonest about these things - it's just that women, for some reason, optimistically believe that they can alter the behavior they don't much like once they're actually sharing a bathroom.

If you stop to think about it, it's really pretty unreasonable to expect great interpersonal communication skills *after* marriage from a guy who never displayed any evidence whatsoever that he possessed such skills *beforehand*. You might as well expect an engineer to write poetry...odds are pretty high that, if he's any good at being an engineer, he doesn't have the right brain chemistry to write poetry.

On the other hand, no sane guy marries a woman with long, sexy hair, in stiletto heels and size eight skirts, hoping that in ten years she'll be a short-haired porker decked out in baggy pants and Birkenstocks (a unique style of footwear guaranteed to make any woman walk like Daffy Duck), and women certainly never *warn* them of the possibility, yet all too often that's exactly what happens.

Talk about bait-and-switch. And yet the majority of divorces are still initiated by women, which I suspect says something positive about men.

Another myth that needs to die is the old saw that "Opposites attract." Turns out it's pretty much bullshit. Geneticists have long known that mating in any species (including ours) is not random, but rather *assortative,* although for some unknown reason they never bothered to share this information with women.

What this means is that, like all other animals, we unconsciously tend to choose as mates partners with whom we share a common physical or personality trait or two. And, generally, they're positive rather than negative ones. (Women with a hot temper or a big butt, for example, rarely find these same traits appealing in a man, which is a good thing for their future offspring, who will often get a double dose of the traits their parents share, genetically speaking.)

Dog breeders, who've used this principle of matching up similar positive attributes deliberately for years, call them "like-to-like" pairings, and they generally produce the best offspring.

What this means is that, even without consciously trying, women tend to marry men with whom they have something positive in common, and this can work out well if they can just get past the parts that drive them crazy long enough to remember what it originally was that attracted them to him in the first place...

And it's a *whole* lot easier to put up with that which makes you crazy if you understand its biochemical underpinnings, instead of viewing it as something somebody could change if only they really *wanted* to, or *loved* you enough, or *worked* at it a little harder.

WELL, NOTHING I DO DON'T SEEM TO WORK, IT ONLY SEEMS TO MAKE MATTERS WORSE...
— MICK AND KEITH AGAIN

What to do?

Hey, remember the line **"You can train a pig to point but that don't make him a pointing dog"**?

It applies here. As the old bird dog trainers figured out years ago, you actually *can* teach a pig to point (with enough corn), but because he has no genetic aptitude for it, the *only* training method that will work is positive reinforcement. (For non-dog trainers, "positive reinforcement" is a training method that sets the trainee up to do the *right* thing and then rewards him for it, rather than allowing him to do the *wrong* thing and then correcting him for it.)

But it's important to remember that because you are fighting genetics here and operating at the mercy of something called "instinctive drift", even when he's trained to point, a pig is inclined to be unreliable at it. And it *still* won't make him a pointing dog. Better to get yourself a pointing dog in the first place if that's what you really want.

And if you've got the pig already...well, you can certainly try positive reinforcement, which really can be used successfully to alter a few specific *behaviors* (like leaving the toilet seat up), but making the relationship work is also ultimately dependent upon learning to simply accept his exasperating *personality traits* (like discomfort discussing emotions or the inability to cuddle without automatic sexual arousal) which are a direct result of his individual male brain chemistry and which you simply can't do anything about. Get *over* it - you'll both be happier.

Men, for some reason, are generally better at this - there are a lot of behaviors (like rearranging furniture) and personality traits (like the need for extensive communication with someone they're seeing the next day anyway) displayed by women that make no earthly sense to them whatsoever, but men are more likely to be amused by them than irritated.

Since I'm really not remotely qualified to be in the marital advice business and we seem to be drifting in that direction - *the Rolling Stones' Guide to Relationships??? Trust me, unless Charlie Watts wrote it, it probably wouldn't be worth reading* - it has occurred to me that right here might be a pretty good place to quit. And since I've never been any good at coming up with snappy exit lines, I'm just going to borrow from Huck Finn's, which besides being hard to beat as an exit line for a book pretty much sums up my own feelings:

"...and so there ain't nothing more to write about, and I am rotten glad of it, because if I'd a knowed what trouble it was to make a book I wouldn't a tackled it and I ain't agoing to no more."

A Disclaimer, An Apology, a few Acknowledgements, and a Friendly Warning

Now, way at the very beginning of this book (in the Introduction I think, although I'm too lazy to actually go back and check) I stated very clearly that I hadn't done any real research before I wrote it, which was pretty much true, technically speaking. As I explained, I'm a dog breeder, and occasionally a dog *writer,* but I'm not a researcher by a long shot.

However, in the course of breeding, training, and writing about dogs over the years, I *have* read a whole lot of stuff on genetics, psychology, brain chemistry, and pack order written by real live serious researchers, some of which I've actually remembered. The problem with my memory, as any of my friends can tell you, is that it's pretty eidetic, which is what people used to call "photographic", until it occurred to someone that Mozart had it in his ears...

Anyhow, what happens to people who have this sort of memory is that they're often accused of plagiarism. (Unless they're Mozart, in which case people are simply impressed.) So if you are a serious researcher reading this - *and for the life of me I can't understand why any serious researcher would bother* - and you happen across a phrase that sounds eerily familiar because maybe you *wrote* it, it was totally unintentional and I am truly sorry. So is Stephen Ambrose.

This list of experts in their respective fields, whose stuff I've read, possibly plagiarized, and certainly extrapolated wildly from includes (but is not limited to) James Dabbs, Simon Baron-Cohen, Tom Insel, Larry Young, Matt Ridley, Floyd Allport, Robert Hare, Peter Dawkins, Herbert Simon, Clarence Pfaffenberger, Goran Bergman, Konrad Lorenz, Robert Hinde, Doug Smith, L. David Mech, Jane Goodall, Frank Ervin, Roberta Palmour, Elaine Peskind, Richard Ebstein, and Xiodong Zhang, all of whom are (or *were* if they're dead) really careful and thorough researchers of one sort or another, and many of whom have written some fascinating books well worth tracking down. I'd like to take this opportunity to thank them all.

I'd also like to take this opportunity to thank Keith Murphy PhD, Brilliant Scientist and Junkyard Dog extraordinaire, for all the help on the genetics and biochemistry end, and for attempting (albeit with minimal success) to stress upon me the virtues of scientific accuracy, which can be neatly summed up, as far as I can tell, by the phrase "appears to be". (Sorry, Murph...I know you tried your hardest.)

And, of course, my undying gratitude goes out once again to Joanne Baldwin DVM, for her unflagging support as well as for her formidable proofreading, editing, and formatting skills, without which this whole thing would still be a Word document filled with a bunch of accidentally embedded fonts. And *neotenous* is too a word - trust me, I probably stole it from somebody with a PhD.

And finally, I'd personally like to thank Keith Richards, quintessential poster boy for the virtues of decadence and my personal role model in that regard, for still being alive, sexy, and a hell of a rhythm guitar player at the ripe old age of 63

Oh, yeah, and the promised Friendly Warning:

If you happen to be a male clinical psychologist or some such silly thing who's actually gotten this far (in spite of my clear warning that you should NOT read this book if you have a Y chromosome) and you really *loathe* the whole premise and feel compelled to write a scathing review on Amazon similar to the one that some dork wrote trashing **The Female Brain**, all I can say is...

DON'T BOTHER.

If you do (and I'm only telling you this to save you from embarrassment) you're gonna end up looking like a total jackass to a whole bunch of women who'll probably figure you for a Fearbiter and who will, most likely, be right. (You just can't *win* this one, sorry.)